The Gardening Which? Guide to

Successful Propagation

The Gardening Which? Guide to
Successful Propagation

Edited by
Alistair Ayres

CONSUMERS' ASSOCIATION

Which? Books are commissioned and researched by
Consumers' Association and published by Which? Ltd,
2 Marylebone Road, London NW1 4DF

Distributed by The Penguin Group:
Penguin Books Ltd, 27 Wrights Lane, London W8 5TZ

First edition 1988
Reprinted 1988, 1989, 1990
Revised edition August 1993
Reprinted January 1995

British Library Cataloguing-in-Publication Data
A catalogue record for this book is available from
the British Library

ISBN 0 85202 561 0

Typeset by Vantage Phototypesetting Co. Ltd
Eastleigh and London
Printed and bound in Great Britain by
Jarrold Printing, Norwich

CONTENTS

ACKNOWLEDGEMENTS

Illustrations by:
  Sophie Allington

Design by:
  Sara Mathews

Design assistance:
  Grant Boston
  Paul Holloway

Cover illustration by Carolyn Jenkins
Cover design by Linda Blakemore

With contributions from:
  David Antill (Efford Research Station)
  Kathleen Dryden (Alpine Garden Society)
  Philip Damp (National Dahlia Society)
  David Mason
  Kay Sanecki (National Council for the
        Conservation of Plants and Gardens)

The Editor would like to thank all the professional
and keen amateur gardeners and the members of
staff at horticultural research stations, horticultural
colleges and arboretums who helped in providing and
checking the information for this book.

Photo credits: All photographs are the copyright of
Gardening Which? with the exception of that on
page 103, which is reproduced by kind permission of
Michael Warren.

ABOUT THIS BOOK

You may have met gardeners who can seemingly
break off any piece of shoot and get it to root; such
gardeners are deemed to have 'green fingers'. But
anyone can acquire 'green fingers'. For example, if
you know that cuttings are more likely to root at a
certain time of year, or if taken in a particular way,
you can greatly improve your chances of success.

   To produce this book, we have consulted many
professionals, experts and specialists so that you can
find all the information you need to propagate a
particular plant. Most plants can be propagated
from seed, cuttings, layers or divisions, and none of
the techniques described in this book require any
special equipment. More complicated techniques,
such as grafting and mist propagation, have far more
applications for the professional nurseryman and
have not been dealt with here.

Rosa rugosa *'Roserie de la Hay' makes
an attractive hedge. Plants are easily
raised from hardwood cuttings.*

LOTS OF PLANTS QUICKLY

When buying plants, have you ever thought about the possibilities of propagating from them before they are even planted? Take fuchsias and geraniums as prime examples. The peak sales time is May and June, just as the plants are coming into flower. But if you buy your plants earlier, say March, you can produce as many as 30 to 50 new plants from a single purchase and have them all in flower by June or July. When you buy the plant, trim it right back (using the trimmings for cuttings) and keep it in the warm. The plants will then produce a flush of new growth, from which more cuttings can be taken (see pages 104 and 106 for more details).

The same principle can be used for shrubs that are easy to root from soft cuttings, such as hebes.

Many shrubs root from cuttings taken in September or October. If you are buying deciduous shrubs at this time, you could be really mercenary and take as many cuttings as possible before planting. Most shrubs will benefit from this hard pruning and produce bushier plants as a result.

You could also extend this idea to shrubs in the garden. Take dogwoods (*Cornus* spp), for example. These are normally pruned hard back in spring to produce a new lot of coloured stems. But if you are willing to forgo the first winter's display and prune in late autumn, you could have half a dozen plants by the following winter from hardwood cuttings. Another possibility would be to use the nurserymen's technique of stooling (see page 46).

HERBACEOUS PLANTS

If you want a number of herbaceous perennials, there are two techniques you can use. For those types that can be propagated from basal cuttings in spring (see pages 77 to 94), pot up the plants in autumn and keep them in the cold frame or cold greenhouse over winter. In early spring, cuttings can be taken as for chrysanthemums (see page 104) over a month or so.

Perennials with fibrous roots can be divided a lot more ruthlessly if you pot up the divisions in individual pots or boxes of compost and keep them in the cold frame for a month or two before planting out. The best time for this is late February.

If you are buying perennials in early spring, it may also be worth looking for the largest plants you can find at the garden centre. Before planting, you should be able to remove shoots or root portions for cuttings, or split them up into at least 5 (possibly up to 30) new plants.

From basal cuttings

Achillea (yarrow)
Anthemis tinctoria
Delphinium
Erigeron (fleabane)
Limonium latifolium (statice, sea lavender)
Lupinus (lupins)
Lythrum (loosestrife)
Michaelmas daisies
Monarda (bergamot)
Nepeta (catmint)
Polygononum affine
Salvia x *superba*
Scabiosa (pin-cushion flower)
Sedum (iceplant)
Solidago (golden rod)

From root cuttings

Acanthus (bear's breeches)
Anchusa azurea (*A. italica*)
Anemone x *hybrida* (Japanese anemone)
Catananche caerulea (cupid's dart)
Dicentra (Dutchman's breeches)
Eryngium (most) (sea holly)
Papaver orientale (Oriental poppy)
Phlox paniculata
Verbascum (mullein)

By division

Acanthus (bear's breeches)
Achillea (yarrow)
Agapanthus (African lily)
Aster novi-belgii (Michaelmas daisy)
Bergenia (elephant's ear)
Brunnera macrophylla
Chrysanthemum maximum
Doronicum (leopard's bane)
Epimedium (barrenwort)
Erigeron (fleabane)
Geranium
Helenium (sneezeweed)
Hemerocallis (day lily)
Hosta (plantain lily)
Iris sibirica (and varieties)
Kniphofia (red hot poker)
Liatris (blazing star)
Oenothera
Potentilla (cinquefoil)
Pulmonaria (lungwort)
Pyrethrum
Sidalcea
Solidago (golden rod)
Stachys lanata (lamb's ear)
Sedum 'Autumn Joy'
Tradescantia (trinity flower)
Trollius (globe flower)

LOTS OF ALPINES

Some of the more invasive alpines can be treated just like herbaceous perennials. However, if you want to use them for ground cover – to colonise gaps between paving, for instance – it would be worth buying large plants and propagating before planting.

● **By division**
Acaena microphylla
Ajuga reptans and varieties (bugle)
Campanula cochleariifolia
Cotula potentillina
Geranium (alpine types)
Gentiana sino-ornata (gentian)
Raoulia australis
Viola cornuta, Viola hederacea
Saxifrage (mossy types)

● **From stem cuttings**
Arabis and *Aubrieta*
Diascia cordata
Origanum vulgare (and varieties)
Phlox subulata, Thymus (thyme)

● **From root cuttings**
Crepis incana
Geranium cinereum 'Ballerina'
Geranium subcaulescens

● **From offsets**
Saxifraga longifolia
Sedum, Sempervivum (houseleek)

QUICK RESULTS

The main disadvantage of raising your own plants rather than buying them is that they can take some time to become established. A tiny rooted cutting, for example, can look very out of place in a shrub border, and it could easily become smothered with weeds. There are two ways around this problem. If you are raising a number of plants, you can plant them out in a nursery bed. A part of your vegetable plot would be ideal – if you are stocking your garden, growing your own ornamentals will save you a lot more money than growing vegetables. The plants can be lined out in rows at quite close spacing. To save having to weed and water the plants and to encourage rapid growth, cover the soil with a sheet of black polythene, firmly secured around the edges, and plant through this. Trees and shrubs, in particular, will grow much faster if treated this way.

If you want quick results, it may be worth growing plants on under protection for the first season. Trees and shrubs raised from seed or cuttings may put on twice as much growth if kept on a capillary bench in the greenhouse through the summer than if they were kept outdoors. For example, a silver birch raised from seed could put on up to 1.8m (6ft) of growth in one season in the greenhouse.

If you want to raise a number of plants, it may be worth investing in a cheap polythene greenhouse just for this purpose. Forcing plants in this way does not result in weak plants, provided you keep them watered and fed and don't let them make too much soft growth. You must also harden them off properly before planting out. If you intend to plant in the autumn, start hardening off the plants and moving them outside in late summer.

SAVING SPACE

If you want to take lots of softwood cuttings but don't really have the space to root them, try the following method.

• Cut a piece of polythene into a long strip. The width should be 1½ times the length of your cuttings.
• Place a line of damp sphagnum moss along the strip of polythene.
• Place your prepared cuttings every few inches along the polythene so that the bases sit in the sphagnum moss. The bottom third of the polythene can then be folded over and the strip rolled up and secured with an elastic band.
• The roll of cuttings can then be kept out of direct sunlight at a suitable temperature until they have rooted.

If you haven't got room to pot them up indoors, improve the soil in a small area of your garden by raking in sand and peat. The cuttings can then be planted out in this and covered with polythene or a cloche and kept well shaded. You can then gradually harden them off. Once growing strongly, they can be transplanted in final positions.

Lay out a long strip of polythene and insert the base of prepared cuttings into a line of damp sphagnum moss (as sold for hanging baskets).

Fold over the polythene, roll up the cuttings and secure with an elastic band. Keep somewhere warm, out of direct sunlight, until the cuttings root.

WHAT YOU CAN ACHIEVE

The illustration on this page shows you what you can expect to achieve with the help of this book. Successful propagation has nothing to do with having 'green fingers'. Anyone can be good at raising plants provided they follow a few basic rules.

Don'ts

● Don't be put off by failures. They are part of the learning process. Even top nurserymen rarely get a 100 per cent success rate, and you should always start with more seed or cuttings than you need to allow for losses.

● Don't try to propagate from poor or unhealthy plants. If the parent plant is poor, you can't expect its offspring to be any better. Pests and diseases will also be carried by cuttings.

● Don't use blunt blades, as ragged cuts will be a source of infection.

● Don't use dirty pots or garden soil as a cheap substitute for compost. This is a sure way of encouraging disease.

● Don't ever let seed or cuttings become dry. Even if this doesn't kill them, they will receive a severe check to growth from which they may never fully recover.

● Don't keep seed in warm humid conditions, such as in the greenhouse, prior to sowing. Even fresh seed can lose its viability within several weeks under such conditions. Store seed somewhere cool and dry.

Climbers
p47

Conifers
p54

Junipers are among the easiest conifers to grow from cuttings.

Honeysuckles are not too difficult to raise from cuttings at the right time of year.

Shrubs
p18

Pond plants
p107

To keep your plants healthy, regular division is essential.

This tubful could easily be raised from seed for a few pounds.

Herbs
p123

Rock plants
p95

Some rock plants can be grown from seed; take cuttings from the choice types.

Do's

● Do propagate plants at the right time of year. Most cuttings will root much more easily at certain times; some may not root at all if taken at the wrong time.
● Do provide the right conditions of warmth and humidity. You can achieve a lot with a polythene bag and a shelf above a radiator.
● Do take cuttings from young plants where possible, as they usually root more easily.
● Do feed cuttings and seedlings after potting on – the compost will contain enough fertiliser for a month or so.

Trees
p36

Silver birches are very easy to grow from fresh seed.

Hedges

Raising your own plants from cuttings can save a fortune.

Wild flowers are raised from seed just like garden flowers.

Fuchsias
p104

Wild flowers
p110

Dogwoods are very easy to propagate from hardwood cuttings.

Buy a few plants in early spring and have lots in flower by the summer.

Vegetables
p118

For earlier crops, try sowing outdoors under a sheet of polythene.

Bulbs
p68

Border plants
p74

You need only a few perennials to propagate enough to fill the border.

Save money by propagating expensive bulbs, like lilies, from scales.

TREES AND SHRUBS: CUTTINGS

For most shrubs and quite a few trees, the simplest method of propagation is from cuttings. The Tables on pages 19 to 30 show when you stand the best chances of rooting a particular shrub and what type of cutting to take. You can find similar information for broad-leaved trees on pages 36 to 41 and conifers on pages 54 to 57.

WHEN TO TAKE CUTTINGS

Cuttings of different shrubs and trees can be taken throughout the season at different stages of growth.

Softwood cuttings

Softwood cuttings are usually taken in May and June from young shoots before they start to become woody. They need to be kept constantly moist and frequently need a fair amount of warmth to root. While commonly used commercially for certain shrubs, where they can be rooted in a mist unit, softwood cuttings are of limited use to the amateur except for easy-to-root specimens such as fuchsias, hebes and potentillas.

Hardwood cuttings

Hardwood cuttings are taken in autumn and winter from the past season's growth. Timing is less critical than with cuttings taken at other times of year, but rooting is often more successful with those taken in early autumn, immediately after leaf fall in the case of deciduous shrubs, when the soil is warmer. Hardwood cuttings taken in mid-winter are more prone to forming shoots before they root in spring and may die as a result.

Semi-ripe cuttings

Also known as semi-hardwood cuttings, these are taken just as the current season's shoots start to harden at the base. As a test, bend a shoot between your fingers. If it breaks, the shoot is either too soft or too hard. If it springs back when you let go, the shoot is at the right stage. Semi-ripe cuttings of deciduous shrubs are usually taken between mid-June and August; evergreens often root better in September or October. With some shrubs, timing is quite critical.

WHAT TYPE OF CUTTING?

As well as taking cuttings at the right stage of growth, how well they are likely to root can be greatly affected by where you make your cut.

The best types of cuttings for individual shrubs are given in the Tables on pages 19 to 30 and the techniques are described below.

Basal cuttings

Cut through the base of young shoots where it joins the main stem. You will often see a slight swelling at this point, and you should cut through this with a sharp knife.

Heel cuttings

Take hold of the shoot between your fingers and pull it downwards so it is detached with a tail of old wood. This tail of old wood is then trimmed with a sharp knife to about 1–3cm ($\frac{1}{2}$–1in), depending on the size of the cutting. Heeled cuttings were traditionally recommended for many shrubs, but they can be disfiguring if a number of cuttings are taken from one plant. Research over the years has shown that basal cuttings usually root as well as heeled cuttings for slightly more difficult subjects.

. . . and trim the heel of old wood.

Make your cut through the swelling at the base of the stem.

Gently pull off the cutting . . .

Nodal cuttings

Trim the base of the cutting at right-angles through the slight swelling that occurs below a leaf joint and remove the lower leaves.

Cut just below a leaf joint and remove lower leaves.

Internodal cuttings

Make your cut at right-angles to the stem about half way between two leaf joints.

Cut between two leaf joints.

Stem cuttings

You can make your cut anywhere along the stem (below or between a leaf joint) as long as the cutting is about the right size.

Leafbud cuttings

These are useful for rooting shrubs such as camellias and mahonias. Look for a bud between the main stem and leaf joint and trim the stem just above the leaf and a few centimetres below it, leaving the bud intact. Large leaves, such as camellias', can be rolled up and secured with an elastic band, or leaves can be cut to a half or a third their size. Insert the cutting into the compost so that the bud is level with the surface. Rooting hormones should never be used on leaf bud cuttings as they prevent the bud from growing once the cutting has rooted.

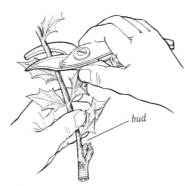

bud

Leafbud cuttings of mahonia: cut the stem above and below the leaf joint and trim the leaf to 3 or 4 leaflets.

Root cuttings

Some shrubs and trees, notably *Aralia*, Californian tree poppy (*Romneya*) and sumach (*Rhus*), won't root readily from shoot cuttings, but can be propagated quite easily from small sections of root carefully lifted in the dormant season. The technique is exactly the same as described for herbaceous plants on page 76.

Thin roots, such as those of Romneya, are cut into 3cm (1in) sections and planted horizontally in trays. For thicker roots, see illustrations on page 76.

TAKING CUTTINGS: STEP-BY-STEP

Soft and semi-ripe cuttings

1. Select healthy shoots at the right stage of growth for the particular tree or shrub (see Tables). Basal cuttings need to be cut in the right place. Other types of cuttings can be taken over-length and then trimmed up. As you take the cuttings, put them in a plastic bag to prevent them drying out and keep them out of the sun. If you can't prepare the cuttings immediately, you can keep the bag in the salad compartment of the fridge for a short period.
2. Trim the cuttings as appropriate (see preceding page) and remove the lower leaves. Most cuttings should have 2 to 4 leaves.
3. To prevent diseases, immerse the cutting in a solution of benomyl and drain off.
4. Treat the cutting with rooting hormone (if necessary), being careful to cover the wound (it doesn't matter if you get it all around the base of the stem).
5. Make sure the rooting medium is thoroughly moist before inserting the cuttings, but don't make the compost too wet or the cuttings may rot. Stand pots in a

Nodal and internodal cuttings can be taken over-length and then trimmed up.

Remove tender tips which wilt readily. Most cuttings should have 2 to 4 leaves.

bowl of water for 15 minutes and allow to drain off.
6. If rooting cuttings in pots, you should be able to get up to 6 cuttings in a 10cm (4in) pot. Many cuttings taken in spring and summer can be rooted under a plastic bag. Use three sticks or two hoops of wire to support the bag, and seal it below the rim of the pot with an elastic band.
7. Place the pots somewhere warm and out of direct sunlight. Check cuttings to make sure the compost has not dried out – stand the pot in water for a short while if this happens. Once you see signs of new growth, ventilate the cuttings by removing the elastic band and gradually give them more air over the next few days. Once hardened off, pot them up immediately into a potting compost. If you can't do this immediately, give them a liquid feed as a temporary stopgap.

Hardwood cuttings

1. Select suitable stems, generally about pencil thickness, and trim to appropriate length (20–30cm/8–12in). With deciduous shrubs, wait until the leaves fall. With many hardwood cuttings, where you make the cut isn't important, though for some types basal or nodal cuttings root better (see Tables).
2. Remove any soft growth at the top of the stem and make the top cut at a slight angle so that it sheds the rain. With evergreens and semi-evergreens, such as privet and some roses, leave the top three or four leaves.
3. Select a suitable site. It should be reasonably sunny and the soil should not become waterlogged. In exposed gardens, erect a temporary netting windbreak to protect the cuttings from drying winds through the first year.
4. Using a spade, open up a furrow to the depth of the cuttings so that one side is vertical. Line the bottom of the furrow with sharp sand to improve drainage and aeration at the base of the cuttings. The cuttings can be spaced 8–15cm (3–6in) apart, depending on how vigorous the plants are.
5. Insert the cuttings to two-thirds their length so that they sit on the sand against the vertical side of the furrow. Replace about two-thirds of the extracted soil and press down firmly with your foot. The rest of the soil should be loosely replaced. Give the cuttings a gentle pull to make sure they are firm – if they are loose they will be lifted by frost. In cold exposed areas it would be better to treat your hardwood cuttings as recommended for lots of cuttings

(see next page).
6. During the following summer, keep the cuttings weeded and water them in dry weather. They should be ready for transplanting by the autumn.

Remove lower leaves and tender tips from evergreen and semi-evergreen cuttings such as privet and roses.

Insert the cuttings against the straight side of the trench.

Lots of hardwood cuttings

If, for example, you want to start a hedge from hardwood cuttings and want 100 or more plants, the following method may save disappointments and is more reliable on a heavy soil.

1. Having taken the cuttings, bundle them up – into 25s, say – and secure them with an elastic band. Bury them in moist sand in a sheltered position over winter.

2. In early spring, look for callusing (slight irregular swellings) at the base of the cuttings. Those that have callused can be planted out. The others can be thrown away as they are unlikely to root.

GUARDING AGAINST DISEASE

To prevent cuttings from rotting or going mouldy before they root, you can treat them with a solution of the fungicide benomyl. Mix one teaspoonful of benomyl in 4.5l (1 gal) of water, fully immerse them for a few seconds and then drain off. However, this is not recommended if you are using a rooting hormone as the reaction between the different chemicals can inhibit rooting.

You will most likely find benomyl (Benlate) sold in sachets together with separate sachets of a liquid fertiliser. When using this fungicide for cuttings, do not add the fertiliser.

Immerse all cuttings in a benomyl solution to avoid disease problems.

IMPROVING YOUR CHANCES

Some cuttings will root freely, given the right conditions, without any special treatment. But with others you can greatly improve your chances of success by either treating them with a rooting hormone or wounding the base of the cuttings.

Tip a small amount of hormone powder into an old lid to treat cuttings.

Rooting hormones

Rooting hormones contain synthetic hormones similar to those occurring naturally in plants to induce root formation. Rooting hormones are available as powders, liquids or gels. However, more important is what they contain. Research in America, Holland and Ireland has shown that preparations containing IBA (indole butyric acid) are more reliable and effective on a wider range of plants than those containing NAA (naphthylacetic acid), though the latter may give just as good results on some plants. Unfortunately, the rooting hormones currently available to amateurs contain only NAA.

When treating cuttings, always tip a small amount of rooting hormone into a small container, such as an old lid, to avoid contamination. Rooting hormones should always be stored in sealed containers out of direct sunlight and in a cool place.

Wounding

If you have difficulty rooting cuttings of a particular plant, try removing a shallow slice of wood a few centimetres long from one side of the cutting or scoring the base of the cutting with a sharp knife. This technique can prove effective for difficult-to-root cuttings such as magnolias and rhododendrons.

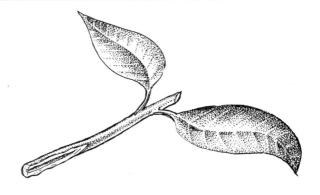

WHERE TO ROOT CUTTINGS

Depending on what type of cuttings you are taking, the time of year and what facilities you have, there are a number of options. Advice on the best place to root cuttings for individual trees and shrubs is given in the Tables on pages 19 to 30 and 36 to 41.

Pots covered with a polythene bag

This is the most convenient method for cuttings taken between May and August (though it can be used at other times), particularly when you want just a few plants. You should be able to insert at least 6 cuttings around the edge of a 10cm (4in) pot. Make a framework from 2 hoops of wire or use 3 sticks to support the bag. Pull the bag down over the rim of the pot and secure with an elastic band. Keep the pot out of direct sunlight until the cuttings have rooted, under the greenhouse staging say, or in a covered porch. If cuttings need heat to root, you can stand the pot on a radiator shelf or a heated propagator base, but make sure that the compost doesn't dry out. Water by standing the pots in a bowl of water for about 15 minutes if this

Bag supported with wire hoops – made from an old coat hanger, say.

happens. Once the cuttings show signs of growth, they can be hardened off. Start by making holes in the polythene, and after several days remove the elastic band. After a week or so, remove the cover completely and pot on the rooted cuttings individually into 8cm (3in) pots.

Polythene tunnels

If you want to root a number of cuttings, a convenient method is to use a small polythene tunnel in the garden. This method is particularly useful for cuttings taken between June and August, and has the advantage that you can leave rooted cuttings until the following spring instead of potting them on. The soil needs to be reasonably well drained, but it should not dry out too quickly. Improve heavy soils by digging in peat and sand and light soils by digging in peat. Get rid of all perennial weeds, and cover the soil with 3–5cm (1–2in) of 2 parts moss peat to 1 part coarse sand. Lightly work this into the soil when inserting the cuttings. You can

make your own tunnels from a white polythene bag (to provide some shade) slit along two sides and supported with wire hoops made from coathangers. Weight down the edges with bricks. This will take 50 or more cuttings.

Most cuttings will root in about 2 months using this method. Check the cuttings periodically during this time to make sure the soil is not too dry. If there are any signs of mould, remove infected cuttings and water with benomyl. Once cuttings have rooted, gradually increase the ventilation over several days before removing the cover. Evergreens and conifers can be re-covered over the winter.

Sealed plastic bags

This is very similar to the pot and bag method, but you have no worries about drying out and you can see the roots once they are well formed. Take a polythene bag and fill the bottom with about 8–10cm (3–4in) of moist rooting medium and insert your cuttings into this. Inflate the bag and hold the top closed with two rulers or pieces of wood. Finally, run a flame along the top of the bag to seal it. The bags can then be hung up on wires or a length of washing line in a shaded greenhouse until they have rooted.

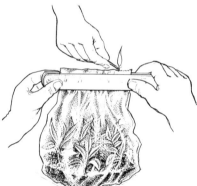

You may find two pairs of hands useful to seal the bag without letting the air out.

Jars of water

This is a simple but limited method for shrubs, though perfectly adequate for semi-hardwood cuttings of fuchsias and willows. Cover the top of the jar with foil to support the cuttings and place the jar out of direct sunlight. Keep the water topped up and replace it with fresh water if it becomes discoloured. Once the cuttings have formed roots, pot up into potting compost. Be careful, as the roots can be very brittle.

In the cold frame

This is the traditional method for rooting cuttings taken in September and October. Cuttings can be put in pots, but it's better to root them direct into the cold frame as you can get more cuttings in and they'll be less prone to drying out or freezing. Replace up to 13cm (5in) of soil in the frame with the rooting medium (2 parts moss peat to 1 part sand is suitable for most cuttings). The frame will need shading, so paint the glass with a greenhouse shading wash. Even in February, the sun can be strong enough to scorch cuttings. Most cuttings should have rooted by April or May.

The cold frame with polythene

You can also use the cold frame to root cuttings taken from April to June if you cover them with a sheet of thin (no more than 100-gauge) clear polythene. The edges of the polythene should be buried or weighted down with pieces of wood or bricks to keep in the moisture. Good shading is essential, and it may be necessary to cover the frame with netting, as well as a shading wash, during very hot sunny weather. Once the cuttings have rooted, harden them off and pot them up and overwinter them in the frame or in a cold greenhouse. This method is best for large numbers of cuttings.

In the propagator

A heated propagator provides warm, humid conditions and is useful for difficult cuttings, particularly early in the year. Most tree and shrub cuttings root well if the compost is around 13–15°C (55–60°F) – use a thermometer to check that the propagator doesn't get too hot, as few cuttings will root above 24°C (75°F). The cuttings can either be rooted in 8–10cm (3–4in) deep trays or in pots. Keep the propagator out of direct sunlight in a shaded greenhouse. Once the cuttings have rooted, start to give them some ventilation. Once hardened off, transfer the cuttings to potting compost.

Warm bench with plastic

To root a large number of cuttings it might be worth installing soil warming cables on the greenhouse bench. The cuttings can be rooted in deep trays or you can cover the sand bed with 8–10cm (3–4in) of sand and peat. To maintain humidity, cover the cuttings with thin (100-gauge or less) polythene, and seal the edges. Apply a shading wash to the greenhouse and suspend netting above the bench. Once a week, turn the plastic and shake off excess moisture. At the same time, make sure that the compost is moist and remove any dead or unhealthy cuttings. Once the cuttings have rooted, start to harden them off by cutting holes in the polythene.

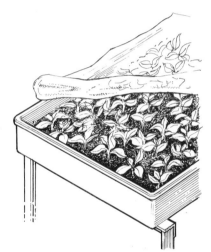

Polythene from dry-cleaners is ideal for this method.

Mist propagator

A mist propagator has soil warming cables or a heated base to supply the necessary bottom heat and overhead nozzles that send out bursts of mist to prevent the cuttings from wilting. The frequency of misting may either be controlled by a light-sensitive mechanism or an 'electronic leaf' that turns the mist on when it dries out and off again when it gets wet. Mist propagators are expensive to buy and can be expensive to install. However, with a mist propagator you could root cuttings of azaleas, camellias, Japanese maples (*Acer palmatum* varieties), magnolias and rhododendrons, which can be difficult to root by other methods. You could also root other types of cuttings much more quickly than by other methods and propagate many shrubs from softwood cuttings early in the year, which otherwise would not be possible.

All the shrubs have been listed under their Latin names in common with garden centres, nursery catalogues and other reference books. Common names are also given where widely used. In most cases, different species and varieties of a particular shrub can be propagated in exactly the same way, and these have been noted only where different methods of propagation are required, as with viburnums for example.

Most shrub cuttings can be rooted in equal parts of moss peat and sharp sand. Where reference is made to sandy compost, use 1 part moss peat to 2 parts sharp sand; similarly with peaty compost – use 2 parts moss peat to 1 part sharp sand.

Both these Eleagnus pungens *'Maculata' were bought at a garden centre. By careful pruning, nine cuttings were taken from the one on the right before planting. Of these, four or five should root to give extra plants.*

Key to how easy
- ●●● Quite easy, should be successful
- ●● More difficult, but reasonable chance of success
- ● Worth trying, but be prepared for failures

species	how	when	hor-mone*	what to do	how easy
A					
Abelia grandiflora	hardwood cuttings	Sep	yes	Take cuttings 10–20cm (4–8in) long and root in a cold frame. Pot up or plant out the following spring.	●●●
Aralia elata	root cuttings	Dec to Jan	no	Insert 5cm (2in) sections of roots in sandy compost. Pot up once strong shoots formed and plant out in autumn. Rooted suckers can also be transplanted March to April.	●●●
Amelanchier (snowy mespilus)	seed	Sum	-	Remove from berries and sow immediately outdoors or in pots. If allowed to dry out, seed needs a warm and cold period to germinate.	●●
	layering	Aut	-	Should root by the following autumn. You may also be able to detach rooted suckers.	●●●
Arundinaria (bamboo)	division	late Spr	-	Cut down clumps to about 30cm (lft) before lifting. A mattock or an axe is the best tool for splitting up old clumps. Don't worry when top growth dies down – new canes will soon sprout up as long as the roots did not dry out.	●●●
	basal cane cuttings	any time	no	Inspect the base of established canes and look for a ring of small roots starting to form at the base. It is important to catch the roots at the right stage, before they start to die back. Having selected a suitable cane, chop it off at ground level (below the new roots) and shorten the top of the cane to 15cm (6in). Plant in a cold frame in boxes of soil. Plant out in autumn or spring once rooted.	●●
	rhizome cuttings	Mar	no	Lift runners before shoots form and cut young healthy rhizomes into 30cm (1ft) sections. Replant immediately in final position, laying sections of runners horizontally in 10cm (4in) trenches. Not suitable for *Arundinaria anceps*, or other species forming tight clumps.	●●●
Aucuba japonica (spotted laurel)	basal cuttings	Oct to Nov	no	Take young shoots near the base about 10–15cm (4–6in) long and plant out in a shady part of the garden. Slow growing in the first 2 years.	●●●
Azalea (deciduous)	layering	July	yes	Wound stem (see page 43) before treating with rooting hormone. Remove any flower buds that form on layered shoots the following spring. Layers should root by the second autumn. You could also try air layering (see page 44).	●●
	basal cuttings	June	yes	Take 10cm (4in) soft wood cuttings and root in peat. They really need bottom heat (20°C/68°F) to root, though you may be lucky with a plastic bag.	●
Azalea (evergreen)	layering	July	yes	As for Azalea (deciduous), but easier as there are usually plenty of shoots to choose from near ground level.	●●●
	nodal or internodal cuttings	July	yes	Take 10cm (4in) semi-ripe cuttings and root as for deciduous azalea, above. Pot up and keep in a cold frame for 2 seasons. Trim over in second summer to ensure a bushy plant.	●●
Azara	hardwood cuttings	Oct to Nov	yes	Take 15cm (6in) basal cuttings and root in a cold frame. Plant out in spring or the following autumn.	●●
	layering	Spr	no	Work plenty of sand into the soil before pegging down layer. Sever and transplant the following spring.	●●

*Hormone means a rooting powder or solution   For an explanation of the different types of cuttings, see page 12

species	how	when	hor-mone*	what to do	how easy
B					
Berberis (deciduous)	basal, heel or nodal cuttings	Sep to Oct	yes	Take 15–20cm (6–8in) semi-ripe cuttings (5–10cm/2–4in for dwarf types), remove spines from bottom 5cm (2in) and root in a peaty compost in a cold frame. Cover with polythene and bury the edges to keep out all draughts. Pot on or plant out the following spring.	●●●
	heel or mallet cuttings	July	yes	Follow the same method as above. Pot on in autumn and plant out in spring.	●●
	seed	Sep to Oct	-	Sow ripe berries in pots of peat and sand and leave outside over winter. Once seeds show signs of germination, pot up or sow directly in an outdoor seedbed. Seedlings can easily reach 30–45cm (12–15in) in first year. Varieties won't come true.	●●
Berberis (evergreen)	hardwood cuttings	Sep to Nov	yes	Prepare cuttings and root as for Berberis (deciduous), above. Pot on or plant out in spring.	● to ●●
	seed	Sep to Oct	-	As for Berberis (deciduous), above.	●●
Buddleia (butterfly bush)	hardwood cuttings	Nov	no	Take 20–25cm (8–10in) lengths of one-year-old shoots and bury bottom two-thirds in the garden. Quick growing, so can be rooted in final position.	●●●
	nodal cuttings	June to July	no	Take 10cm (4in) cuttings of soft or semi-ripe wood and root in pots covered with plastic bags.	●●●
Buxus	hardwood cuttings	Sep to Nov	no	Use 8–15cm (3–6in) lengths of one-year-old wood (remove any soft tips) and leave the top 3 or 4 leaves intact. In mild districts root in open ground; otherwise in peaty compost in a cold frame. Plant out in spring.	●●●
	division	Spr	-	*Buxus sempervirens* 'Suffruticosa' can be lifted, pulled into several pieces and replanted.	●●●
C					
Callicarpa	seed	Mar to Apr	-	Sow in pots in the cold frame. Grow on for planting the following spring.	●●
	nodal cuttings	June to July	yes	Take 10cm (4in) tip cuttings and root in a pot covered with a plastic bag. Plant out in a sheltered position in autumn.	●●
Callistemon (bottle brush)	seed	Feb	-	Sow on surface of peat and sand and cover lightly with sharp sand or grit, or damping off may be a problem. When seedlings have 3 true leaves, prick out into sandy compost.	●●●
	basal cuttings	June	yes	Take cuttings of soft growth about 10cm (4in) long. Needs bottom heat and plenty of moisture, so best in a heated propagator. However, they are expensive to buy so worth trying with a pot covered with a plastic bag.	●●
Calluna				See Heathers, page 52.	

*Hormone means a rooting powder or solution   For an explanation of the different types of cuttings, see page 12

species	how	when	hor-mone*	what to do	how easy
Camellia	shoot tips or leaf bud cuttings	Feb to July	yes / no	Slow unless you have a heated propagator or a mist unit. Root in peaty compost. Pot up and keep under glass until the following summer.	●
	layering	Feb to Mar	no	Layers should root by following autumn.	●●●
Caryopteris	basal or nodal cuttings	June	no	Take 8–10cm (3–4in) cuttings from new growth. Insert in a cold frame and cover with polythene, or in a pot covered with a plastic bag. Pot up once rooted (3 to 4 weeks) and plant out in autumn or spring.	●●●
Ceanothus (deciduous)	basal or heel cuttings	Sep to Oct	yes	Take 10–13cm (4–5in) semi-ripe cuttings and root in a cold frame. Plant out in spring.	●●
Ceanothus (evergreen)	stem cuttings	June to Aug	no	Take 10–15cm (4–6in) semi-ripe cuttings and root in a pot covered with a plastic bag. Pot up once rooted and grow on in a cold frame. Plant out in spring.	●●
Ceratostigma	basal cuttings	June to July	no	Root 5cm (2in) cuttings in a pot covered with a plastic bag. Pot up once rooted and grow on in a cold frame until spring.	●●●
Chaenomeles (flowering quince)	basal cuttings	June	yes	Take 5–8cm (2–3in) cuttings of soft growth and root in pots of peaty compost and cover with plastic bags. Alternatively, root in a cold frame and cover with a polythene sheet. Pot up once rooted (about 4 weeks) and plant out the following spring.	●●
	root cuttings	Jan	no	Plant 8cm (3in) lengths of thin root (from near main stem) and plant horizontally in boxes of compost. Pot up once strong shoots are formed. Don't propagate grafted plants this way.	●●
Chimonanthus (winter sweet)	layering	July to Aug	yes	May take 2 years to root and a further 7 years to reach flowering size.	●
Choisya ternata (Mexican orange blossom)	basal cuttings	June	yes	Take 10cm (4in) semi-ripe cuttings and root in pots covered with plastic bags. Plant out in autumn or spring.	●●●
	basal cuttings	Oct	yes	As above, but root in a cold frame or, in mild districts, in the garden.	●●●
Cistus	basal or nodal cuttings	Sep to Oct	yes	Take 8cm (3in) semi-ripe cuttings and root in pots of sandy compost in the cold frame. Plant out in spring.	●●●
Clerodendron	suckers	Spr	no	Remove suckers with a spade and transplant.	●●●
	root cuttings	Dec	no	Plant 8cm (3in) sections of root horizontally in boxes of sandy compost. Keep under glass until several shoots appear from each root section and pot up or plant out.	●●
Colutea arborescens	seed	Feb to Mar	-	Sow in pots in the greenhouse and grow on for autumn or spring planting. Plants from seed can be longer lived than those from cuttings.	●●●
	basal cuttings	July to Aug	yes	Root 10cm (4in) cuttings in a pot covered with a plastic bag or under a sheet of polythene in the cold frame. Pot up and grow on in the cold frame for spring planting.	●●

*Hormone means a rooting powder or solution   For an explanation of the different types of cuttings, see page 12

species	how	when	hor-mone*	what to do	how easy
Convolvulus cneorum	stem cuttings	Sep	no	Take 10cm (4in) semi-ripe cuttings and root in sandy compost in a cold frame. Pot on in spring and plant out in autumn.	●●
Cornus (dogwood)	hardwood cuttings	Nov	no	Take 20cm (8in) stem cuttings and insert in open ground. Lift the following autumn. Suitable only for *Cornus alba* and *Cornus stolonifera* and their varieties. Variegated varieties may prove more difficult.	●●●
	layering	Spr	no	Suitable for all types of dogwood, including *Cornus kousa* and *Cornus mas.*	●●●
Corylopsis	layering	Spr	yes	Should root by autumn.	●●
Cotinus coggyria (smoke bush)	layering	Spr	no	If you want several plants, try French layering (see page 45). Layers should root by autumn and may have formed shoots up to 60cm (2ft) tall. Prune hard back after planting to prevent plants becoming leggy.	●●●
	suckers	Nov to Mar	no	Detach rooted suckers with spade and transplant any time during the dormant season.	●●●
Cotoneaster	hardwood cuttings	Oct	yes	Take basal cuttings (or nodal cuttings for prostrate evergreen types) and root in peaty compost in a cold frame. Plant out in April.	●●
	seed	Spr	-	Pick the berries as soon as ripe, put them in a plastic bag and crush them with a rolling pin. Mix the crushed berries with sand and leave outside for the winter and then sow in a seedbed in spring. With some species, such as *C. horizontalis* and *C. microphyllus*, germination is usually better after two winters.	●●
Cytisus (broom)	seed	Feb	-	Home-saved seed germinates very readily if sown under glass in late winter or early spring. Prick off into deep pots or peat blocks. Harden off and plant out when seedlings reach about 10cm (4in) in height. Pinch out growing tips at this stage to encourage bushy plants. Not suitable for named varieties.	●●●
	basal cuttings	July	no	Take 8cm (3in) semi-ripe cuttings and root in a cold frame or in a pot covered with a plastic bag. Once rooted (4 to 6 weeks), pot on into deep pots and overwinter in a cold greenhouse or cold frame. Plant out in spring.	●
D–E					
Daboecia				See Heathers, page 52.	
Daphne cneorum	layering	June	yes	Work peat and sand into the soil before pegging down layers. Layeral shoots should be covered with at least 5cm (2in) of soil. Detach and transplant rooted layers the following spring.	●●
	nodal cuttings	Sep	yes	Take semi-hardwood cuttings 5–8cm (2–3in) long and root in a pot covered with a plastic bag or in a cold frame.	●
Daphne mezereum	seed	Aut	-	Sow in pots or trays as soon as ripe. Keep pots in a shady place outdoors. A few seedlings may emerge in the first spring, but the majority won't germinate until they have undergone two winters. Protect plants with netting, or birds may eat seed before it is ripe.	●●
Desfontainea spinosa	hardwood cuttings	Oct	no	Take basal cuttings 8–10cm (3–4in) long and root in the cold frame. Pot on or plant out in spring.	●●

*Hormone means a rooting powder or solution   For an explanation of the different types of cuttings, see page 12

Cotoneaster frigidus *has a spectacular display of red berries, which can also be used to raise extra plants.*

species	how	when	hor-mone*	what to do	how easy
Deutzia	hardwood cuttings	Oct	yes	Take 10–15cm (4–6in) heeled cuttings and root in a cold frame or in a pot covered with a plastic bag, using a peaty compost. Plant out in late spring.	●●
Elaeagnus	hardwood cuttings	Feb to Mar	yes	Take 15cm (6in) nodal cuttings. Best rooted in a heated propagator at around 21°C (70°F), although you could try a pot and plastic bag over a radiator. Pot on once rooted (4 to 6 weeks) and grow on in a cold frame until autumn.	●
Enkianthus	seed	Feb	-	Collect seed in December and sow in a heated propagator at 13–15°C (55–60°F). Prick out into pots of lime-free compost and harden off in late summer.	●●
Erica				See Heathers, page 52.	
Escallonia	hardwood cuttings	Oct to Nov	no	Use 23–30cm (9–12in) lengths of one-year-old wood and bury bottom third in a sand-lined trench. Root in final position or transplant in autumn. Not in cold districts.	●●●
	basal, heel or nodal cuttings	July to Oct	yes	Take 10–15cm (4–6in) semi-ripe cuttings and root in a pot covered with a plastic bag. If you want a number, for a hedge say, root in a cold frame and cover with a polythene sheet.	●●●
Euonymus (all types)	basal or nodal cuttings	Sep to Oct	yes	Take 10cm (4in) cuttings of semi-ripe wood and root in peaty compost in the cold frame. Plant out the following spring.	●●●
Euonymus europaeus (spindle bush)	seed	Aut	-	Best method if you want a number of plants, for a hedge say. Remove orange seed coat, sow in trays of moist sand and leave in a cold frame all winter. Prick out seedlings and harden off and plant out when they are several inches tall.	●●●
Exochorda	basal cuttings	Apr	yes	Not worth trying unless you have a heated propagator or mist unit. Take softwood cuttings and wound them before treating with rooting hormone. Very slow growing in first few years.	●

*Hormone means a rooting powder or solution   For an explanation of the different types of cuttings, see page 12

species	how	when	hormone*	what to do	how easy
F−G					
Fatsia japonica	nodal cuttings	June to Aug	yes	Take 10cm (4in) from shoot tips with at least one leaf attached and insert singly into 8cm (3in) pots. Best rooted in a propagator with bottom heat of 18−21°C (65−70°F).	●●
	seed	Apr	-	Sow in greenhouse and grow on under glass until the following spring.	●●
Forsythia	nodal or basal cuttings	June to July	no	Take 10cm (4in) cuttings of soft growth and root in a pot covered with a plastic bag. Plant out in autumn and spring. Prune back in spring to get a bushy plant.	●●●
	hardwood cuttings	Oct	no	Take 20cm (8in) basal cuttings and root in the open ground or cold frame. Transplant in spring and prune as above.	●●●
Fothergilla	layering	Aug	no	Transplant rooted layers in second autumn.	●●
Fuchsia				See page 104 for taking cuttings.	●●●
Garrya elliptica	hardwood cuttings	Oct to Nov	no	Take 10−15cm (4−6in) basal cuttings and root in the open ground or cold frame. In the cold frame they may root by spring – leave outdoor cuttings until the following autumn.	●●
Gaultheria	basal cuttings	Aug	no	Insert 5−13cm (2−5in) cuttings in a pot covered with a plastic bag or in a cold frame.	●●
	division	Spr	-	Line out divisions in a shady part of the garden and keep moist.	●●
	suckers	Aut	-	As for division.	●●●
	seed	Feb	-	Collect ripe seed, remove flesh and store dry. Sow in pots in the greenhouse. Harden off seedlings when 3cm (1in) high and line out in a shady position.	●●●
Genista (Spanish gorse)	basal cuttings	June	no	Take 5−8cm (2−3in) cuttings of new growth and root in a pot covered with a plastic bag. Pot on when rooted (in August or September), overwinter in a cold frame and plant out the following spring.	●●●
	basal cuttings	Oct	no	Take 10cm (4in) long cuttings of semi-ripe wood and root in a cold frame. Pot on in spring and plant out the following autumn.	●●●
	seed	Mar	-	Gather the seed when the pods start to turn black (late summer) and store until spring. Sow under glass and pot on when seedlings are 5cm (2in) tall. Plant out in June. Stake young plants to prevent them from becoming too floppy.	●●●
Griselinia	hardwood cuttings	Oct to Nov	no	Take 20−30cm (8−12in) nodal cuttings and bury bottom third in ground. In cold areas root in a cold frame. Transplant to final positions in late spring.	●●●
H					
Hamamelis (witch hazel)	layering	Spr	yes	Bend down shoots of one-year-old wood. Twist and slit shoots about 20cm (8in) from top. Tie shoot tip to a cane. Layers should root by the following spring.	●●
Hebe (shrubby veronica)	stem cuttings	Sep to Oct	no	Take 8−15cm (3−6in) semi-ripe cuttings (depending on species) and root in a cold frame. Pot up or plant out the following spring. May also root easily from softwood cuttings taken in May or June.	●●●

*Hormone means a rooting powder or solution   For an explanation of the different types of cuttings, see page 12

species	how	when	hor-mone*	what to do	how easy
Hibiscus	stem cuttings	July to Aug	no	Root 15cm (6in) cuttings in sandy compost in the cold frame. Pot up in spring and plant out the following spring.	●●
	seed	Spr	-	Sow in the open or in a cold frame. Move to final positions in autumn.	●●●
Hippophae rhamnoides (sea buckthorn)	seed	Aut	-	Sow ripe orange berries in trays. Leave outside over winter and bring into greenhouse or cold frame as soon as they start to germinate in spring. Prick out seedlings and grow on in a greenhouse or cold frame for autumn planting.	●●
	suckers	Win	-	Detach with spade and replant.	●●●
Hydrangea	stem cuttings	June to Aug	no	Take 10cm (4in) semi-ripe cuttings and root in a pot covered with a plastic bag. Hortensias and lacecaps (varieties of *H. macrophylla*) root more readily than other species.	●●●
Hypericum calycinum (rose of Sharon)	division	Spr	-	Lift with a spade to sever the tangle of creeping roots.	●●●
	rooted cuttings	Apr to May	no	Sever new shoots which have a few roots attached below ground level and then heap peat around the plant. Transplant once cuttings established. Use this method if you want lots of plants, for ground cover say.	●●
	seed	Aut	-	Collect when ripe in autumn and store dry. Sow in trays in the greenhouse, prick out when 5cm (2in) and transfer to a cold frame. Plant out in autumn.	●●
Hypericum (tall shrubby types)	cuttings	July to Nov	yes	Take 10cm (4in) semi-ripe cuttings and root in a cold frame. Pot on or plant out in spring.	●●●
I–K					
Ilex (holly)	nodal cuttings	Sep to Oct	yes	Take 10cm (4in) semi-ripe cuttings and wound the base before treating with rooting hormone. Root in peaty compost in the cold frame. To improve results, cover cuttings with polythene sheeting and bury the edges. Pot on in spring. It may take several years before cuttings are large enough to plant out.	●●
Indigofera	nodal cuttings	July	yes	Take 8cm (3in) semi-ripe cuttings and root in a pot covered with a plastic bag. Pot on when rooted (September) and overwinter under glass. Plant out in spring and trim back shoots to ensure bushy plants.	●●
Itea	basal cuttings	Sep	yes	Take 15–23cm (6–9in) semi-ripe cuttings, wound the base before treating with rooting hormone, and root in the cold frame. Pot on or plant out in spring.	●●●
Kalmia	layering	Spr	yes	Work peat and sand into the soil before bending down layer. Takes 2 years to root.	●
Kerria japonica	suckers	Spr	-	Detach with a spade and replant.	●●●
	hardwood cuttings	Oct to Nov	no	Take 20cm (8in) stem cuttings and bury bottom two-thirds in open ground. Transplant the following autumn.	●●●
Kolkwitzia amabilis	nodal cuttings	Aug	yes	Take 15cm (6in) semi-ripe cuttings and root in a cold frame. Pot on cuttings that have rooted in autumn and plant out the following spring.	●●

*Hormone means a rooting powder or solution   For an explanation of the different types of cuttings, see page 12

species	how	when	hor-mone*	what to do	how easy
L					
Laurus nobilis (sweet bay)				See Herbs, page 136.	
Lavatera olbia (shrubby mallow)	basal cuttings	June to July	no	Take 13cm (5in) semi-ripe cuttings and root in peaty compost in a cold frame. Pot up or plant out in autumn.	●●●
	nodal cuttings	Sep to Oct	no	As above. Plant out in spring.	●●●
Lavendula (lavender)				See Herbs, page 137.	
Leptospermum	hardwood cuttings	Oct to Nov	yes	Take 8cm (3in) basal cuttings and root in a cold frame. Plant out in spring.	●●●
	self-sown seedlings	Spr	-	In mild districts leptospermum may self-seed. Select those with the darkest foliage for growing on, as they usually have best colour flowers.	●●●
Leycesteria	seed	Aut	-	Sow fresh seed in trays in a cold frame. Prick out in spring and plant out when they reach a reasonable size.	●●●
	hardwood cuttings	Nov to Dec	no	Insert 20–25cm (8–10in) cuttings in a sand-lined trench. Should root by the following spring.	●●
Ligustrum (privet)	hardwood cuttings	Oct	yes	Take 30–38cm (12–15in) nodal cuttings. Remove soft tips, but leave a few leaves at the top and bury to two-thirds depth in open ground. Transplant the following autumn.	●●●
	nodal cuttings	July	yes	Take 10–13cm (4–5in) semi-ripe cuttings and root in peaty compost in a well-shaded cold frame. Plant out in autumn.	●●●
Lippia citriodora (lemon-scented verbena)	basal or nodal cuttings	May to July	no	Take 10cm (4in) semi-ripe cuttings and root in a pot covered with a plastic bag. Pot on after rooting (around 6 weeks) and overwinter in a frost-free greenhouse or in a cool room.	●●●
Lonicera nitida (and non-climbing honeysuckles)	hardwood cuttings	Oct to Nov	no	Take 20–25cm (8–10in) stem cuttings and root in sandy compost in a cold frame or, in mild districts, in open ground. Pot on or plant out in spring.	●●●
	basal or nodal cuttings	June to July	no	Take 10cm (4in) semi-ripe cuttings and root in a pot covered with a plastic bag. Pot on or plant out in autumn.	●●●
M					
Magnolia	layering	Spr	no	Layers from one-year-old shoots should root by late autumn. You can also layer in August using current year's shoots, but rooting will take 2 years.	●
Mahonia	leaf bud cuttings	Feb or Sep to Oct	no	Root in peat compost in a heated propagator at 15°C (60°F). May be worth trying in a pot covered with a plastic bag over a radiator indoors.	●●●

*Hormone means a rooting powder or solution   For an explanation of the different types of cuttings, see page 12

species	how	when	hor-mone*	what to do	how easy
Myrtus communis (common myrtle)	basal cuttings	Nov	no	Take 10–15cm (4–6in) semi-ripe cuttings and root in a cold frame. Plant out in spring.	●●
N–O					
Nandina	hardwood cuttings	Nov to Dec	no	Take 10–15cm (4–6in) basal or nodal cuttings of one-year-old wood and root in a cold frame. Plant out the following autumn.	●
Olearia (daisy bush)	hardwood cuttings	Oct	no	Take 15–20cm (6–8in) heeled cuttings and root outdoors or in a cold frame. Transplant or pot on in early summer.	●●●
Osmanthus	hardwood cuttings	Oct	yes	Take 15–20cm (6–8in) heeled cuttings and root in a cold frame. Pot up or plant out in late spring.	●
	layering	Aut	no	Should root by following autumn or spring.	●●
P					
Pachysandra	division	Spr	-	Split up clumps and replant 20cm (8in) apart.	●●●
Paeonia, tree	seed (species only)	Aut	-	Sow as soon as ripe in pots or boxes in the cold frame. Roots will form the first year, but shoots won't appear until the second spring.	●●
Parrotia persica	layering	Spr	-	As for Hamamelis, page 24.	●●
Pernettya mucronata	division	Spr	-	Replant about 60cm (2ft) apart.	●●●
	basal cuttings	June to July	no	Root in peat in the cold frame and cover cuttings with clear polythene. Overwinter in the cold frame and plant out the following autumn.	●●●
Perowskia (Russian sage)	nodal or heel cuttings	July to Aug	yes	Take 10cm (4in) semi-ripe cuttings and root in a pot covered with a plastic bag. Pot on and overwinter in the cold frame.	●●
Phlomis fruticosa (Jerusalem sage)	nodal cuttings	Sep	no	Take 8–10cm (3–4in) semi-ripe cuttings. Root in a cold frame and plant out in spring.	●●●
Philadelphus (mock orange)	nodal cuttings	June to July	yes	Take 10cm (4in) semi-ripe cuttings and root in a pot covered with a plastic bag. Pot on and overwinter in a cold frame.	●●●
	internodal cuttings	Sep	yes	As above, but root in a cold frame. Pot on or plant out in spring.	●●●
	hardwood cuttings	Nov to Dec	yes	Take 20cm (8in) heel cuttings and bury bottom two-thirds in ground. Transplant the following autumn.	●●●
Phormium (New Zealand flax)	division	Spr	-	Cut up roots with a sharp knife and pot up or replant. Each portion should have a strong root attached.	●●●
	seed	Spr	-	Sow under glass at 18°C (65°F) for good germination. Prick out when large enough to handle and gradually harden off and move to a cold frame. Plant out the following spring. Seedlings will show some variation.	●●
Photinia	nodal cuttings	July to Aug	yes	Take 10cm (4in) semi-ripe cuttings and root in a pot covered with a plastic bag. Pot up and overwinter in the cold frame.	●●

*Hormone means a rooting powder or solution   For an explanation of the different types of cuttings, see page 12

species	how	when	hor-mone*	what to do	how easy
Pieris	layering	Aut	no	Mix sand and peat into soil before pegging down shoots of current year's growth. Twist stem to aid rooting, which should be the following autumn.	●●●
	basal cuttings	July to Aug	yes	Root in peat in a heated propagator at 21°C (70°F). Pot up in autumn and overwinter in a cold frame.	●●
Piptanthus	seed	Feb to Mar	-	Collect ripe seed pods in late summer or autumn and extract seeds. Store in a cool place and sow under glass in spring. Prick out seedlings into individual pots and grow on under glass for autumn planting.	●●
Pittosporum	basal cuttings	Oct	yes	Take 8–10cm (3–4in) semi-ripe cuttings and wound the base before treating with rooting hormone powder. Insert cuttings in a cold frame and cover with clear polythene. Check cuttings regularly from early spring and harden off and pot as soon as they have rooted.	●
	seed	Oct	-	Collect ripe seed in October and treat as for Piptanthus, above. Plant out when about 3cm (1ft) tall.	●●●
Potentilla fruticosa	basal cuttings	Sep	yes	Take 8–15cm (3–6in) semi-ripe cuttings, remove any flower buds and root in the cold frame. Pot on or plant out in spring.	●●●
	nodal or basal cuttings	June to July	yes	Take 10–15cm (4–6in) cuttings from new shoots and root in a pot covered with a plastic bag. Pot on once rooted (4 to 6 weeks) and plant out in autumn.	●●
Prunus laurocerasus and P. lusitanica (laurels)	basal cuttings	Sep	yes	Take 10cm (4in) semi-ripe cuttings and root in a cold frame. Pot on or plant out in late spring.	●●●
Pyracantha	heel cuttings	Sep	yes	Take 10–15cm (4–6in) semi-ripe cuttings and root in a cold frame. Pot up in spring and grow on under glass for autumn or spring planting.	●●
R					
Rhamnus	heel cuttings	July to Aug	yes	Take 10–15cm (4–6in) cuttings in pots covered with plastic bags or in a cold frame covered with a sheet of polythene. Variegated forms are more difficult.	●
Rhododendron	layering	Spr or Aut	no	Slit stems of young shoots about 15cm (6in) from tip to make a tongue. Incorporate peat and sand in soil before pegging down. Lift after 1½ to 2 years.	●●
	nodal cuttings	June to July	yes	Take 10–13cm (4–5in) semi-ripe cuttings and root in a pot covered with a plastic bag using a peaty compost. Remove growing tip and, with large-leaved species, cut the leaves in half. Pot up into lime-free compost and grow on under glass for a year or so.	●
Rhus	suckers	Aut or Spr	-	Scrape away the soil around the base of the shrub and detach rooted suckers with a spade or sharp knife. Transplant immediately.	●●●
	root cuttings	Dec	no	Insert 3cm (1¼in) root sections the right way up in individual pots. Keep under glass and pot on or plant out in late spring.	●●
Ribes	hardwood cuttings	Oct	yes	Take 20–25cm (8–10in) cuttings and bury bottom two-thirds in the ground. Root in final position or transplant in spring or autumn. Trim back in second spring to encourage branching.	●●●

*Hormone means a rooting powder or solution   For an explanation of the different types of cuttings, see page 12

species	how	when	hormone*	what to do	how easy
Romneya	root cuttings	Dec	no	Cut thin roots into 3cm (1in) sections and plant horizontally in trays of sandy compost. Keep under glass and pot on or plant out in early summer (several months after first shoots appear).	●●
Rosa (roses)	hardwood cuttings	Oct	yes	Select 23–30cm (9–12in) cuttings of about pencil thickness and bury bottom two-thirds in the ground.	●●●
Rubus cockburnianus	root cuttings	Nov	no	Take 3cm (1in) root sections and pot up individually and keep in greenhouse over winter. Grow on in pots for planting out in autumn. Suckers can also be detached in dormant season.	●●
Rubus tricolor	tip layering	any time	no	See Blackberries, page 115, for method.	●●●
Ruscus aculeatus (butcher's broom)	division	Spr	-	Separate creeping roots with a sharp knife and replant.	●●●
Ruta graveolens (rue)	cuttings	July	no	Tips of semi-ripe shoots will root easily in a pot covered with a plastic bag. Pot up once rooted and plant out in spring.	●●●
S					
Salix, dwarf (willow)	hardwood cuttings	Jan to Feb	no	For dwarf species, such as *Salix helvetica* and *S. lanata* (wooly willow), root 5–10cm (2–4in) cuttings in pots in the cold frame.	●●●
Sambucus nigra (elder)	hardwood cuttings	Jan to Feb	no	Take 20–30cm (8–12in) heel cuttings and bury bottom two-thirds in the ground. Root in final position or transplant the following autumn.	●●●
Santolina (cotton lavender)	stem cuttings	Sep	yes	Take 8cm (3in) semi-ripe cuttings and root in a cold frame. Pot on or plant out in spring.	●●●
Sarcococca	suckers	Spr	-	Lift established clumps just as they are showing signs of growth, divide with a sharp knife and replant immediately.	●●●
	hardwood cuttings	Oct	yes	Take 8–10cm (3–4in) basal cuttings of one-year-old wood and root in a cold frame. Pot on or plant out in late spring or early summer.	●●
Senecio greyi (S. 'Sunshine', S. laxifolius)	basal or nodal cuttings	Aug to Oct	yes	Take 10–15cm (4–6in) semi-ripe or hardwood cuttings and root in a cold frame using a sandy compost. Plant out in spring.	●●●
Skimmia	hardwood cuttings	Sep	yes	Take 15cm (6in) basal cuttings and root in a cold frame. Pot on or plant out the following spring. For berries you need 1 male variety to every 3 female varieties.	●●●
	nodal tip cuttings	June	no	Trim shoot tips below the first leaf node. Root in a pot covered with a plastic bag using a peaty compost. Alternatively, root in a cold frame and cover with polythene. Pot on or plant out in late summer or early autumn.	●●
Spartium junceum (Spanish broom)	seed	Aut or Spr	-	Collect seed in autumn and store in cool conditions for sowing under glass in spring. Pot on when seedlings are around 15cm (6in) and plant out in summer.	●●●
Spirea	hardwood cuttings	Aut	no	Take 15–20cm (6–8in) stem cuttings. Either plant in final position or move the following autumn.	●●
	nodal cuttings	June to July	no	Root 5–8cm (2–3in) cuttings in a pot covered with a plastic bag. Pot up once rooted and plant out in autumn or spring.	●●●

*Hormone means a rooting powder or solution   For an explanation of the different types of cuttings, see page 12

species	how	when	hormone*	what to do	how easy
Stranvaesia	seed	Aut		Collect berries before they are fully ripe. Extract seed, sow in pots and leave outside over winter. Once you see signs of germination, bring pots into a cold frame.	●●
Symphoricarpus	hardwood cuttings	Oct	no	Plant 15–20cm (6–8in) cuttings with bottom two-thirds buried in ground. Move to final positions the following autumn.	●●●
Syringa (lilac)	layering	Spr	no	Beware of layering shoots of *S. vulgaris* varieties, as these are often grafted on to the common lilac. To be sure you are propagating the desirable variety, try air layering (see page 44).	●●●
T–Y					
Tamarix (tamarisk)	hardwood cuttings	Nov	no	Take 20–25cm (8–10in) cuttings and either root in final position or transplant the following autumn.	●●●
Ulex europaeus (gorse)	basal cuttings	Sep	yes	Take 10–15cm (4–6in) semi-ripe cuttings and root in pots of peaty compost in the cold frame. Pot up or plant in spring.	●●●
Viburnum (deciduous)	hardwood cuttings	Oct	yes	*V. x bodnantense, V. fragrans/V. farreri,* and *V. tomentosum.* Take 13cm (5in) sections of stem, trimming each one below a node. Root the cuttings in peaty compost in the cold frame, burying them so just the top is showing. Give a liquid feed every two weeks through spring and summer and plant out in autumn.	●●
	layering	Spr	no	Easy for *V. opulus* and *V. tomentosum,* which produce low branches. Layers should root by the autumn.	●●●
	basal cuttings	July to Aug	yes	*V. carlesii, V. x juddii, V. carlcephalum.* Take 10–15cm (4–6in) semi-ripe cuttings and wound the base before treating with a rooting hormone. Root in a pot covered with a plastic bag.	●
Viburnum (evergreen)	basal cuttings	Sep	yes	Take 13cm (5in) semi-ripe cuttings and remove any flower buds. Root in a cold frame using a peaty compost. Pot on or plant out in spring. Suitable method for *V. davidii* and *V. tinus.*	●●●
	stem cuttings	June to July	yes	Take 8cm (3in) cuttings from young shoots. Wound the base before treating with a rooting hormone and root in a pot covered with a plastic bag. Pot on in early autumn and overwinter in a cold frame.	●●
Vinca (periwinkle)	division	Spr	no	Split up into small pieces and replant immediately.	●●●
	stem cuttings	Oct	no	Take 8–10cm (3–4in) cuttings and root in peaty compost in the cold frame. Plant out in spring.	●●
Weigela	hardwood cuttings	Oct to Nov	yes	Take 23cm (9in) cuttings and wound the base before treating with a rooting hormone. Root in final positions or transplant the following autumn. Trim back to get bushy plants.	●●●
	basal cuttings	June	yes	Take 13cm (5in) soft or semi-ripe cuttings and root in a pot covered with a plastic bag using a peaty compost. Pot on or plant out in autumn.	●●●
Yucca	offsets	Spr	no	Young offsets with a few roots can be carefully severed with a sharp knife. Grow on in a sandy compost until well rooted.	●●●
	toes	Spr	no	Lift the plant and look for small swollen buds at the tips of the roots. These can be removed with a sharp knife, potted up and grown on in the greenhouse.	●●

*Hormone means a rooting powder or solution   For an explanation of the different types of cuttings, see page 12

Raising trees and shrubs from seed can be very worthwhile if you want a number of plants, for a hedge say, or for plants that are difficult to propagate by other methods, such as daphnes. In the case of many trees, seed is often the only practical method, and in most instances you can grow for little or no cost specimens which in two or three years will be as large as those available at garden centres.

The limitation with growing from seed is that you are restricted to the species, as seed from varieties usually produces variable results. Certain varieties of mountain ash, such as *Sorbus latifolia* 'Majestic', however, do breed true from seed, and with Japanese maples you may get a lot of colour variation but most will be garden-worthy plants.

Japanese maples are well worth raising from seed as, although the seedlings won't be identical to the parent plant, you can get some very attractive colour variations. For best results, sow fresh seed straight from the tree.

OBTAINING THE SEED

The first decision is whether you buy the seed or collect your own.

Saving your own seed has a number of advantages:

● You can see what the plant is like beforehand. Collect seed only from strong healthy plants.
● The offspring of plants growing locally are likely to do well in your garden.
● You can collect the seed at exactly the right stage. In most cases fresh seed gives the best results and is absolutely essential for some trees, such as chestnuts and oaks.

Collecting your own seed is not always easy, though. You may be in competition with birds and rodents, and you may need a ladder or pole pruner.

Buying seed is only worthwhile for certain trees (see Tables on pages 36 to 41) and the seed's performance is very dependent on how fresh it is and how well it has been stored. Unfortunately, this is often impossible to determine beforehand.

The advantages in buying seed are that you don't have to locate a mature tree in order to collect the seed, and it is the only way of getting seed for trees that don't seed in this country.

Tree and shrub seed is available from several large seedsmen and bonsai nurseries. You may also be able to get reasonably fresh seed through seed distribution schemes run by horticultural societies, such as the Alpine Garden Society, the Northern Horticultural Society and the Royal Horticultural Society (see Useful Addresses).

SPECIAL TREATMENTS

Some tree and shrub seeds, such as brooms and eucalyptus, can be sown in the spring in the greenhouse without any problems. Most trees and shrubs, however, require, or will germinate more reliably, if given some form of special treatment. Details for individual species are given in the Tables for shrubs (pages 19 to 30), deciduous trees (pages 36 to 41), conifers (pages 54 to 57) and climbers (pages 48 to 51). The techniques are described below.

Cold and warm treatments

Some seeds have what is called double dormancy and need a period of warmth followed by a period of cold in order to germinate. The wayfaring tree (*Viburnum lantana*), for example, has been known to give best results if the seed is mixed with moist sand and kept at 20–30°C (68–86°F) for 2 to 4 weeks, then in a fridge at 3°C (40°F) for 16 weeks.

Cold treatments

Many shrubs and trees come from areas of the world which have cold winters, and their seeds often require a period at around 1–3°C (34–38°F) before they will germinate.

To simulate winter, mix seeds with moist peat in a polythene bag and put them in the fridge for 6 to 8 weeks. Don't forget to label the seeds.

Fresh seed With home-saved seed, the easiest way to provide a cold period is to sow in autumn as soon as it's collected. Small quantities of seed are best sown in pots or trays in the cold frame, as it's easier to guard against rodents. Alternatively, you can mix the seed with peat in a plastic bag and keep it in the fridge over winter for spring sowing. Seed that requires exposure to two winters in order to germinate is best stratified (see hard seeds, opposite page).

Bought or stored seed So long as the seed is not adversely affected by drying out (see details under individual plants), the seed can simply be placed in paper bags in the fridge for 6 to 8 weeks prior to sowing. Check seed regularly and sow immediately if it germinates prematurely. Otherwise, mix the seed with moist peat first, as for fresh seed. Spring sowing is still best as high temperatures – above 25°C (80°F) – later in the season can induce secondary dormancy in many tree seeds, and they will then require a further cold period in order to germinate.

Hard seeds

Some seeds develop a hard seed coat if dried, in storage for example, or if allowed to mature fully on the tree. This hard seed coat prevents the seed absorbing moisture.

Dormancy can be overcome in a number of ways, depending on how hard the seed coat is:

● Seed of plants such as laburnum and piptanthus can be soaked in warm water for 24 hours, in a thermos flask say, prior to sowing. Any seed that sinks will have taken up water and should germinate once sown.

● Other seeds, such as cercis, cytisus and gleditsia, will respond to soaking in near-boiling water. Let the water cool and then remove the seeds that sink. Repeat up to five times until you have sufficient seeds to sow.

● With seeds such as robinia the hard seed coat can be broken down by scarification (rubbing it away). The easiest way to do this is to line a jar with sandpaper, place the seeds inside, screw the lid on tight

and give it a good shake for at least 10 minutes or so. You can then soak the seed for up to 24 hours. If the seed sinks, you know you've done the trick. If it floats, try a further period in the jam jar.

With larger seed it may also be possible to make a nick in the seed coat with a nailfile or a sharp knife as an alternative to the sandpaper method. However, it is easy to damage the seed or slip and cut your finger if the seed is very hard.

● Some seeds, such as hawthorns and yew, have such hard seed coats that it is not possible to break them down mechanically. To overcome dormancy, the seed is stratified over two winters so that the seed coat can break down naturally. All this means is that the seed is mixed with moist sand and peat and left outside for 18 months prior to spring sowing. An old biscuit tin with drainage holes in the bottom is best, as it will keep out birds and rodents. Place the box somewhere cool, such as at the foot of a north-facing wall.

Softening the hard seed coats with near-boiling water.

Berries

Most berries are very attractive to birds, so if you want to save seeds it is advisable to place a net over a well-laden branch well before they show colour. Some berries, such as daphnes, are best collected when green and sown immediately before the seed coat hardens.

Most berries can be sown or stratified as they are (in some cases the temperature lift provided by the composting flesh can aid germination). Seed that is stratified can easily be separated out prior to sowing. Many people, however, prefer to extract the seed. The easiest way to do this is to place the berries in a polythene bag on a hard surface and gently squash them with a piece of wood. If you are extracting a lot of seed, place the pulp in a bucket of water – in a day or so viable seeds should sink to the bottom and can be removed for sowing.

Rubbing down seed coats with sandpaper in a jar.

Nicking the seed coat with a sharp knife.

SOWING

If you want **a number of plants**, for a hedge say, you can sow in a seedbed outdoors in the autumn provided you have a reasonably well-drained soil. On heavy soil you could construct a raised bed, with four railway sleepers say, and fill it with equal parts of sharp sand, peat and soil. Fine seed is usually sown broadcast on the surface of the soil and then covered with a thin layer of sharp sand and firmed down. Large seed can be sown 8–10cm (3–4in) apart.

Cover the seedbed with wire netting to keep off birds, and put down traps for mice. Treat the seed with a combined insecticide and fungicide dressing to guard against soil pests and diseases.

Most conifers and several shrubs and trees tend to

germinate very early in spring from autumn sowings. Unless you can provide cloche protection, it's better to sow in the cold frame or delay sowing until spring. Don't thin the seedlings – wait until autumn, then grow them on at a wider spacing or plant out.

If you want only **a few plants**, sow in trays or pots in the cold frame. Once the seeds start to germinate, you could bring them into a warm greenhouse to encourage growth. Once they are large enough to handle, the seedlings can be potted up individually in 8cm (3in) pots. For many species you can get rapid results if you keep them on a capillary bench in the greenhouse for several months, and then harden them off for autumn planting.

COLLECTING TREE SEEDS

Correct timing is critical when collecting tree seeds. With maples (*Acer* spp), for example, germination can be delayed for a year if you wait until the winged seeds become hard and dry. With berries, you are in competition with birds, so collect them as soon as they show colour. The illustrated guide on these two pages tells you when to collect seed for a selection of trees. Full sowing and cultivation details can be found on pages 36 to 41.

Acer palmatum (*Japanese maple*)
Collect ripe seed Aug–Nov and sow immediately.

Acer platanoides (*Norway maple*)
Collect seed as soon as it turns yellow (Sep/Oct) and sow immediately.

Aesculus × carnea (*red chestnut*)
Collect ripe conkers Sep–Oct and sow immediately.

Alnus glutinosa (*alder*)   Collect seed as it starts to turn brown from Sep. Sow immediately.

Betula pendula (*silver birch*)   Collect seed from Aug onwards. Best sown immediately.

Carpinus betulis (*hornbeam*)   Collect as wings turn yellow and sow immediately.

Castanea sativa (*sweet chestnut*)
Collect chestnuts Oct–Nov and sow immediately.

Cercis siliquastrum (*Judas tree*)
Collect ripe seed from Sep onwards. Store for spring sowing.

Corylus avellana (*hazel*)   Collect nuts in Oct and sow immediately.

Crataegus crus-galli (*cockspur*)   Collect ripe berries in Sep–Oct and stratify over two winters before sowing.

Davidia involcrata (*handkerchief tree*)
Collect seed in Oct and stratify for two winters.

Fagus sylvatica (*beech*) *Collect beech nuts Sep–Oct and sow immediately.*

Tilia europaea (*lime*) *Collect seed while still green in Sep and sow immediately.*

Fraxinus excelsior (*ash*) *Collect winged seed just before it turns brown, from Aug onwards.*

Juglans regia (*walnut*) *Collect walnuts in autumn, remove husk and stratify in fridge over winter.*

Laburnum alpinum *Collect seed in Sep–Oct and store for spring sowing.*

Morus nigra (*mulberry*) *Extract seed from ripe fruits in late Aug and stratify in fridge over winter.*

Nothofagus procera (*southern beech*) *Collect seed in Sep–Oct and sow immediately.*

Prunus avium (*bird cherry*) *Pick ripe fruits in July before the birds eat them and stratify over winter.*

Quercus robur (*oak*) *Collect acorns as soon as they are ripe in Sep–Oct and sow immediately.*

Sorbus aucuparia (*rowan*) *Pick berries as soon as they show colour (July–Sep) and sow immediately.*

Sorbus aria (*whitebeam*) *Pick berries as soon as they show colour (July) and sow immediately.*

species	how	when	what to do	how easy
A				
Acer (maples) *Note:* Although acers can be propagated from cuttings, they are generally very difficult to root unless you have a mist propagator. For amateurs, seed is probably the best method.	fresh seed	Aut	Seed is best collected fresh before it starts to dry out and harden (for most maples this will be when the winged seeds turn yellow). Sow immediately in trays in the cold frame. Once they germinate in spring, growth will be more rapid if you bring them into a warm greenhouse. Once they have their first few leaves, pot individually. For quicker results, grow on in the greenhouse until autumn – many species can make 1m (3ft) of growth in the first year. If you can't sow immediately, mix the seed with moist peat in a plastic bag and keep it in the fridge over winter, then sow in the cold frame in spring. Most species maples will come true from seed (though some, such as *A. hersii*, readily hybridise and can produce variable results), but varieties of Japanese maples will produce a very mixed bunch of seedlings. Sow a lot more than you need and select the best forms.	●●●
	bought seed	Aut or Spr	With some species, such as *A. davidii*, *A. grosseri* and *A. hersii*, bought seed should germinate if treated as above and kept in the fridge for 6 to 8 weeks. Many other species, including Japanese maples, need exposure to 2 winters before they will germinate if not sown fresh. If bought seed is more than a year old or has been poorly stored, germination is likely to be very poor indeed.	● to ●●
	air layering	Spr	As Japanese maples are so expensive to buy, air layering a single branch (see page 44) is worthwhile if you have a good form. Done in spring, you should be able to prune off and plant the rooted layer in autumn.	●●
Aesculus (horse chestnut)	seed	Aut	*A. x carnea* (red chestnut), unlike most others, will not outgrow a reasonably sized garden, and, although a hybrid, breeds relatively true from seed. However, the seed only fully matures in a good summer, and only the conkers that turn completely brown are suitable for sowing. Sow conkers as soon as they drop, either in deep pots in the cold frame (best in cold areas) or outdoors. In both cases protect from mice. Treat with a seed dressing if sowing outdoors.	●●●
	root cuttings	Dec to Jan	*A. parviflora* is the best horse chestnut for gardens, as it barely reaches 3m (10ft). Carefully excavate the soil around the plant and remove a root. Cut into 8cm (3in) sections, making a straight cut at the top and a slanted cut at the bottom. Bury the cuttings *upside down* in moist sand outdoors, and plant them out the *right way round* in April. Cuttings will make little growth the first year, but may reach 60cm (2ft) or more by the second year. Any suckers can also be detached and transplanted.	●●
Ailanthus (tree of heaven)	root cuttings	Dec to June	Take root cuttings as for *Aesculus* above and pot the right way up in peat and sand in the cold frame. Once cuttings have well-developed shoots, pot up and grow on for planting out in autumn.	●●
	bought seed	Spr	Bought seed may germinate without special treatment, though a few weeks in the fridge can improve results. Sow in spring in a cool greenhouse or cold frame. Seedlings may reach 30cm (12in) or so in the first year. Expect fairly poor germination from bought seed. One disadvantage of seed-raised plants is that you will not know what sex they are – male plants give off an unpleasant odour when in flower.	●●
Alnus (alder)	fresh seed	Aut to Win	Alder seeds are borne in cone-like strobiles, and the best method of collection is to cut branches just as the cones start to turn brown and hang them up to dry. The branches can be shaken at intervals and the seed collected on a cloth below. Seed is best sown when fresh, though some should still germinate if you delay until spring. Sow in pots or deep trays. Spread the seeds thinly on the surface and cover with a thin layer of sharp sand. Pot on when a few inches high and grow on for autumn planting, when they should be 30cm (12in) or more in height.	●●

species	how	when	what to do	how easy
B–D				
Betula (birch)	fresh or bought seed	Aut to Win	The seed is borne in strobiles, like *Alnus*, and these can be picked off before they are ripe and spread out to dry. When dry, rub the strobile between your fingers to separate the seed. There will still probably be a lot of debris among the seed, but it is easier to sow the whole lot. The seed is best sown in the autumn, as for *Alnus*. If spring germination is poor, bring the seeds into the warmth. If seed is stored without winter chilling (as is the case with bought seed), it then needs light in order to germinate. Sow on the surface of compost, cover the pots or trays with glass and keep out of direct sunlight. The seeds should start to germinate by June. With fresh seed sown in autumn, you can easily expect 1m (3ft) or more of growth in the first year.	●●●
Carpinus (hornbeam)	fresh seed	Aut	The winged seeds are best collected before they ripen, just as the wings turn yellow. If sown in pots, as for *Alnus*, and left outside over winter, you should get reasonable germination in spring.	●●
	bought seed	Spr	If seeds are harvested when hard and dry, or if seed is bought, it may take 2 winters before the seed germinates.	●
Castanea (sweet chestnut)	fresh seed	Aut	Sow ripe nuts outdoors or in pots. Check that seed is viable and pest free by placing it in water – discard any that float. Provided seed has not had a chance to dry out, germination in spring should be good, though you will have to wait around 30 to 40 years before the tree produces nuts. Protect seed against mice over winter.	●●●
Cercidiphyllum	bought seed	Spr	As for *Cercis*, above.	●●
	basal cuttings	June	Take cuttings from young shoots about 15cm (6in) long and root in a pot covered with a polythene bag. Pot on rooted cuttings in July or August and plant out in autumn.	●●
Cercis siliquastrum (Judas tree)	fresh or bought seed	Spr	Sow in trays in the cold frame or cold greenhouse. Pot up seedlings when about 8cm (3in) and grow on for planting out in autumn. Seedlings are likely to reach 15cm (6in) or so in the first year. As long as bought seed is reasonably fresh, you should have few problems.	●●
Cornus mas, Cornus kousa	bought seed	Aut	Bought seed is likely to take 2 winters before it germinates. Rubbing down the seed coat with sandpaper (see page 33) may help germination, but the seed will still need overwintering outdoors or 6 weeks in the fridge prior to sowing (mix with moist peat in a plastic bag).	●●
Corylus avellana, Corylus maxima (cobs, filberts and hazelnuts)	layering	Spr	Peg down young shoots about 30cm (12in) from tip and twist stem sharply to aid rooting and tie to cane. Layers should root by the following spring.	●●
	seed	Aut	Gather seed in autumn before the squirrels get it and store in damp sand over winter. Sow outdoors in spring. Germination can be erratic.	●●
	suckers	Aut	Remove rooted suckers with a spade and replant immediately.	●●●
Crataegus species (hawthorns)	fresh seed	Aut	Collect ripe berries of species only and mix with moist peat in a biscuit tin with drainage holes at the bottom. Leave outside for 2 winters and sow early in the second spring before seed starts to germinate.	●●
Davidia involucrata (handkerchief tree)	fresh seed	Aut	Collect the ripe fruits in early autumn and mix with damp peat in a biscuit tin with drainage holes in the bottom. Leave outside until the following autumn, by which time they will have started to form roots. The individual seeds can then be carefully sown in pots and left outside for the winter. Shoots should emerge the following spring.	●

species	how	when	what to do	how easy
E–F				
Eucalyptus (gum trees)	bought seed	Spr	Sow under glass in early spring at around 18°C (65°F). Prick out seedlings into individual pots and grow on for planting out in summer or autumn. They can easily grow 1m (3ft) in the first year.	●●●
Eucryphia x nymanensis	heel cuttings	June to July	Take cuttings from 8cm (3in) side shoots and treat with a rooting hormone. They should root in 5 to 6 weeks in a heated propagator. Pot up and keep in a cold frame or cool greenhouse over winter.	●●
	bought seed	Feb	The species *E. cordifolia* and *E. glutinosa* (from which *E. x nymanensis* was derived) can be grown from seed. Sow under glass in February, prick out seedlings individually in small pots and, for quickest results, grow on under glass until the following spring.	●●●
Fagus sylvatica (beech)	fresh seed	Aut	Sow ripe nuts straight away. They can be sown outdoors, but they are easier to protect from rodents if sown in pots in the cold frame. Germination in spring should be good provided the seed did not have chance to dry out prior to sowing. Purple-leaved forms, while not true from seed, should produce a proportion of coloured-leaved seedlings (though some may revert later).	●●●
Fraxinus excelsior (ash)	fresh seed	Aug to Sep	Collect the winged seed before it turns brown and sow immediately. They can be sown outdoors but are best sown in pots in the cold frame as seeds germinate in early spring and can be susceptible to frost damage. If you wait until seeds turn hard and brown, it may take 2 winters before they germinate.	●●
G				
Ginkgo biloba (maidenhair tree)	bought seed	Spr	As long as the seed has been harvested the previous autumn and stored under the correct conditions, it will germinate rapidly if sown under glass at a temperature of 18°C (65°F) in early spring. Seedlings can easily reach 30cm (12in) in the first year. However, if seed is a year or more old, germination may be extremely poor.	● to ●●●
Gleditsia triacanthos (honey locust)	bought seed	Spr	Seed has a very hard coat. It should be abraided in a jar with sandpaper (see page 33) and then soaked in warm water for an hour or so prior to sowing. Seed is best sown in a greenhouse in spring as seedlings are frost tender.	●●
J–K				
Juglans regia (walnut)	fresh seed	Aut	Collect fruit from the ground and rub away fleshy husk (wear gloves, as the flesh stains). Dip in a fungicide solution to prevent moulds, mix with peat in a polythene bag and keep in the fridge over winter (though check regularly and sow immediately if it starts to germinate). Sow in pots in the cold frame in spring.	●●
Koelreuteria paniculata (golden rain tree)	bought seed	Spr	The seed stores well over several years, so you can expect reasonable results from bought seed. Soak seed for 24 hours prior to sowing or treat with near-boiling water and allow to cool. Best sown in trays in the cold frame in early spring. Prick out seedlings into individual pots and grow on for planting out in autumn, when they may be 60cm (2ft) high.	●●●
L–N				
Laburnum	hardwood cuttings	Jan to Feb	Take 15–23cm (6–9in) cuttings and plant in a sand-lined trench outdoors. Cuttings should root by the following autumn and can be transplanted to final positions.	●●●
	fresh or bought seed	Aut	Suitable method for common laburnum (*L. anagyroides*) and Scotch laburnum (*L. alpinum*). Shell seed from the pods and store dry for sowing in spring. Soaking the seed for 24 hours prior to sowing will aid germination. Seedlings can be transplanted to final position in autumn.	●●

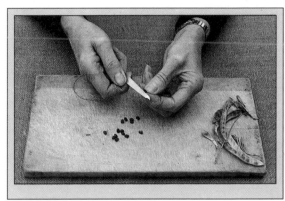

Top left: To extract seeds, place berries in a plastic bag and crush with a rolling-pin. Separate the pulp in a bowl of water. Bottom left: To stratify berries, place them in layers of peat in a pot. Cover the pot with bubble polythene and mesh, then place outside.

Top right: With hard seeds, you can make a small nick in the seed coat using a nailfile so they can take up water. Bottom right: A quick test to see if seeds are likely to germinate is to place them in a bowl of water. Use the ones that sink and reject the ones that float.

species	how	when	what to do	how easy
Ligustrum lucidum	hardwood cuttings	Oct to Nov	Although a privet, it is quite slow to root from cuttings. Take 25–30cm (8–12in) nodal or heel cuttings of current year's shoots. Remove soft tips, but retain 3 or 4 leaves at the top. Treat with a liquid rooting hormone and plant out in sand-lined trenches outdoors or, in exposed areas, in the cold frame. Cuttings should root by the following autumn.	●●
Liquidambar styraciflua	bought seed	Win	Seed has to be bought and will need cold treatment before it germinates. Either stratify the seed or mix it with moist peat in a plastic bag and keep it in the fridge for at least 12 weeks. Sow in trays on the surface of the compost and cover with a fine layer of sharp sand or grit. Keep the seed in the cold frame and bring into warmth once it starts to germinate to harden growth. Pot on seedlings and grow on until large enough to plant out. Germination is likely to be poor, especially if seed is not fresh.	●
	layering	Oct to Nov	Peg down shoots of current season's growth about 15cm (6in) from the tip. Incorporate sharp sand into the soil below the layer and twist shoot to aid rooting. Move to final position the following autumn.	●●

species	how	when	what to do	how easy
Liriodendron (tulip tree)	bought seed	Spr or Sum	Once seed has dried, it needs a period of warmth and a period of cold in order to germinate and is best stratified in moist peat and left outside for 2 winters. Sow conventionally in trays the second spring. Germination is likely to be very poor – you may get 2 or 3 seedlings from a packet. Prick out seedlings and grow on until large enough to plant out.	●
Morus nigra (mulberry)	fresh seed	Aug to Sep	Ripe fruit can be mashed up and placed in water. The pulp should float while seed sinks to the bottom. For best results, mix the seed with moist peat in a plastic bag and put in the fridge for 4 weeks prior to sowing. Seed can be sown in trays or an outdoor seedbed. They are quite fast growing and can be planted out in permanent positions in autumn.	●●●
	hardwood cuttings	Oct to Nov	Take 30–60cm (12–24in) cuttings, treat with a rooting hormone and insert 15–20cm (6–8in) deep in a cold frame. Plant out the following autumn and grow on for 2 years before moving to final position. Cuttings root quite easily, but young plants often succumb to disease. Fruiting takes around 10 years.	●●
Nothofagus (southern beech)	fresh seed	Aut	Collect the fresh seed, which is very similar to beech nuts, and sow 2 to a small pot. Leave outdoors in a cold frame over winter; if both germinate, remove one. The seedlings can be planted out when they are around 15cm (6in) high. By autumn they may be 30–60cm (12–24in). Seed deteriorates rapidly on drying, so buying seed is probably not worthwhile.	●●●
P				
Paulownia (foxglove tree)	bought seed	Spr	Needs no special treatment. Sow in trays under glass in early spring and prick out seedlings individually into small pots. They are best grown on under glass until mid-summer and then hardened off for autumn planting. Seedlings may reach 45cm (18in) or more in the first year.	●●●
Platanus (plane)	hardwood cuttings	Oct to Nov	After leaf fall take 25–30cm (8–12in) lengths of current season's wood and insert in open ground. Move to final position the following autumn.	●●●
Poplar	hardwood cuttings	Oct to Nov	As for *Platanus*, above.	●●●
Prunus (flowering cherries, plums and almonds)			Most trees are produced by grafting, and while Japanese flowering cherries can be grown from cuttings, this is not really a job for the amateur. However, a few flowering cherries and plums can be propagated quite simply – see below.	
Prunus avium (bird cherry), P. padus, P. sargentii	fresh seed	Sum	Pick ripe fruit as soon as available and stratify whole in moist peat. Leave outside and separate the seed for sowing outdoors or in pots in spring. Bought seed should be all right as long as it is not too old. Mix with moist peat and keep it in the fridge for 4 to 6 weeks prior to sowing.	●●
Prunus cerasifera (myrobalan plum)			See Fruit, page 116.	
Q−R				
Quercus (oak)	seed	Aut	Although oaks grow rather large for most gardens, they can be trained as hedges, particularly *Q. ilex*, the evergreen or holm oak. Collect acorns as soon as they are ripe and sow *immediately* in deep pots, as used for sweet peas, or in cardboard tubes filled with compost. Keep in a cold frame over winter and protect against rodents. Seedlings can be planted out when about 10–15cm (4–6in) high.	●●●

species	how	when	what to do	how easy
Robinia pseudoacacia (false acacia) *Note*: 'Frisia', the golden-leaved form, can be propagated only by grafting.	suckers	Aut	Separate with a spade and replant.	●●●
	root cuttings	Aut	Take 3cm (1in) sections of root and plant in pots in the cold frame.	●●●
	seed	Spr	Bought seed should give reasonable success. Soak seed in warm water for 24 hours and sow in pots or outdoors.	●●
S–T				
Salix (willows)	hardwood cuttings	Aut to Win	Cuttings of up to 3m (10ft) or more will root in open ground. However, those grown for their coloured stems, such as *S. alba* 'Britzensis', are best rooted from 30cm (1ft) cuttings. Cut the trees right back every year in spring to give a plentiful supply of new coloured stems. See page 29 for dwarf varieties.	●●●
Sorbus (whitebeam and mountain ash or rowan)	seed	July to Sep	Pick berries as soon as they show colour, extract seed and sow immediately in trays in the cold frame. If you wait until the seed is too ripe, germination may take 2 or 3 years, but with fresh seed sown before the seed coat hardens you stand a chance of getting reasonable germination in the first spring. Mixing the seed with moist peat and keeping it in the airing cupboard for the winter and then in the fridge for 3 months before sowing has been said to give good germination. Once germinated, mountain ashes are worth growing on in the greenhouse, as this way they can put on 1m (3ft) or more of growth in time for autumn planting. Unlike most plants, several of the varieties and hybrids, such as *S. latifolia* 'Majestica' and *S.* 'Joseph Rock', will come reasonably true from seed.	● to ●●
Stewartia pseudocamellia	bought seed	Spr	May germinate after soaking for 24 hours prior to sowing in the cold frame. For more reliable results, sow in pots, cover with a polythene bag and keep in the warm for 6 to 8 weeks and in the fridge for a further 8 to 12 weeks prior to sowing.	● to ●●
	heel cuttings	early June	Take 10cm (4in) cuttings from semi-ripe side shoots and root in a heated propagator. Pot up once rooted and keep under glass until the following spring.	●●
Styrax japonica	seed	Spr	Fresh seed can be stored dry over winter and sown in pots in the cold frame in spring. Lightly cover the seed with compost and cover the film with clinging film to prevent the seeds from drying out.	●●
Tilia (lime)	fresh seed	late Sum/ Aut	Germination can be poor and seed may need exposure to 2 winters before it will germinate. However, good results have been obtained by collecting the seed while it is still greenish and sowing before it starts to harden and dry out. If you can collect the seed at exactly the right time, it may give good germination the following spring.	●
	air layering	Spr	Commercially, young plants are pruned right back to produce suitable shoots for layering, though air layering (see page 44) would be worth trying. Allow up to 2 years for rooting.	●
U–Z				
Ulmus glabra 'Camperdownii' (Camperdown elm)	layering	Aug	This elm makes a small weeping tree. When shoots reach the ground they can be layered in the normal manner. The layer should form a good root system within 2 years.	●●●
Zelkova (Chinese elm)	bought seed	Spr	Bought seed can produce very variable results. Store in the fridge for 6 to 8 weeks before sowing. Sow in trays in the greenhouse. Pot on seedlings and grow on for autumn planting.	● to ●●
	fresh seed	Sep	If you can get it, seed collected while still green and sown immediately should produce good germination in the spring.	●●●

There are several ways to layer plants – which one you use will probably depend on the plant (the Table on page 46 lists the best methods to use for a selection of trees and shrubs). Whichever method you use, the plant that you are propagating from must be healthy, and you must provide suitable soil or compost. Always choose stems that are vigorous, and never use any that are showing pest or disease problems.

A bold group of Cornus alba *'Sibirica' brightens up the garden in winter. To propagate a number of plants, try French layering (see page 45).*

Most shrubs have some strong, vigorous stems that can be brought down to soil level, but sometimes it may be necessary to prune the bush or tree to obtain vigorous shoots for layering. Roots will not form readily in dry or poorly aerated soil. On the other hand, the soil should also have good moisture-holding capacity. Dig the soil deeply where simple or serpentine layers are to be buried, and work in peat to lighten the soil and improve moisture-retention. Grit will also help to lighten heavy soil.

For French layering only, just loosen the top 8–10cm (3–4in), as the soil must be firm enough for the pegs to hold the branches in position.

Layers will be more likely to root if the plant is in an open, sunny position, where the soil is likely to be warmer than in a shady spot.

Even if you are not in the habit of watering and feeding your shrubs, it's worth doing so while the layers are rooting. Water in dry weather and apply a balanced fertiliser such as Growmore to the parent plant at 140g a sq m (4oz a sq yd). Also remove any flowers that form on layered shoots.

Simple layering

Simple layering is probably the easiest and most effective method for a wide range of ornamental plants. For most plants it is best done in autumn or early spring. You need strong, actively growing shoots close to the ground.

How it's done
● Prune some low branches on an established plant during the dormant season to promote vigorous growth in spring. This is necessary only if you don't have any suitable branches.
● Cultivate the area around the plant, adding peat and grit.
● When you have selected a shoot, trim off side shoots below the growing point to make layering easier, and remove any leaves that would otherwise be buried (so that they don't rot). Pull the stem to the ground and mark a position on the soil 15–30cm (6–12in) behind the tip.

● Use a spade to remove a shallow trench 8–15cm (3–6in) deep with one straight side and a sloping side pointing towards the parent plant.
● Bend the stem at right-angles 20–23cm (8–9in) behind its tip, being careful that it doesn't snap, and peg it into position against the straight side of the trench using a piece of stiff wire bent into a peg, or use some other suitable anchor. This may be all that's necessary, as the V-shape into which the branch is bent will stimulate most plants to root. For more difficult plants, however, such as parottia, it may be necessary to injure the stem too. You can do this by making a slit on the underside of the stem, or by twisting the stem to injure it. You can also use a combination of both and make a cut on the upper side, then twist the stem at the cut to bring the tip upright. Another way of injuring

the stem is to use a method called girdling. This involves removing a narrow strip of bark about 2mm ($\frac{1}{6}$in) wide right around the stem. Winding copper wire tightly around the stem has a similar effect to girdling.
● Return the soil to the trench to bury the stem. If necessary, you can tie the tip to a cane to keep it upright. Water well.
● Plants layered in autumn or early spring will probably have rooted by the autumn, though much depends on the species. If they have rooted, sever the rooted layer from the parent plant in August or September. Cut back the growing tip by about 8–10cm (3–4in) if the plant is very vigorous and, 3 or 4 weeks later, lift the plant if sufficient roots have formed. If it does not seem to have rooted well, leave it in position for another year before lifting the layer.

Remove leaves and wound stem at the point where you are going to peg down the shoot.

Peg down the layer with a piece of bent wire and then tie the shoot to an upright cane.

Air layering

Air layering (also known as Chinese layering or marcottage) is quite often used by gardeners on leggy rubber plants, but the method can also be used on many trees and shrubs, and can be useful for climbers such as wisteria. It is best done in spring on wood that has matured the previous year, or in late summer on the hardening shoots of the current season's growth. Air layering is a useful method of propagation where there are no branches to bring down for simple layering – on large magnolias and some rhododendrons, for example.

How it's done
● Select a suitable stem and trim off any side shoots for 15–30cm (6–12in) below the tip.
● Remove a strip of bark 1–2.5cm ($\frac{1}{2}$–1in) wide right around the stem. Scrape the exposed surface. Alternatively, you can make an upward slanting cut about 5cm (2in) long towards the centre of the stem. To keep this apart, push a little sphagnum moss or peat, or a small pebble, into the slit.
● Dust a hormone rooting powder on to the stem or cut surface to speed rooting. Work the wet

sphagnum moss into a ball about 8cm (3in) in diameter, then split the moss into two halves and place around the stem. If sphagnum moss is not available, you could use damp peat instead, but it must not be too wet.
● Hold the moss or peat in place with a square of black polythene held securely with insulating tape. It's important to make the seal as tight as possible to prevent the moss or peat drying out or becoming waterlogged. Use black rather than clear polythene as darkness encourages rooting. The layered stem will take anything from a few months to more than a year to root, depending on the species. When adequate roots have formed, cut the stem just below the point of layering, using secateurs, then remove the polythene. Loosen the moss or peat ball and pot up carefully. *Suitable plants* Hamamelis (witch hazel), hydrangea species, *Magnolia*, rhododendron species – though the technique will work with most trees and shrubs.

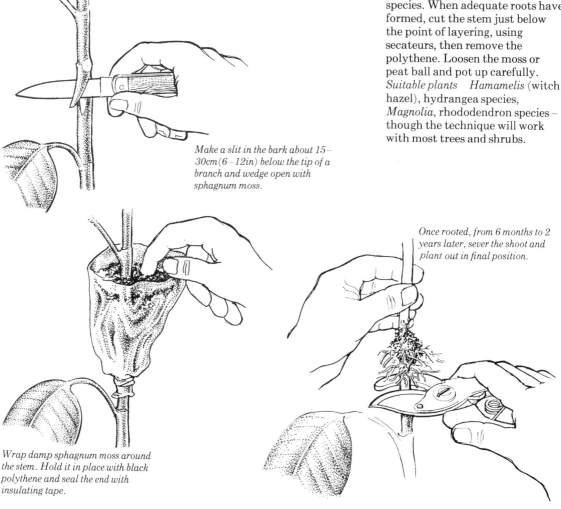

Make a slit in the bark about 15–30cm (6–12in) below the tip of a branch and wedge open with sphagnum moss.

Wrap damp sphagnum moss around the stem. Hold it in place with black polythene and seal the end with insulating tape.

Once rooted, from 6 months to 2 years later, sever the shoot and plant out in final position.

Serpentine (compound) layering

This is the variation of simple layering in which the branch is alternately covered and exposed along its length. It is used for plants with long, pliable shoots, especially climbers.

How it's done
● In late winter or early spring, prepare the plant as if you were about to embark upon simple layering.
● At each point that is going to be buried, wound the lower part of the stem (but be careful if the stem is thin). You must ensure that exposed sections have at least one bud so that they can develop new shoots. Each layered point should be as near vertical as possible.

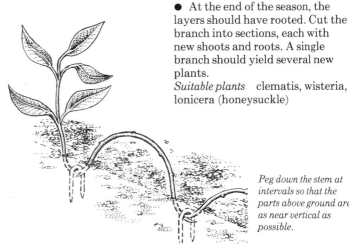

● At the end of the season, the layers should have rooted. Cut the branch into sections, each with new shoots and roots. A single branch should yield several new plants.
Suitable plants   clematis, wisteria, lonicera (honeysuckle)

Peg down the stem at intervals so that the parts above ground are as near vertical as possible.

French layering

French layering (also known as continuous layering) produces an annual crop of rooted layers. The shrubs must be well established before you try this method, and there must be plenty of room around them. This means that French layering is not usually a practical method for shrubs in borders, and you really need to plant specifically for this type of layering.

How it's done
● Grow on a rooted layer for a year (or buy a young plant), then cut the stems down to 3–5cm (1–2in) above the ground in early winter. You could try cutting down a more established plant if you have one.
● Once the new stems have grown in the spring, thin them out to leave 8 to 10 on the plant. After the leaves have fallen in autumn, cut the growing tips back so all the stems are around the same length. This will encourage buds to form along the stems.)
● In early winter, peg down the stems horizontally along the ground. This will induce a more even bud break in spring.

● In spring, once the new shoots on the stems are about 5–8cm (2–3in) long, lift the stems, dig over the ground beneath them, and make a 5cm (2in) deep trench for each one. Arrange the stems like the spokes of a wheel, radiating from the centre of the plant. Remove the tip from each new shoot before covering with soil.
● As the new shoots grow, earth them up. Use a mulch of moist peat and soil for the first covering, as this will encourage root formation. Earth up at intervals, always leaving the top 5cm (2in) of growth exposed until the mound is about 15cm (6in) high.
● Late the following winter or in early spring, carefully draw the soil away from the shoots. Remove the pegs and lift and cut each layer into individual plants. Each piece should have a shoot and a portion of roots. Leave the shoot nearest the parent stump to continue the process next year. The parent plant can immediately have another 8 to 10 new shoots laid down, leaving the same number to develop for next year's layers.
See the Table overleaf for suitable plants.

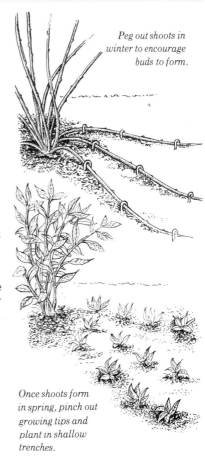

Peg out shoots in winter to encourage buds to form.

Once shoots form in spring, pinch out growing tips and plant in shallow trenches.

Stooling

Stooling (sometimes called mound layering) could be used for all the plants listed for French layering in the Table below and is particularly useful for heathers (see page 52).

How it's done

● Take a one-year-old plant and cut it down to 3–5cm (1–2in) above the ground during the dormant season.

● In spring, the new shoots should be earthed up as they appear. Mix in moist peat with soil to encourage rooting.

● As soon as the new shoots put on 8–10cm (3–4in) of growth, mound up again with soil, until it is 23–30cm (9–12in) high. Don't earth up into a peak as the rain may wash the soil away; flatten the top. Keep the plants watered in very dry weather.

● In early winter, fork the soil away carefully to expose the stool and new rooted shoots. You can now cut them off flush with the original stool. Replant or pot up those stems that have rooted; discard those that haven't.

● If you want, you can repeat the process next spring, but fork excess soil away from the stool and leave exposed through the winter to encourage bud formation.

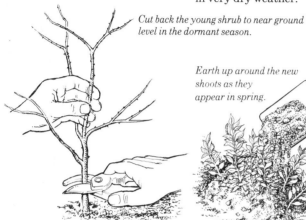

Cut back the young shrub to near ground level in the dormant season.

Earth up around the new shoots as they appear in spring.

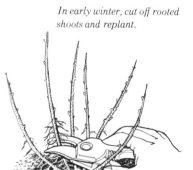

In early winter, cut off rooted shoots and replant.

LOTS OF PLANTS BY LAYERING

plant	type of layer	timing	rooting (months)	expected success %	no. of plants per layer	no. per plant
Acer spp	French	Dec to Feb	12	85	4–5	30–50
Azalea spp	serpentine	Dec to Feb	6–9	80	5–6	[1]
Camellia spp	serpentine	Dec to Feb	6–9	80	5–6	[1]
Cornus alba varieties	French	Dec to Feb	12	85	4–5	30–50
Hydrangea paniculata	French	Dec to Feb	12	85	4–5	30–50
Magnolia	serpentine	Dec to Feb	6–9	80	5–6	[1]
Prunus tenella	French	Dec to Feb	12	85	4–5	30–50
Rhododendron spp	serpentine air	Sep to Apr Sep to Apr	6–9 6–18	80 90	5–6 1	[1] [1]
Syringa spp	stooling, serpentine	Dec to Feb	6–9	80	5–6	[1]
Viburnum spp	serpentine	Dec to Feb	6–9	80	5–6	[1]
Viburnum x bodnantense	French	Dec to Feb	12	85	4–5	30–50

Species clematis like this Clematis macropetala *can be raised from seed.*

Most climbers are shrubs, but herbaceous and annual climbers have also been included in this section. All the plants are listed alphabetically under their Latin names, as with a few exceptions these are the most commonly used. You can find sweet peas under *Lathyrus odoratus* and climbing nasturtiums under *Tropaeolum*. Unless raised from seed, different species and varieties of particular climbers can usually be propagated in exactly the same way. Any exceptions have been noted.

Key to how easy
- ●●● Quite easy, should be successful
- ●● More difficult, but reasonable chance of success
- ● Worth trying, but be prepared for failures

species	how	when	hor-mone*	what to do	how easy
A					
Actinidia kolomikta	nodal cuttings	June to July	yes	Take 15cm (6in) cuttings of soft or semi-ripe wood, wound base and insert into a sandy compost. Choose shoots with greenest leaves for propagation as those that are predominantly cream tend to die. Root in a pot with a polythene bag or in a heated propagator. Harden off once rooted and keep in the cold frame until the following spring.	●
Akebia quinata (chocolate vine)	nodal cuttings	Aug to Sep	yes	Take 15cm (6in) cuttings of semi-ripe wood and root in individual pots in a heated propagator at 20–25°C (70–80°F). Keep in the same pot and start feeding once rooted, as they transplant badly. Keep cool over winter.	●
	layering	Mar to Sep	no	Bring down shoot to soil level and tie to a cane.	●●
Ampelopsis	cuttings	July to Aug	yes	Root 5–10cm (3–4in) softwood cuttings in a pot covered with a polythene bag. Pot up and overwinter in the cold frame.	●●●
C–H					
Campsis (trumpet vine)	hardwood cuttings	Oct to Nov	no	Take 25–30cm (10–12in) cuttings and root in the cold frame. Suitable only for the hardier species, *C. radicans*.	●●
	nodal or double leaf bud cuttings	July	no	Root in a heated propagator at 15–18°C (60–65°F). Pot up and keep in greenhouse over winter. See Clematis, below, for how to take double leaf bud cuttings.	●●
	root cuttings	Dec to Feb	no	Cut roots into 5cm (2in) sections and plant vertically. Keep at a temperature of 10–15°C (50–60°F) until shoots have formed (possibly indoors on the windowsill and then in the cold frame) in the summer. Pot up, providing a stick for support, and grow on for planting the following spring.	●●
	layering	Oct to Nov	no	Rooted layers can be transplanted into compost the following autumn.	●●●
Celastrus	root cuttings	Dec to Feb	no	Cut roots into 5cm (2in) sections and pot vertically so that tops are just above the compost.	●●
	nodal cuttings	July	yes	Take 10cm (4in) cuttings of ripe wood and root in a pot covered with a polythene bag. Pot up and overwinter in the cold frame.	●●
	leaf bud cuttings	Mar to June	yes	Root in a heated propagator at 15–18°C (60–65°F). Pot up and overwinter in the cold frame.	●
	layering	Aug	no	Select current year's shoots for layering. Layers should root by the following autumn.	●●●
	seed	Aut	-	Sow fresh seeds in pots or trays and leave outside over winter. Bring them into the greenhouse or cold frame at first signs of germination in spring. You will get berries and seeds only if you have a male and female plant or if you are lucky enough to have a hermaphrodite clone.	●●

*Hormone means a rooting powder or solution   For an explanation of the different types of cuttings, see page 12

species	how	when	hor-mone*	what to do	how easy
Clematis	double-leaf bud cuttings (see illustration)	June to July	no	Thin stems on young plants root more readily than those on older plants. You could try rooting cuttings in a pot covered with a polythene bag, but best in a heated propagator. Spray with fungicide at 10-day intervals to avoid problems. Pot once well rooted (5 to 7 weeks) and grow on in the cold frame for spring planting.	●●

If you are short of space in the propagator, remove one set of leaves.

Double-leaf bud cutting: trim the cutting just above a leaf pair and about 3–5cm (1–2in) below.

If you want lots of cuttings from a few plants, you can double up the number by slicing each one down the middle.

species	how	when	hor-mone*	what to do	how easy
	layering	Spr to Aut		If you want several plants, use the serpentine layering method (see page 45). Rooted layers can be moved in spring or autumn.	●●
	hardwood cuttings	late Feb	yes	Take small inter-nodal cuttings with a pair of buds at either end and root in a frost-free greenhouse. Keep in greenhouse until mid-summer before planting out.	●●●
	seed	Sep to Nov	-	Collect fluffy seeds, separate as far as possible and sow in trays in the cold frame (or outdoors under glass) and bring into warmth at first sign of germination. Pot up seedlings and grow on for autumn or spring planting. This method is only suitable for species, not the large-flowered hybrids. *C. armandii* is difficult to propagate by cuttings or seed.	●●●
Cobaea scandens (cup and saucer vine)	seed	Feb to Mar	-	Treat as half-hardy annual or greenhouse perennial. Soak seeds for 24 hours and sow individually in small pots. At 18°C (65°F) germination should take 18 to 21 days. Plant out after last frosts.	●●●
Eccremocarpus scaber (Chilean glory vine)	seed	Feb to Mar	-	Sow under glass. At 13°C (55°F) germination should take about 21 to 28 days. Prick out into small pots and provide stick for support. Plant out after last frosts. Treat as an annual or short-lived perennial.	●●●
Fremontodendron (Californian glory)	bought seed	Spr	-	Sow in the greenhouse in early spring. Soak seed for 48 hours prior to sowing and germinate at 18°C (65°F). Grow on in pot for first year and overwinter in the greenhouse. Plant out in a warm, sheltered position late the following spring.	●●●
Hedera (ivies)	stem cuttings	Oct to Nov	no	Take 13cm (5in) cuttings from ripe wood and root in the cold frame. Pot up or plant out in late spring. Cuttings taken from very hard woody shoots are harder to root and resultant plants will be reluctant to climb.	●●●
	nodal or leaf-bud cuttings	June to July	no	Take 8–10cm (3–4in) cuttings of semi-ripe wood or use single leaves with 3cm (1in) or so of stem attached and root in a pot covered with a polythene bag. If you want a number of cuttings, for ground cover say, root the cuttings in the cold frame and cover them with thin polythene until rooted.	●●●
	layering	Spr or Aut	no	Ivies grown as ground cover very often layer themselves. Almost any shoot weighted down with a stone should root. Transplant rooted layers in autumn or early spring.	●●●

*Hormone means a rooting powder or solution   For an explanation of the different types of cuttings, see page 12

species	how	when	hormone*	what to do	how easy
Humulus japonicus (*H. scandens*, ornamental hop)	seed	Spr	-	Treat as hardy annual. In mild districts, providing soil not too heavy, it can be sown in autumn for earlier establishment. The variegated form, *H. japonicus* 'Variegatus', is attractive.	●●
Humulus lupulus (brewer's hop)	leaf bud or stem cuttings	June to Aug	no	Use 8–10cm (3–4in) shoot tips or individual leaves with 3cm (1in) of stem. Root in pots covered with a plastic bag or in a heated propagator. Pot up and overwinter in the cold frame.	●●
Hydrangea petiolaris (climbing hydrangea)	basal cuttings	Apr	yes	Take 3–8cm (1–3in) cuttings from soft new growth, either from side shoots or shoot tips, of non-flowering shoots (these are thinner than flowering shoots), and root in a pot covered with a polythene bag or in a heated propagator. Pot on once rooted (about 6 weeks or so) and grow on in the cold frame or greenhouse for planting out the following spring.	●
	layering	Spr	no	Peg long shoots to the ground. When upright shoots develop and reach about 10cm (4in), earth up around the layer. Keep moist. Lift the following spring.	●●
	seed	Spr	-	Sow under glass in tray of peaty compost and cover with paper until seedlings appear. Germination variable.	●●
I–R					
Ipomea (morning glory) half-hardy annual	seed	Feb to Mar	-	Sow several seeds to a pot and thin out to one seedling. Germination should take up to 21 days at 21°C (70°F). Plant out after last frosts.	●●●
Jasminium officinale and J. nudiflorum (summer and winter jasmine)	hardwood cuttings	Nov	no	Take 15–20cm (6–8in) cuttings of one-year-old wood and root in the open ground or, in cold districts or in heavy soils, in the cold frame. Move to final position in late spring.	●●●
	basal cuttings	June to July	no	Take 8–10cm (3–4in) cuttings of semi-ripe side shoots and root in a pot covered with a polythene bag, a cold frame or polythene tunnel. Pot up rooted cuttings in late summer and overwinter in the cold frame. Cuttings under a polythene tunnel can remain in the ground until spring.	●●●
	layering	Spr	no	Rooted layers can be planted out or potted up by autumn.	●●●
Lathyrus odoratus (sweet peas) hardy annual	seed	Sep or Mar	-	Keep seed between moist blotting paper for 24 hours prior to sowing. Any seed that doesn't swell should be nicked with a sharp knife. For best results sow outdoors in autumn (South only) or in pots of peat-based compost in spring.	●●●
Lonicera (honeysuckles)	hardwood cuttings	Oct	yes	Take 13cm (5in) basal or nodal cuttings and root in a peaty compost in the cold frame. Pot up or plant out in late spring.	●●
	leaf-bud cuttings	June to July	yes	Trim stems about 3cm (1in) on either side of a leaf joint. Root in a pot covered with a polythene bag. Pot up in early autumn and overwinter in the cold frame.	●●
Parthenocissus (Virginia creeper)	stem cuttings	July to Sep	yes	As for *Amelopsis* (page 48) but note that not all leaf axils contain buds. Each cutting should have at least 2 buds.	●●
	hardwood cuttings	Feb	yes	Take cuttings with a single bud and root in a propagator at 15–18°C (60–65°F). Make a sloping cut directly above bud and a straight cut 3cm (1in) below. Pot as soon as they root.	●●
	layering	Spr to Aut	no	As for Clematis, page 49.	●●●

*Hormone means a rooting powder or solution   For an explanation of the different types of cuttings, see page 12

species	how	when	hor-mone*	what to do	how easy
Passiflora (passion flower)	nodal cuttings	July to Aug	no	Take 10–15cm (4–6in) semi-ripe cuttings and root in uncovered pots or even jars of water. Pot up once rooted (3 to 6 weeks) and overwinter in the cold frame or greenhouse.	●●●
Pileostegia	tip cuttings	Spr	yes	Root in a heated propagator at 15–18°C (60–65°F).	●●
Polygonum baldschuanicum (Russian vine)	basal cuttings	July to Aug	no	Take 8–10cm (3–4in) cuttings from new shoots and root in a pot covered with a polythene bag. Pot up once rooted and overwinter in the cold frame for spring planting.	●●
	hardwood cuttings	Oct to Nov	no	Take 20–25cm (8–10in) cuttings from past year's growth and root in open ground or in the cold frame.	●●●
Rosa (climbing roses)	hardwood cuttings	Oct	yes	As for Roses (page 29).	●●●
S–W					
Schizophragma	cuttings	June to Aug	yes	Snap off 8–10cm (3–4in) shoots at base and root in a pot covered with a polythene bag or in a heated propagator at 21°C (70°F). Pot on and keep under glass over winter.	●●●
	layering	Spr	no	Peg down layer into a pot and tie shoot tip to a cane.	●●●
Solanum crispum (potato vine)	basal cuttings	June to July	yes	Take cuttings from 10–15cm (4–6in) side shoots and root in the cold frame. May be killed if conditions too moist once rooted.	●
Thunbergia alata (black-eyed Susan)	seed	Spr	-	Treat as half-hardy annual and sow in the greenhouse in March to April. Germination should take 3 to 4 weeks at 21°C (70°F). Soaking seeds overnight aids germination.	●●●
Trachelospermum (star jasmine)	cuttings	Aug	no	Take 8cm (3in) cuttings from semi-ripe side shoots and let them dry off thoroughly before potting as they will exude a milky white sap. Root in a heated propagator at 21°C (70°F) and keep under glass for the first season.	●
	layering	Spr to Aut	no	Can also be layered as for Clematis (page 49).	●
Tropaeolum majus and T. peregrinum (climbing nasturtium and canary creeper)	seed	Spr	-	Treat as hardy annuals. For earlier flowers, sow 2 or 3 seeds in small pots in the cold frame in March and thin out to strongest seedling. Soaking overnight prior to sowing aids germination. Plant out in April with root ball intact.	●●●
Tropaeolum speciosum (Scotch flame flower)	root division	Spr	-	Carefully lift the root ball, which may be 23cm (9in) deep. Cut the roots into several sections with a sharp knife and replant.	●●●
Tropaeolum tuberosum (flame flower)	offsets on tubers	Spr	-	Lift in autumn and store in frost-free conditions. Separate offsets from tubers before replanting in March.	●●●
Vitis coignetiae	layering	Spr	-	Layers should have rooted by the following autumn. Other ornamental vines can be propagated as for Grapes (page 116).	●●●
Wisteria	layering	Spr	no	Transplant or pot up in autumn and stake. Move to final position after 2 or 3 years. Flowering will take 7 to 8 years.	●●●
	basal cuttings	June to July	no	Take 10–15cm (4–6in) cuttings from side shoots and root in peaty compost, ideally in a heated propagator. Pot up in late summer and overwinter in the greenhouse.	●

*Hormone means a rooting powder or solution   For an explanation of the different types of cuttings, see page 12

HEATHERS: TECHNIQUES

Heathers are very easy to propagate by a number of methods. Which method you choose depends on how many plants you want and the condition of the plants.

Take 3cm (1in) basal or nodal cuttings.

Insert in 2 parts moss peat to 1 part sharp sand.

Pot up individually once rooted in lime-free compost.

Cover pot with polythene bag.

From cuttings

The best time to take cuttings is in July or August. Cuttings taken earlier from softer wood are prone to wilting, and some species are reluctant to root from harder wood. Heel cuttings are traditionally recommended, but 3cm (1in) basal or nodal cuttings (see page 12) should root just as well. Insert cuttings in pots of 2 parts moss peat to 1 part sand. The cuttings should be buried to half their depth without removing the lower leaves. Place the cuttings in a cold frame or cover the pot with a polythene bag and keep well shaded. Pot up into a lime-free (ericaceous) potting compost once they show signs of growth, keep in the cold frame over winter and plant out in spring.

Layering

Layering is an ideal method of producing a few more plants from an established plant. Although it may take up to a year before rooted layers are ready for planting out, it requires very little effort and no special facilities. Select a vigorous young shoot and replace the soil where the layer is to be pegged down with a mixture of sand and peat. Several layers can be pegged down from one plant without detracting from its appearance.

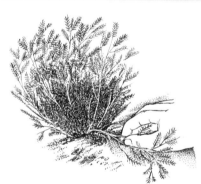

Pull down vigorous young shoots . . .

. . . and weight with a heavy stone.

Stooling or mound layering

This technique is discussed on page 46 and the procedure is basically the same as for other shrubs. One useful modification is to make a wooden frame with 4 old bits of wood to place around the plant. This can then be filled with moss peat and sand as the new shoots grow and avoid any problems with the compost being washed away by the rain.

Dropping

This is a good way of dealing with an old plant that has become bare at the base.
● Prune the plant in the dormant season to encourage new growth.
● In spring, dig a large hole and drop in the plant so that only the top 3cm (1in) of the stem tips are showing. Refill the hole with sand and peat.
● Keep watered during the summer, and in autumn lift and separate the rooted portions.

From seed

Best done for fun, as most heathers are named varieties and won't come true, though you could raise an interesting plant.

Remove the sprigs once the seed capsules turn brown and lay them on sheets of paper indoors until they release the seeds. Sow in autumn following the same method as for alpines (see page 96). Chilling hastens germination but is not essential. Pot up seedlings in spring and grow on until large enough for planting.

Many conifers can be propagated at home either from cuttings or from seed. Cuttings will produce identical plants to the parent, and this is the way to propagate named varieties. Raising from seed is a good way of growing conifer species, especially if you want a number of plants, but named varieties often give mixed results. Seed from golden or blue forms usually produce green plants. The best method of propagating individual conifers is given in the Tables on pages 54 to 57. The basic principles are discussed below.

From cuttings

Many forms of juniper, cypress, cryptomeria, thuja and some smaller genera are quite easily raised from cuttings. Pines, cedars, spruces and firs are notoriously difficult to propagate in this way, partly because of the high secretion of resin from the cut surfaces.

Conifer cuttings will root quicker and more reliably if the cuttings are taken from vigorous young specimens. Some cultivars, such as *Chamaecyparis lawsoniana* 'Elwoodii', retain their juvenile foliage indefinitely instead of developing the flattened sprays of foliage seen on ordinary Lawson's cypress. Such forms are particularly easy to root from cuttings. On the other hand, a few forms of this cypress, such as the golden 'Stewartii' and the blue 'Triomphe de Boskoop', are not so easy, though you may have more success by using a liquid rooting hormone rather than a powder.

There are two periods when conifer cuttings root best: February to April and August to October. The cuttings should be severed from the parent plant at the base of the past season's growth. Though it is often recommended that cuttings should be taken with a heel of older wood, trials have shown that those cut through a node give as good if not better results and do less damage to the tree.

Once rooted, give the cuttings good growing conditions. For quicker results, grow on rooted cuttings in the greenhouse and feed them regularly with a dilute liquid feed. Given such conditions, a 10cm (4in) cutting of *Chamaecyparis lawsoniana* 'Elwoodii' can reach 30cm (12in) in its first year. Dwarf cultivars will be slower, a rooted cutting of *Cryptomeria japonica* 'Vilmoriniana' perhaps putting on 2cm (¾in) of growth in one season, whereas a grafted plant can grow to 23cm (9in).

From seed

There is no essential difference between raising conifers and raising other trees from seed. The main problem is in collecting the cones, which can be high up in the tree. In many cases a ladder or a long-handled pruner will be needed.

Cones of pines often take more than one year on the tree to mature. Ideally they should be gathered when the scales show signs of opening. Cones of pines, spruces, larches and also the tiny cones of cypress, thuja and hemlock spruce may be left on trays in a moderately warm place for the scales to separate and allow the seeds to be shaken out. Cones of fir (*Abies*) and cedars fall to pieces on the tree on maturity and so should be collected as soon as they show signs of disintegration. Junipers and yews have berry-like fruits, to be collected when they soften and show colour. Any of the standard composts are suitable for sowing the seeds. Two or three months after germination, the seed leaves will be fully developed and the seedlings ready for pricking out into potting compost, preferably into single pots. Never let the seedlings become pot-bound or the tap root will encircle the root ball and never straighten. To avoid the chances of this happening, sow conifer seeds in deep trays or deep pots such as those used for tomatoes and sweet peas.

As with cuttings, you will get quicker results if you grow seedlings on in the greenhouse for the first season and feed them regularly with a dilute liquid feed while growing.

Leave cones of pine, larch and spruce on trays in a moderately warm room until they open up. The seeds can then be shaken out.

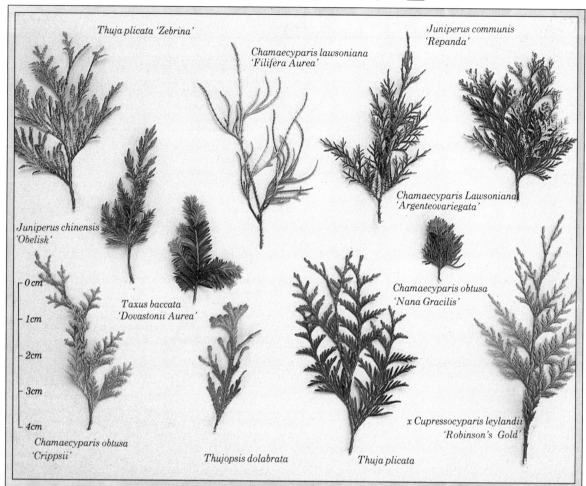

Thuja plicata 'Zebrina'

Chamaecyparis lawsoniana 'Filifera Aurea'

Juniperus communis 'Repanda'

Chamaecyparis Lawsoniana 'Argenteovariegata'

Juniperus chinensis 'Obelisk'

Taxus baccata 'Dovastonii Aurea'

Chamaecyparis obtusa 'Nana Gracilis'

0cm

1cm

2cm

3cm

4cm

Chamaecyparis obtusa 'Crippsii'

Thujopsis dolabrata

Thuja plicata

x Cupressocyparis leylandii 'Robinson's Gold'

Key to how easy ●●● Quite easy, should be successful
●● More difficult, but reasonable chance of success
● Worth trying, but be prepared for failure

species	how	when	hor-mone*	what to do	how easy
A					
Abies (firs)	fresh seed	Aut	-	Sow fresh, as seed deteriorates within a few months. Collect the cones as soon as they start to disintegrate on the tree and keep indoors on a tray until they are easily pulled apart. Sow in trays in the cold frame and prick out when seedlings are a few inches tall, by about June. Smaller species for the garden include *A. koreana*, which forms cones when 1m (3ft) high, and *A. forestii* and *A. procera*, which form cones when 3m (10ft) high. Only species will breed true from seed.	●●
	layering	Spr	no	Suitable for dwarf varieties such as *Abies balsamea* 'Hudsonia'. For best results peg 2-year-old shoots in autumn. Wound stem. Rooting may take 2 years.	●
	basal cuttings	Aug to Sep	yes	Dwarf varieties and seedlings can be rooted from 8cm (3in) cuttings in a heated propagator at 15–18°C (60–65°F). Can also take cuttings January to February.	●

* Hormone means a rooting powder or solution   For an explanation of the different types of cuttings, see page 12

species	how	when	hor-mone*	what to do	how easy
Araucaria araucana (monkey puzzle tree)	fresh seed	Sep	-	The cone-shaped winged seeds can be collected from the ground. Mix with moist sand or peat and sand and store in a polythene bag over winter for spring sowing. If sown in autumn, the seeds can germinate early and the seedlings may be killed by frost. Sow individually in pots and grow on under glass for several years before planting out. Growth is slow for the first few years.	●●
C					
Calocedrus (Libocedrus, incense cedar)	fresh or bought seed	Oct to Mar	-	Cones can be collected just before they start to open and dried to extract seed. Alternatively, bought seed should give reasonable results. There are no dormancy problems, but seed sown in the cold frame in February, exposed to a brief period of chilling, may improve results. Prick out seedlings into individual pots and grow on for autumn planting, when they should be up to 15cm (6in) high.	●●●
Cedrus (cedars)	fresh seed	Aut		Cones disintegrate on the tree, as with *Abies*, and should be treated similarly. Only the species, all of which have green leaves, will come true, but the blue forms should produce some blue seedlings.	●●
	layering	Spr	no	Named varieties are usually grafted, though you can layer young plants as for *Abies*. This may be worth trying with dwarf prostrate forms such as *Cedrus libani* 'Sargentii'.	●
Cephalotaxus (plum yew)	heeled cuttings	Oct	yes	Take 8–10cm (3–4in) cuttings from semi-ripe wood and root in the cold frame. Pot on in early summer for planting out the following spring. A useful garden tree, being shade tolerant and never reaching more than about 4m (13ft).	●●
Chamaecyparis lawsoniana (larger varieties) and Cupressus	basal cuttings	Sep to Oct	yes	*Chamaecyparis lawsoniana* varieties that retain their feathery sprays of juvenile foliage are generally very easy to root. Others, such as 'Stewartii' and 'Triomphe de Boskoop', are more difficult. Take 10cm (4in) cuttings from semi-ripe wood and remove them as close to the old wood as you can. Root in a cold frame and pot up in early summer. With more difficult to root types, try dipping the cuttings in a liquid rooting hormone for 24 hours prior to potting.	● to ●●●
	basal cuttings	Feb	yes	If you have a heated propagator (or a warm bench and plastic) you can root cuttings taken as above in about 3 months at around 18°C (65°F).	●●
Chamaecyparis (dwarf varieties)	basal cuttings	Mar	yes	Most of the dwarf varieties will root within 10 weeks from cuttings in the cold frame. However, for the very dwarf varieties, such as *Chamaecyparis lawsoniana* 'Minima Glauca' and *Chamaecyparis obtusa* 'Nana Gracilis', the cuttings may be only 2cm (¾in) long and it may take 4 or 5 years before they are large enough to plant out.	●●
Cryptomeria japonica	cuttings	Feb	yes	The variety 'Elegans' will reach around 10cm (30ft) after 20 years and can be propagated from 8–13cm (3–5in) cuttings of semi-ripe wood in a cold frame. Cuttings can be potted up in spring. After several years they should be about 1m (3ft) high and ready for planting out. Dwarf types, such as 'Vilmoriniana', can also be propagated similarly, though wounding the cuttings may increase success. Growth will be slow, and it may take 5 or more years before they are a reasonable size.	●●

* Hormone means a rooting powder or solution   For an explanation of the different types of cuttings, see page 12

species	how	when	hor-mone*	what to do	how easy
Cupressocyparis leylandii (Leyland's cypress)	stem cuttings	Oct	yes	Take 10–15cm (4–6in) cuttings ideally from young plants, when leaf nodes at the base are turning brown. Wound the cutting before treating with rooting hormone and insert in a cold frame and cover with thin polythene (see page 17). Rooted cuttings can be potted up by June and planted out in autumn. They can grow up to 45cm (18in) in the first year.	●●to ●●●
	nodal cuttings	Feb	yes	Cuttings as above rooted in a heated propagator or warm bench and plastic can root in as little as 10 weeks.	●●●
J–M					
Juniperus (junipers, including the many dwarf varieties)	basal cuttings	Apr	yes	Remove side shoots as near to the stem as possible (the size of cutting depends on the plant). Root in a cold frame and cover with thin polythene (see page 17) or in a pot covered with a polythene bag. Rooting should take 8 to 12 weeks.	●●●
	basal cuttings	Sep to Oct	yes	Cuttings as above can be rooted in a cold frame without the polythene cover, though they will take 8 months to root with a higher proportion of failures.	●●●
Larix (larch)	seed	Aut	-	Seeds are shed in the first winter, but the empty cones remain on the tree (although a few seeds may remain in older cones). Store seed in trays somewhere cool and dry over winter and sow in a cold frame in spring. Keep in the cold frame and prick out seedlings the following spring.	●●
Metasequoia glyptostroboides (dawn redwood)	hardwood cuttings	Feb	yes	Take 8–15cm (3–6in) cuttings with a heel of old wood attached and root in pots in a cold frame. Feed once shoots start growing and plant out in autumn. Cuttings will reach about 60cm (2ft) in 3 years.	●●
P					
Picea abies (Norway spruce, Christmas tree) and Picea omorika	fresh or bought seed	Aut	-	The seed is dispersed in autumn but empty cones remain on the tree. Collect cones before they ripen and place them on a sunny windowsill. Shake out the seed once they open. Sow in autumn in a cold frame or store dry in a sealed container in the fridge over winter and sow in spring. Prick out seedlings when large enough to handle and plant in early autumn. Mix bought seed with moist peat and keep in the fridge for about 6 weeks prior to sowing. It will take about 4 years to grow a 1.2m (4ft) Christmas tree from seed.	●●
Picea breweriana	fresh or bought seed	Aut	-	Can be raised from seed as above, but very slow growing in the early years. It can take 15 to 20 years before it starts to develop its weeping habit.	●●
Picea, dwarf forms	basal cuttings	July to Aug	yes	Root in a heated propagator at 21°C (70°F). Wait at least 2 to 3 months for signs of rooting. Should be large enough for planting out within 3 years.	●
Pinus (pines)	fresh or bought seed	Sep to Oct	-	Unfortunately, the dwarf pines, such as *P. sylvestris* 'Beuvronensis', are all selected forms and can be propagated only by grafting. However, the species can all be raised from seed, and they don't all grow into big trees – *P. leucodermis*, for example, reaches about 3m (10ft) in 20 years and *P. mugo* (mountain pine) can take 40 years or more to reach this size. Collect cones before they open and put on a sunny windowsill to collect the seed. Alternatively, bought seed may give reasonable results. Chilling for about 6 weeks improves germination and can be achieved by sowing in February or keeping the seeds in the fridge. Most species grow quickly in the first year and can be planted out in autumn.	●●

*Hormone means a rooting powder or solution   For details of special seed treatments, see page 32

species	how	when	hor-mone*	what to do	how easy
Pseudotsuga menziesii glauca (blue douglas fir)	fresh or bought seed	late Sum or Aut	-	Unlike the green douglas fir, this one never reaches more than about 3m (10ft) and it also comes true from seed. Collect cones before they open and dry on a sunny windowsill until the seed can be shaken out. Bought seed should also give reasonable results. Sow in autumn or winter in trays in the cold frame or mix the seed with moist peat and store in a polythene bag in the fridge over winter for spring sowing.	●●
S–T					
Sciadopitys (Japanese umbrella pine)	fresh or bought seed	Aut	-	Collect cones as they start to open and dry to extract the seed. Bought seed should give reasonable results. Sow in a cold frame in early winter or mix seed with moist peat and store in the fridge for spring sowing. Seedlings are very slow-growing, and you may have to wait several years before they reach 30cm (1ft) in height.	●
Taxodium distichum (swamp cypress)	hardwood cuttings	Oct	yes	Take 10–15cm (4–6in) cuttings after leaf fall (this is a deciduous conifer) and root in a cold frame. Pot up rooted cuttings and grow on in the cold frame for planting out the following autumn. Cuttings should grow around 45–60cm (18–24in) in 3 years.	●●
	fresh seed	Aut	-	Mature cones can be broken apart once dried. Sow the seed (with debris) in trays in a cold frame not later than February. Prick out seedlings into individual pots and grow on for planting out the following spring.	●
Taxus baccata (yew)	fresh seed	Aut	-	Collect ripe berries, extract the seed and stratify (see page 33) over 2 winters. In the following spring sow the seed outdoors or in a cold frame – most should germinate, but some won't come up until the next spring. Be prepared to wait 8 to 10 years for a 1.5m (6ft) hedge.	●●
Taxus baccata 'Fastigiata Aurea'	stem cuttings	Sep to Oct	yes	This golden form and other dwarf varieties of yew will take from 8–15cm (3–6in) cuttings of semi-ripe wood in a cold frame. Stand the cuttings in a liquid rooting hormone for an hour or two to improve your chances. Cuttings should root by late spring or early summer. The plain green species is very difficult to root from cuttings.	●●
Thuja occidentalis varieties and T. orientalis (including dwarf forms such as 'Juniperoides' and 'Rosedalis')	stem cuttings	Sep to Oct	yes	Take 8–10cm (3–4in) cuttings for dwarf varieties, up to 15cm (6in) for others, and root in a cold frame. Pot up when rooted, in late spring, and grow on for planting out in autumn. Cuttings of faster-growing sorts should reach 25cm (10in) in the first year. The species may also be raised from seed for *T. plicata*.	●●
Thuja plicata (western red cedar)	fresh or bought seed	Aut	-	Collect cones as soon as they turn brown. Dry indoors and shake out the seed. Store cool and dry over winter and sow in trays in a cold frame in spring. Growth is slow in the first year. Keep seedlings in the cold frame and don't prick them out until the second year.	●
Thujopsis dolobrata	seed	Aut	-	As for *Thuja plicata*.	●
	stem cuttings	Sep to Oct	yes	Varieties may be raised as for *Thuja occidentalis*.	●●

*Hormone means a rooting powder or solution   For details of special seed treatments, see page 32

The techniques involved in raising bedding plants are the same as for raising any plants from seed under glass. The most common causes of poor plants are leaving the seedlings too long before pricking out, not feeding plants that have been in their container a long time, and failing to harden off plants properly before planting out.

Sowing techniques are dealt with on the next page, and requirements of individual plants are given on pages 60 and 61.

French marigolds flower eight weeks after sowing, so there is no point in starting them off before mid-April at the earliest.

Sowing techniques

● Fill the trays or pots with compost and work it down into the corners with your fingers so as to get rid of any air pockets. Level off the compost and firm down with a piece of wood or a tamper.

● Water the compost before sowing. Either stand the pot or tray in shallow water until the surface becomes moist and then stand to drain or use a watering can with a very fine rose. To prevent any problems with damping off (a disease that causes seedlings to collapse), add a copper fungicide or Cheshunt compound.

Fill trays with compost, level off and firm down with tamper.

● Sow the seed on the surface of the compost. Large seeds can be sown individually at regular spacing. Long tufted seeds, such as African and French marigolds, are best separated and sown flat on the compost. Small seeds can be sown broadcast by gently tapping the packet, but sow thinly and space the seed as evenly as possible. Very fine seed,

such as begonias and lobelias, can be mixed with fine sand to aid even sowing.

● After sowing, cover the seed with the required depth of compost – usually 6–12mm ($\frac{1}{4}$–$\frac{1}{2}$in) for large seeds and 3–6mm ($\frac{1}{8}$–$\frac{1}{4}$in) for small seed. Very fine seed usually requires light to germinate. A fine covering of vermiculite will help keep the seed moist without inhibiting germination. If this is not available, leave uncovered.

Sow seed on surface and cover with required depth of compost.

Cover tray with glass and newspaper (so long as seeds don't require light).

● If you are not using a propagator, cover the pots or seed trays with a sheet of glass, clinging film or a polythene bag pulled taut over the top. So long as the seeds do not require light, cover the glass with brown paper or newspaper. Remove the paper as soon as the seeds germinate or they will become drawn. Seeds that require light must be kept out of direct sunlight – under the greenhouse bench, say.

● If seeds are covered, you may not need to water again before they germinate. However, if compost does dry out always water fine seeds from below. Larger seeds can be watered with a mist sprayer. Use warm water to avoid any check to growth.

● Prick off seedlings into new trays or pots as soon as possible – ideally when the first true leaves have unfolded (these look different from the seed leaves that appear first). Fine seeds, such as begonias and lobelias, will probably be too small to handle at this stage, though lobelias can be pricked off in small clumps if congested. Always handle seedlings by the leaves and never by the stem. Water with warm water, as cold water can cause a check to growth.

● Harden off seedlings in the cold frame or by increasing ventilation in the greenhouse for a week or so prior to planting out.

BEDDING PLANTS FROM CUTTINGS

Helichrysum petiolatum, a grey-leaved trailing plant which is ideal for hanging baskets or to trail among flowers in a bedding scheme, cannot be raised from seed. However, it is very easy to raise from 8–10cm (3–4in) stem cuttings taken in late summer and overwintered in a frost-free greenhouse.

It may also be worth propagating some of the expensive F1 varieties of bedding plants from cuttings. Worth trying, if you heat your greenhouse over winter anyway, are *Dianthus heddewigii*, bedding geraniums, impatiens and pansies.

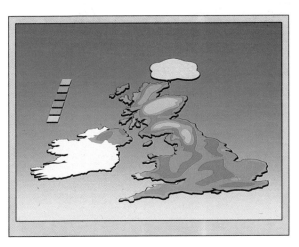

*When to plant out
Last frosts:*
☐ *early to mid-June*
■ *late May*
■ *early to mid-May*
■ *mid-Apr to early May*
☐ *mid-Apr*
☐ *almost frost free*

Sow late and save money

Some bedding plants, such as fibrous-rooted begonias and bedding geraniums, need relatively high temperatures to germinate and a long growing season, starting in January or February. However; many bedding plants can be sown in April or even early May without delaying flowering by more than a few weeks. You will probably still have to provide some heat initially, but as you will be using your greenhouse heating for a much shorter period you can make considerable savings. Late-sown plants are also likely to benefit from better light and be less affected by sudden cold snaps. And as the plants are transplanted at a younger, more vigorous stage, the plants are likely to be stronger.

The Chart opposite shows the results of a late sowing trial conducted by *Gardening Which?* in the north of England. The safest candidates for late sowing are alyssum, calendulas, godetias and French marigolds. But as the trial showed, other bedding plants are worth sowing late, though you can get caught out in a bad summer.

BEDDING PLANTS: LATE SOWING CHART

	MARCH		APRIL			MAY				JUNE				JULY				AUGUST			
WEEK	1	2	3	4	5	6	7	8	9	10	11	12	13	14	15	16	17	18	19	20	21	22
Alyssum 'Snowdrift'						✻	✻	✻	✻													
Aster 'Milady'																				✻	✻	✻
Dianthus 'Snow Fire'															✻	✻	✻					
French marigold 'Pascal'								✻	✻	✻	✻											
Nemesia 'Carnival'													✻	✻	✻							
Pansy 'Majestic Giants'												✻	✻				✻					
Petunia 'Serene'								✻	✻	✻	✻											

✻ = *first flowers*

Using the Table below
Sowing dates Sowing within the recommended dates should produce results at times given in the Table.
Germination temperature Seed may germinate at lower temperatures than recommended, but will be slower and less reliable. Higher temperatures may inhibit germination.
Notes Seed that needs light to germinate should be sown on the surface of the compost.

BEDDING PLANTS: A – Z

plant	when to sow	temp.	days to germinate (approx)	in flower	notes
Ageratum	Feb to Apr	18°C	5 to 14	June to Sep	Needs light to germinate.
Alyssum	Mar to Apr	15–18°C	7 to 10	May to Sep	Can also be sown outdoors April to May for July flowering.
Antirrhinum	Feb to Mar	15–18°C	14 to 21	July to Oct	Germinates best in light. Can also be sown in cold frame July to September.
Begonia semperflorens	Dec to Feb	18–21°C	12 to 28	June to Sep	Needs light to germinate. Will flower for most of year under glass. Grow on at 15°C (60°F).
Canna	Jan to Feb	21°C	21 to 28	June to Sep	Rub down seed coat with sandpaper and soak in warm water for 24 hours prior to sowing. Can be overwintered at 7°C (45°F) in greenhouse. Usually flowers in second year.
Cineraria maritima	Jan to Feb	18°C	5 to 21	silver foliage	Needs light to germinate.

plant	when to sow	temp.	days to germinate (approx)	in flower	notes
Cosmos	Mar to May	18°C	7 to 14	July to Sep	In mild areas can be sown outdoors in April and May.
Dahlia	Feb to Apr	15–18°C	7 to 14	July to Oct	Early sowing doesn't necessarily mean earlier flowering as it is dependent on day length.
Dianthus	Jan to Apr	18°C	7 to 10	July to Oct	Once germinated, keep cool – around 10°C (50°F).
Gazania	Feb	15–18°C	14 to 21	July to Sep	'Ministar' series best for bedding.
Heliotrope	Feb to Mar	21°C	14 to 21	June to Oct	Seedlings hate draughts.
Impatiens	Mar to Apr	21°C	5 to 21	June to Sep	Needs light to germinate.
Kochia	Mar to Apr	15–18°C	5 to 10	bright green foliage	Cover with 3mm (⅛in) of compost. Can also be sown outdoors in April or May.
Lobelia	Jan to Mar	15–18°C	12 to 24	May/ June to Oct	Needs light to germinate. Seedlings can be pricked out in clumps.
Marigold, African	Feb	18°C	2 to 14	June to Oct	It is best to separate the seed and sow flat on the surface of the compost and then cover.
Marigold, French	Apr	18°C	2 to 7	May to Oct	Sow as above. Can also be sown outdoors in May for July/August flowering.
Mesembryan-themum	Feb to Mar	18°C	14 to 21	June to Sep	Germinates best in total darkness.
Mimulus	Feb to Apr	15–18°C	7 to 21	June to Sep	Germinates better in light.
Nemesia	Mar to Apr	18°C	14 to 21	June to Aug	Germinates best in total darkness. Higher temperatures will reduce germination rate. Sowing too early can result in straggly plants.
Nicotiana	Feb to Apr	18°C	7 to 14	June to Sep	Choose F1 hybrids, such as 'Nicki', for bedding. Needs light to germinate.
Pansy	Mar to Apr	15–18°C	5 to 21	May to Oct	Germinates best in total darkness.
Pelargonium (geranium)	Sep to Oct	18–28°C	14 to 21	June to Oct	Overwinter at 7°C (45°F).
	Jan to Feb	18–21°C	14 to 21	June to Oct July* to Aug*	*March sowings. Grow on at 12°C (55°F) after hardening off seedlings for best results.
Perilla	Jan to Mar	21°C	14 to 28	July to Aug	Grown mainly for purple foliage. Germinates best in light.
Petunia	Mar to Apr	18–21°C	7 to 14	June to Oct	Germinates best in light.
Phlox drummondii	Mar to Apr	10–18°C	7 to 14	June to Aug	Germinates best in total darkness.
Portulaca	Feb to Mar	15–21°C	14 to 21	June to Aug/ Sep	Cover with 4mm (¼in) of compost.
Salvia splendens	Mar to Apr	18–21°C	14 to 21	July to Sep	Germinates best in light.
Stocks, 10-week	Feb to Mar, Mar to May	15–18°C	5 to 14	June to Aug, July to Sep	Germinates best in light. Can be sown outdoors in May.
Verbena	Feb to Mar	21°C	5 to 28	June to Oct	Germinates best in total darkness.
Zinnia	Mar to Apr	18–21°C	5 to 24	July to Sep	Can also be sown outdoors in May in mild areas.

Hardy annuals have fallen from favour in recent years. This may have a lot to do with traditional sowing methods, which involve a lot of hard work and may give disappointing results. They can, however, provide a cheap source of colour in your garden with the minimum of effort if you raise them the right way.

Shirley poppies can be left to self-seed if you rake over the soil in the autumn.

Sowing outdoors

Hardy annuals can be sown outdoors in spring once the soil is in a workable condition. In milder areas, some types can also be sown outdoors in early autumn for early flowering (see Table on page 64), though these would need cloche protection in most areas.

The vast majority of hardy annuals germinate freely and quickly. They have to, because in nature they need to flower and set seed within one season in order to survive from one year to the next. But you still need to prepare the bed carefully, and thin the plants and keep them watered. Hardy annuals do not need fertilisers or good soil – they should flower quickly and prolifically even on poor soil. Rich soil may lead to a lot of leaves and larger plants but fewer flowers. But dig the soil thoroughly and let it settle for a week or two before sowing to give new weeds a chance to emerge and be hoed or killed before sowing.

Sowing in straight rows is much better than sowing broadcast, which makes weeding and thinning a nightmare. But for sowing in patches or irregular 'blocks' you will need to vary the angles of the drills from patch to patch to avoid the appearance of regimented lines. The rows won't be noticeable once the plants have grown.

The areas can be marked out with a stick or cane to start with. Filling in the outlines with sand or vermiculite will help you to visualise the finished plan.

Water the ground thoroughly before you sow if the soil is dry.

If the ground has been watered thoroughly enough you should not need to water again before the seedlings germinate.

Hoe and hand weed until the young plants start to cover the soil. Some plants will need supporting – ideally with twiggy pea sticks – and this should be done early so that the plants can grow through the sticks and completely hide them.

Mark out irregular blocks for different annuals and sow in straight rows .

Sowing under glass

Hardy annuals are a cheap and quick source of colour in the garden, but they can be a big disappointment when sown outdoors. Thinning and weeding can be a problem. In a bad spring, on heavy soils, or in the North, when outdoor sowings have to be delayed, you may not get any flowers until late August when the season is nearly over. In many cases they are best raised in trays in an unheated greenhouse or cold frame in March. They can be planted out to fill gaps or even as bedding, and will flower by June or July. You can even get away without pricking out the seedlings. Once the roots fill the tray, simply cut up the seedlings into 5–8cm (2–3in) squares and plant out in clumps.

Clarkia pulchella is ideal for filling gaps and for cut flowers. Can be sown in autumn for early flowering.

WHAT ABOUT MIXED ANNUALS?

Most seedsmen offer packets of mixed annuals. The pictures on the packets or in the catalogue usually look charming, but what can you expect?

A small pack of mixed annuals is likely to look disappointing and untidy, especially if there is a risk of a few dominant plants swamping the display. Some seedsmen, however, offer separate tall-growing and dwarf mixtures. This is a good idea because it reduces the chance of tall plants swamping the small ones. Even so, some seeds will germinate much more rapidly than others, and some plants will grow much more vigorously and take up more space.

When thinning within the rows, be careful not to remove the smallest seedlings and leave just the largest – you'll be removing the plants that are slower to germinate.

Improving performance

Stopping   You can produce shorter, bushier plants by pinching out the growing tips while the plants are young, and possibly again later. This will delay flowering but may produce better plants. It's worth stopping a few plants as an experiment.

Deadheading   Seed production takes a lot of energy from the plant and may give you problems with self-sown seedlings the following spring. Regular dead-heading will keep the plants looking tidy and also probably keep them blooming longer.

However, it is only worthwhile for small displays, in tubs or window-boxes, say, or where individual flowers are large, such as larkspurs and sunflowers.

Identifying seedlings
Sowing in rows will make seedling identification easier, but you may still have problems. You could, on weedy ground, sow a few seeds of each variety in labelled pots, so that you have a 'reference collection' to help resolve any doubts.

Remove dead flowers to prolong flowering season and to prevent unwanted seedlings.

HARDY ANNUALS: A – C

The Table below contains most of the hardy annuals that you are likely to find in the major seed catalogues. Each plant has been given an overall rating as to its garden merit.

The plant names in the Table are the ones you are likely to find in the catalogues – this may be the common name or the Latin name (or both where different names are used in different catalogues).

Notes:
[1] From a March sowing. Later sowings may flower in less time
[2] ★   Flowering period short or flowers not spectacular
   ★★   Attractive but untidy habit or needs staking
   ★★★   Bold display, long period of interest, no staking
[3] Can be used in dried arrangements
[4] Grown for foliage rather than flowers
[5] Sap is poisonous

	weeks to flower[1]	sowing depth	distance apart	autumn sowing	garden merit[2]	gap filler	edging plant	cut flower	frag-rance	rock garden
Acroclinium	17	6mm(¼in)	23cm(9in)	–	★★★	–	–	[3]	–	–
Adonis aestivalis	14	6mm(¼in)	23cm(9in)	–	★★	–	–	■	–	■
Agrostemma milas	17	surface	23cm(9in)	yes	★	■	–	■	–	–
Alyssum (sweet)	14	6mm(¼in)		yes	★★★	–	■	–	–	■
Anchusa 'Blue Angel'	17	12mm(½in)	30cm(12in)	–	★★★	■	■	■	–	–
Asperula azurea 'Setosa' (A. orientalis)	11	6mm(¼in)	23cm(9in)	yes	★★	–	■	■	–	■
Atriplex hortensis	13	6mm(¼in)	45cm(18in)	–	★★	■	–	[4]	–	–
Bartonia aurea	17	6mm(¼in)	23cm(9in)	–	★★	–	–	■	–	–
Cacalia coccinea	22	3mm(⅛in)	15cm(6in)	–	★	–	–	■	–	–
Calendula	16	12mm(½in)	23cm(9in)	–	★★★	■	–	■	–	–
Calliopsis (coreopsis) (annual)	21	6mm(¼in)	23cm(9in)	–	★★	■	–	■	–	–
Candytuft (annual)	13	6mm(¼in)	10cm(4in)	yes	★★★	–	■	■	–	–
Chrysanthemum carinatum (C. tricolor)	18	6mm(¼in)	30cm(12in)	–	★★	■	–	■	–	–
C. coronarium	17	6mm(¼in)	30cm(12in)	–	★★	■	–	■	–	–
C. indorum 'Bridal Robe'	17	6mm(¼in)	30cm(12in)	–	★★	–	–	■	–	–
C. multicaule	16	6mm(¼in)	30cm(12in)	–	★★	■	–	–	–	–
C. paludosum (miniature marguerite)	16	6mm(¼in)	23cm(9in)	–	★★	■	–	■	–	–
C. spectabile 'Cecilia'	16	6mm(¼in)	30cm(12in)	–	★★	■	–	■	–	–

	weeks to flower[1]	sowing depth	distance apart	autumn spring	garden merit[2]	gap filler	edging plant	cut flower	frag-rance	rock garden
Clarkia elegans	16	6mm(¼in)	23cm(9in)	yes	★★★	■	—	■	—	—
Clarkia pulchella	16	6mm(¼in)	30cm(12in)	yes	★★★	■	—	■	—	—
Convolvulus minor	15	12mm(½in)	30cm(12in)	—	★★	—	■	—	—	—
Cornflower (Centaurea cyanus)	15	12mm(½in)	23cm(9in)	—	★★	■	—	—	—	—
Crepis rubra	14	6mm(¼in)	15cm(6in)	yes	★★	—	—	—	—	—
Cynoglossum	17	6mm(¼in)	30cm(12in)	—	★	—	—	—	—	—
Dimorphotheca aurantiaca hybrids	14	6mm(¼in)	15cm(6in)	—	★★★	■	—	—	—	—
Echium	15	6mm(¼in)	23cm(9in)	yes	★★★	■	■	■	—	—
Eschscholzia	15	6mm(¼in)	23cm(9in)	yes	★★	■	—	—	—	—
Euphorbia marginata	21	6mm(¼in)	30cm(12in)	—	★★	■	—	[4] [5]	—	—
Gilia capitata	14	6mm(¼in)	15cm(6in)	yes	★★	■	—	—	—	—
G. 'Summer Song'	11	6mm(¼in)	15cm(6in)	yes	★	■	—	■	—	—
Godetia	15	6mm(¼in)	30cm(12in)	yes	★★	■	—	—	—	—
Gypsophila elegans	13	6mm(¼in)	15cm(6in)	yes	★★	—	—	■	—	—
Helichrysum	19	6mm(¼in)	30cm(12in)	—	★★	■	—	[3]	—	—
Ionopsidium acaule	8	6mm(¼in)	8cm(3in)	—	★	—	■	—	—	■
Jacobea (Senecio elegans)	15	6mm(¼in)	15cm(6in)	—	★★★	■	—	—	—	—
Kaulfussia amelloides	16	6mm(¼in)	10cm(4in)	—	★★★	—	■	—	—	■
Larkspur	23	6mm(¼in)	30cm(12in)	yes	★★	■	—	■	—	—
Lavatera	17	12mm(½in)	60cm(24in)	—	★★	■	—	■	—	—
Layia elegans	17	surface	15cm(6in)	—	★★	—	—	■	—	—
Leptosiphon	14	6mm(¼in)	5cm(2in)	—	★★	—	■	—	—	■
Limnanthes douglasii	13	3mm(⅛in)	10cm(4in)	yes	★★	—	■	—	—	■
Linaria maroccana	13	3mm(⅛in)	10cm(4in)	yes	★	—	■	—	—	■
Linum grandiflorum	15	6mm(¼in)	10cm(4in)	—	★★	■	—	—	—	—
Lonas inodora	18	6mm(¼in)	15cm(6in)	—	★★	—	—	[3]	—	—
Love-lies-bleeding (Amaranthus caudatus)	21	3mm(⅛m)	60cm(24in)	—	★★	■	—	■	—	—
Lupinus (annual type)	17	12mm(½in)	45cm(18in)	—	★★	■	—	■	—	—
Malope	18	6mm(¼in)	23cm(9in)	—	★★	■	—	—	—	—
Matthiola bicornis (night-scented stock)	12	6mm(¼in)	23cm(9in)	—	★	■	—	—	■	—
Mignonette (Reseda odorata)	17	3mm(⅛in)	10cm(4in)	—	★★	■	—	■	■	—
Nasturtium	15	6mm(½in)	30cm(12in)	—	★★	■	—	—	—	—
Nemophila insignis (N. menzies)	15	6mm(¼in)	8cm(3in)	yes	★★	—	■	—	—	■
Nicandra physaloides	18	6mm(¼in)	30cm(12in)	—	★★★	■	—	—	—	—
Nigella (love-in-a-mist)	16	6mm(¼in)	15cm(6in)	yes	★★	■	—	■	—	—
Phacelia campanularia	16	6mm(¼in)	8cm(3in)	yes	★	—	■	—	—	■
Poppy (various) (Papaver)	16-17	6mm(¼in)	23cm(9in)	yes	★★	■	—	—	—	—
Prince's feather (Amaranthus hypochondriacus)	19	3mm(⅛in)	45cm(18in)	—	★★	■	—	—	—	—
Rhodanthe manglesii (Helipterum)	17	12mm(½in)	15cm(6in)	—	★★	■	—	[3]	—	—
Salvia horminum (clary)	17	6mm(¼in)	15cm(6in)	yes	★★	■	—	■	—	—
Saponaria vaccaria	15	6mm(¼in)	15cm(6in)	—	★★	■	—	■	—	—
Scabious stellata (Scabious 'Drumstick' or 'Paper Moon')	16	12mm(½in)	23cm(9in)	—	★★	■	—	[3]	—	—
Silene armeria 'Electra'	18	12mm(½in)	60cm(24in)	yes	★	■	—	■	—	—
Sunflower (Helianthus anuus)	18	6mm(¼in)	23cm(9in)	—	★★	■	—	■	—	—
Sweet sultan (Centaurea moschata)	17	6mm(¼in)	23cm(9in)	—	★★	■	—	■	—	—
Sweet William (Dianthus barbatus)	17	6mm(¼in)	23cm(9in)	—	★★	■	■	■	■	—
Virginian stock (Malcomia maritima)	11	6mm(¼in)	15cm(6in)	yes	★	—	■	■	—	—
Viscaria occulata	16	6mm(¼in)	10cm(4in)	—	★	■	—	—	—	—
Xeranthemum	19	6mm(¼in)	15cm(6in)	—	★★	■	—	[3]	—	—

The so-called spring bedding plants and a few popular border plants are biennials (or short-lived perennials best grown as biennials), i.e. they are sown one year to flower the next. Most are quite easy to grow from seed, but timing is crucial. Sowing too late can mean plants are killed by autumn frost or will never reach flowering stage.

Details of sowing and flowering dates are given in the Table. If you're raising large numbers from fairly cheap seed, the best method is to sow in rows in a seedbed, thin out as soon as the seedlings are large enough and plant out in final positions in September or October (September in the North). However, germination is usually poorer outside, and you can easily lose vulnerable seedlings in very hot or very wet conditions, or to slugs. Consequently, many gardeners prefer to start their seeds off in trays, transplant them into boxes or pots and then move them outside when they've outgrown these containers. This is certainly worth the effort for pansies, which are slow growing as seedlings, and for polyanthus, which can be expensive and slow to germinate.

When the plants are ready to go outside, line them out in a nursery bed if their final positions are full of summer bedding plants. Most plants should be spaced about 15cm (6in) apart in the nursery bed, though double daisies and pansies need only 5cm (2in) between them. Final spacings are given in the Table.

Brompton stocks are not very hardy, so in most areas it is best to sow in the cold frame and prick out into pots for planting out in March. In mild areas sow thinly in a nursery bed in June or July for planting out in March.

	when to sow	sowing depth	autumn planting distance	in flower	notes
FOR BEDDING					
Brompton stock (*Matthiola incana*)	June to July	6mm (¼in)	30cm (12in)	May to June	Sow in trays. Overwinter under glass and plant in spring.
Double daisies (*Bellis perennis*)	May to June	6mm (¼in)	15–20cm (6–8in)	Mar to July	Self-seeding can be a problem.
Forget-me-nots (*Myosotis*)	May to July	6mm (¼in)	15–30cm (6–12in)	May to July	Self-seeding can be a problem.
Pansies, winter flowering (*Viola* x *wittrockiana*)	June to July	6mm (¼in)	25–30cm (10–12in)	Jan to July	Can also be sown in cold frame September to October for flowers from February.
Polyanthus (*Primula vulgaris elatior*)	May to July	3mm (⅛in)	25–30cm (10–12in)	Jan to July	'Crescendo' is a hardier type.
Siberian wallflower (*Cheiranthus* x *allionii*)	May to July	6mm (¼in)	30cm (12in)	May to July	
Sweet William (*Dianthus barbatus*)	May to June	6mm (¼in)	20–25cm (8–10in)	June to July	'Wee Willie' and 'Roundabout' will flower in same year if sown February to March under glass.
Wallflower (*Cheiranthus cheiri*)	May to June	6mm (¼in)	25–40cm (10*–16in)	Apr to June	Protect with cloches in cold winter. *Spacing for dwarf types.
FOR THE BORDER					
Canterbury bell (*Campanula medium*)	Apr to May	6mm (¼in)	30cm (12in)	May to July	Dead-head for second flush of flowers.
Evening primrose (*Oenothera biennis*)	June to July	6mm (¼in)	30cm (12in)	June to Oct	Self-seeds freely. See page 89 for perennial types.
Foxglove (*Digitalis purpurea*)	June to July	barely cover	40–60cm (16–24in)	June to July	Seed very fine so best started in pots. 'Foxy' will flower in same year if sown under glass in March.
Honesty (*Lunaria annua, L. biennis*)	June to July	12mm (½in)	30cm (12in)	Apr to June	Variegated form comes true from seed. Self-seeds.
Icelandic poppies (*Papaver nudicale*)	May to June	6mm (¼in)	Sow *in situ*, thin to 30cm (12in)	June to Aug	Flowers are poor if left for second year.
Miss Willmott's ghost (*Eryngium giganteum*)	June to July	3mm (⅛in)	60cm (24in)	Aug to Sep	Self-seeds freely.
Sweet rocket (*Hesperis matronalis*)	Apr to May	6mm (¼in)	45cm (18in)	June	Self-seeds.
Teasel (*Dipsacus fullonum*)	June to July	3mm (⅛in)	45cm (18in)	July to Aug	Self-seeds.
Verbascum species (mullein)	Apr	6mm (¼in)	30–60cm (12–24in)	June to Aug	Germinates best below 18°C (65°F). Frequently self-seeds.

BULBS: TECHNIQUES

If you want a number of bulbs for naturalising or to create a drift of a rare or unusual variety, you can save a lot of money by bulking them up yourself. The techniques you can use are described on the following four pages. Details of the best methods for individual bulbs can be found on pages 72 and 73.

BULBLETS, BULBILS AND CORMLETS

Bulblets (also called offsets) and cormlets are small bulbs formed around the base of a parent bulb or corm. Bulbils are very similar, but they are formed either in the leaf axils – as with some lilies – or, in the case of the tree onion and a few other members of the onion family, on top of the flower stem in place of seed heads.

Bulblets, bulbils and cormlets are often about the size of peas, or even smaller, and can be sown in much the same way as seeds. With some bulbs, such as daffodils, however, the offsets are quite large and can be replanted in their flowering positions straight away. Most will take from 1 to 3 years to reach flowering size. All these young bulbs will reach flowering size more quickly if they are fed fortnightly throughout the growing season with a weak liquid tomato feed.

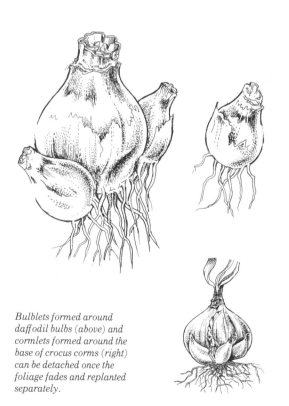

Bulblets formed around daffodil bulbs (above) and cormlets formed around the base of crocus corms (right) can be detached once the foliage fades and replanted separately.

BULBLETS AND CORMLETS

Bulblets are best removed either at the end of the growing season, when the foliage has died down (e.g. bulbous irises), or just as growth is beginning and you're repotting (e.g. lachenalia).

Lift garden bulbs carefully – any damage may result in fungal diseases. Gently pull away the bulblets and remove the old soil and loose outer scales. Grade them for size and, unless replanting immediately, store in shallow trays of sand or peat, almost dry to prevent them from drying out completely, in a cool but frost-free airy place. Before replanting, dig over the ground, remove weeds and stones and incorporate plenty of well-rotted organic material. If your soil is heavy, work in grit as well.

Container-grown plants, such as lachenalias (which are grown as houseplants), need to be carefully eased out of their containers with the rootball intact. Tease away the old potting compost, detach healthy bulblets and repot in fresh compost.

Cormlets   When the foliage has withered and dried off, carefully dig out the corms together with the cormlets. Grade them for size and throw away the very small ones as they'll take too long to reach flowering size. Plant out the largest cormlets – anything over 1.5cm (½in) in diameter – along with the parent corms to bloom the following spring. Set them about 5–8cm (2–3in) deep and 8–10cm (3–4in) apart. Sow the smaller cormlets – pea size to 1.5cm (½in) in diameter – at about the same depth but 3–5cm (1–2in) apart in rows in a nursery bed during July or early August. Grow these on for at least a year before planting out in their flowering positions. For species crocus you can reduce all the measurements given above.

Gladioli cormlets are tender, so overwinter them indoors and plant out in late March about 5–8cm (2–3in) deep in sand-lined drills. A layer of gorse or holly should deter mice. Lightly cover with more sand before covering with soil. Lift the cormlets in autumn to dry off and overwinter indoors again. The following spring plant the largest – those of 2.5–3cm (1–1¼in) in diameter – in their flowering positions. Grow the others on for another year in a nursery bed.

If you have only a few corms, or are afraid of losing track of them, they can be grown on in containers. Place 6 or 7 about 3cm (1in) deep in, say, a 13cm (5in) pot of loam-based potting compost. Keep moist and grow on in a cold frame at least during the first winter.

BULBILS

Stem bulbils form on 4 species of lilies: *L. bulbiferum*, *L. sargentiae*, *L. sulphureum* and *L. tigrinum* (tiger lily). They should be gathered just before they fall – usually about 2 or 3 weeks after the blooms have faded. Plant in a semi-shaded position with the tip just below the soil. Most will flower within 2 or 3 years.

You can encourage a lily to form bulbils by ripping out the flower stem before the buds open and burying it at 45°, half in and half out of some peaty compost. Alternatively, cut the flower stem into 15cm (6in) segments, trim the leaves off (just leaving the stalks) from the bottom 13cm (5in) and plant vertically in peaty compost with the top 2.5cm (1in) showing. Bulbils should form on the stem beneath the compost. This method is worth trying for any lily that forms leaves singly or in pairs on its stem. Avoid propagating from a lily with striping on the leaves as this is a sign of virus disease.

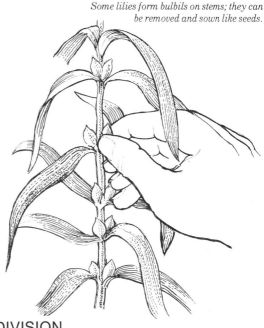

Some lilies form bulbils on stems; they can be removed and sown like seeds.

PODS

Pods, sometimes called pips, are bulbils that form on the flower head as the flowers wither. Leeks and ornamental alliums also produce pods. To propagate, remove them from the flower head and discard any with brown spots – a sure sign of disease. Soak the remainder in a strong solution of benomyl, carbendazim or thiophanate-methyl. Plant them either singly into small pots or 4cm (1½in) apart in trays using a standard potting compost. Keep barely moist in a well-lit, airy spot at about 7–10°C (45–50°F), increasing the temperature to about 13°C (55°F) in January. Gradually increase watering as the plants grow. Harden off in spring before planting out. This will produce leeks ready for harvesting in winter. Ornamental alliums will normally take 2 years before flowering. The number of pods per seed head will vary from 20 to 150 or more.

DIVISION

This method is especially useful for bulbs or corms that form clumps, and is normally best carried out as the plants are starting into growth in spring or when the leaves are withering and yellowing at the end of the season. This often means summer in the case of spring-flowering bulbs, such as scillas and grape hyacinths. Snowdrops and winter aconites should be divided as soon as they have finished flowering, while still green, and replanted immediately. To obtain maximum numbers, gently tease out each bulb so as not to damage the roots and discard any bulbs or bulblets that are withered, shrivelled, soft or rotten.

Another form of division can be carried out on begonias. Prior to planting in spring, cut the tubers in two so that each piece has several buds or eyes. Treat wounds with a fungicide, such as sulphur, before planting.

Dividing a begonia tuber: make sure each half has several healthy buds.

Note: If you intend to lift your bulbs and corms frequently for propagation, it is worth while planting them in plastic mesh baskets, or laying plastic netting under them so they can be lifted *en masse*.

Scoring

This technique is particularly useful for hyacinths, which are otherwise slow to propagate. In autumn, take a flowering-size bulb and clean off any soil, loose scales or roots and then make 2 or 3 deep cuts across the base – up to one-third the depth of the bulb. Half fill a pot with potting compost then put in a 1cm (½in) layer of clean, coarse sand. Set the prepared bulb on this, then add compost until only the top quarter of the bulb is showing. Grow the bulb on for a year, keeping it moist but not too wet, then reduce watering and allow it to die down in the autumn. Keep the compost barely moist in winter. In the spring of the second year, leaves should appear around the outer edges of the bulb. When these turn yellow in about July, gradually dry off the bulb, then ease it out of the pot and carefully remove the young bulblets (from 4 to 20 or more). Pot these up, or set them out in trays of potting compost, and grow on for up to 4 years, until they reach flowering size – a minimum of 4.5cm (1¾in) in diameter in the case of hyacinths. During this period, repot annually.

Apart from hyacinths, scoring can also be used for daffodils, tulips, gladioli and crocuses.

Bulblets formed on the bottom of the scored bulb.

Scooping

This technique is most effective with hyacinths. In autumn, cut away and discard the whole of the base plate and a shallow cone of tissue above it, reaching about a quarter of the way into the bulb. Try to cut cleanly without crushing or bruising the bulb. A woodworking gouge, a scalpel or a sharpened teaspoon make good tools for this, and it's a good idea to practise on an onion first. Dust with fungicide before potting up, and treat as for scored bulbs.

In autumn, use a sharpened spoon to remove the base of the bulb and then plant upside down as described under Scoring.

New bulblets will form in the hollowed-out base of the bulb.

The following spring, leaves should appear. Once they die down in summer, lift the bulb.

Carefully remove the bulblets, pot them up and grow them on until they are large enough to plant out.

Scaling

This method is commonly used for lilies. After flowering, in late summer lift the bulbs and pull off the scales, ensuring that they come away as near the base as possible. Soak the scales in a fungicide solution, mix with vermiculite and follow the same technique as described for chip segments.

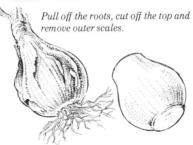

Soak the bulb in fungicide, remove outer scales and replant.

Soak the scales in fungicide, mix with vermiculite and keep in the warm for 12–14 weeks until bulblets form.

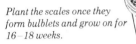

Plant the scales once they form bulblets and grow on for 16–18 weeks.

Once foliage dies down, lift the scales to remove individual bulblets and grow on separately.

Chip segments

This is a modification of scaling which allows a similar technique to be used for other bulbs. Daffodil bulbs are as good as any to try, but the technique is also successful with hippeastrums and could be tried for other bulbs. After lifting, between June and August, select large, firm, healthy bulbs and allow them to dry for a few days indoors.

Hygiene is critical with this method. Brush or rub off any remains of soil, pull off the roots and trim back the top, then peel off all the brown, outer scales. Soak the bulb in a fungicide solution, such as benomyl, for 10 minutes, then, using a clean, sharp knife, cut the bulb into 8 or 16 segments. Each section must have a piece of base plate (the round bit from which roots are formed) attached. Soak the scales in a solution of systemic fungicide such as benomyl and then allow to drain for about 10 minutes. Mix the scales with a small quantity of clean vermiculite – previously soaked in clean water and allowed to cool (the warmth generated can otherwise encourage rotting). Put

Pull off the roots, cut off the top and remove outer scales.

the scales into a clear plastic bag, blow in it to create an air space and seal the top. Keep the bag somewhere warm, such as an airing cupboard, and shake periodically to ensure a good oxygen supply. After 12 to 14 weeks bulblets should have developed on the scales. Once this happens, plant the scales about 5cm (2in) apart into pots or trays of fresh potting compost. Grow on at about 10°C (50°F) for another 16 to 18 weeks. Once leaves die down, remove individual bulblets from the scales and pot up separately. Grow on in an unheated greenhouse or cold frame for another year or 2 before planting in the garden. Expect them to reach flowering size in the next 2 years.

Carefully cut the bulb into segments and treat as for scales, above.

Twin scaling

This is a further modification of chip segments. Follow the previous method, but cut each chip again (see illustration) to form 2 or 4 twin scales, giving you up to 64 plants from one bulb.

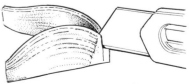

Dividing chip segments.

species	how	when	how long to flowering	new plants per bulb	likely success rate
Allium (ornamental onion)	bulbils	Sum	1–2 years	5–8	75%
	division of clump	Spr, Aut	1–2 years	2–4	65%
	pods	Sum, Aut	2–3 years	30–120	90%
	seed	Spr, Aut	2–3 years	[1]	65%
Anemone, corm-forming types	seed	Sum	2–3 years	[1]	40%
Begonia, tuberous [T]	basal cuttings	Spr	6 months	3–5	80%
	stem cuttings	Sum	12–15 months	4–8	70%
	division of tubers	Spr	3 months	2–3	90%
	seed	Spr	9 months	[1]	55%
Brodiaea [T]	offsets	Aut	2–3 years	2–4	85%
	seed	Spr	3–6 years	[1]	35%
Camassia (quamash)	offsets	Spr, Aut	1–3 years	2–4	80%
	seed	Sum	3–5 years	[1]	35%
Chionodoxa	offsets	Sum, Aut	1–2 years	2–4	90%
	chip segments	July to Aug	2–3 years	4–6	65%
	scoring	July to Sep	2–3 years	4–8	65%
	seed	Sum	2–3 years	[1]	60%
Colchicum (autumn crocus)	offsets	Sum	2–3 years	2–3	90%
	seeds	Sum	3–4 years	[1]	45%
Cyclamen, hardy	fresh seed	July to Aug	1–2 years	[1]	35%
	bought seed	Spr (soak for 24 hours)	2–3 years	[1]	25%
Daffodil (narcissus)	offsets	Sum, Aut	9–21 months	2–3	85%
	twin scaling	Sum	3–7 years	30–60	50%
	chip segments	Aut	3–7 years	12–16	60%
	seed	Sum	3–6 years	[1]	25%
Eranthis (winter aconite)	division	after flowering	2 years	2–3	90%
	seed	Spr (when ripe)	3–5 years	[1]	25%
Erythronium (dog's tooth violet)	offsets	late Sum, Aut	2–3 years	2–3	85%
	seed	Spr	5–7 years	[1]	25%
Freesia [T]	cormlets	Sum	4–6 months	2–3	90%
	seed	Spr, Sum	6–8 months	[1]	60%
Fritillaria imperialis (crown imperial)	offsets	late Sum	4–5 years	2–3	60%
	seed	Sum	6–8 years	[1]	25%
Fritillaria meleagris (snake's head fritillary)	bulblets	late Sum	3–4 years	2–4	60%
	seed	Sum	4–6 years	[1]	30%
Galanthus (snowdrop)	division	after flowering	2 years	2–4	90%
Gladioli [T]	cormlet	Spr	1–3 years	2–8	90%
	scoring	Spr	2–4 years	4–16	70%
	seed	Spr	2–3 years	[1]	60%
Gloxinias [T]	division of tuber	Spr	4–6 months	2–4	85%
	stem cuttings	Spr	4–6 months	2–6	70%
	leaf cuttings	Sum	1 year	20–30	50%
	seed	late Win, Spr	1½–3 years	[1]	25%

[1] Number of plants depends on how many seeds you sow

species	how	when	how long to flowering	new plants per bulb	likely success rate
Hippeastrum [T]	offsets	Aut, Spr	3 years	2–3	75%
	twin scaling	Win	3–5 years	30–60	55%
	chip segments	Win	3–4 years	12–16	60%
	seed	Spr	3–4 years	[1]	35%
Hyacinth	bulblets	Aut, Spr	2–4 years	2–3	70%
	scoring, scooping	Aut	3–5 years	6–12	55%
	seed	Sum	2–4 years	[1]	45%
Iris, bulbous	bulblets	Sum	1–2 years	2–4	60%
	seed	Spr	2–3 years	[1]	40%
Ixia (African corn lily)	offsets	Aut	1–2 years	2–3	65%
	seed	Sum	2–3 years	[1]	55%
Leucojum (snowflake)	division of clump	Sum, Aut	4–5 years	2–3	65%
	offsets	Sum, Aut	3–4 years	2–6	75%
	seed	Sum, Aut	4–6 years	[1]	25%
Lilies	bulbils	Aut	2–5 years	10–12	50%
	bulblets	Aut	2–4 years	2–6	55%
	division of clump	Aut, Spr	2–3 years	2–4	70%
	scaling	Aut, Spr	3–6 years	16–60	50%
	seed	Aut, Spr	3–6 years	[1]	30%
Montbretia (crocosmia)	division of clump	Aut, Spr	6–18 months	2–6	90%
	offsets	Aut	1–3 years	2–4	75%
	seed	Spr	1½–2½ years	[1]	60%
Muscari (grape hyacinth)	division of clump	Sum	1–2 years	4–6	95%
	seed	Sum	2–4 years	[1]	65%
Nerine bowdenii	offsets	Spr, Sum	1½–2 years	4–6	95%
	seed	Spr, Sum	3–5 years	[1]	40%
Ornithogalum (star of Bethlehem)	bulbils	Aut, Spr	1–3 years	2–4	65%
	seed	Aut	3–5 years	[1]	45%
Oxalis adenophylla	division of clump	Spr, Sum	1–2 years	2–4	85%
Ranunculus asiaticus [T]	division of clump	Aut, Spr	1–3 years	3–4	65%
Scilla (squills and bluebells)	division of clump	Sum	1–2 years	2–4	80%
	seed	Sum	3–5 years	[1]	40%
Sparaxis [T]	offsets	Aut	1–2 years	2–3	65%
Sternbergia	offsets	Sum, Aut	1–2 years	2–3	55%
Tigridia [T] (tiger flower)	cormlets	Aut, Spr	2–3 years	2–6	80%
Tropaeolum tuberosum [T]	division of tubers	Spr	1–2 years	3–6	80%
	seed	Spr	1½–2½ years	[1]	50%
Tubergiana	offsets	Aut	2–3 years	2–3	55%
Tulip	offsets	Sum	2–3 years	2–5	75%
	seed (species only)	Aut, Spr	3–5 years	[1]	25%

[T] Tender or not reliably hardy, so lift each autumn and store in frost-free conditions over winter and replant in spring

HERBACEOUS PERENNIALS: TECHNIQUES

Most herbaceous plants need to be divided regularly in order to keep them growing strongly, and this is also a useful way of getting a few more plants. You can also propagate herbaceous perennials from various types of cuttings and from seed. Details of the techniques are given on pages 75 to 76 and the requirements of individual plants are given in the Tables on pages 77 to 94.

Russel lupins will flower in the same year if seed is sown in February. Nick the seed coat or soak the seed for 24 hours to improve germination.

DIVISION

Why divide? Some plants such as Michaelmas daisies are fast growing and could take over less vigorous companions if not divided regularly. Division also improves old established clumps that have old woody centres and an outer ring of young vigorous growth. Division is also a useful method of producing a few extra plants, and many perennials can be divided every few years if you want to increase your stocks.

When? Herbaceous perennials should be divided once flowering declines or clumps start to die out in the middle. It is possible to divide plants successfully throughout the growing season, although spring and autumn are the usual times. The 'ideal' time for most situations is given in the Tables, but a lot can depend on the soil type and the weather. Heavy soils may be too wet in autumn, and plants are often best divided in late spring. On light soils, spring divisions will need regular watering until established.

It is often more convenient to tackle a section of a border all at the same time but, for best results, divide each plant according to its needs.

What to do

Plants with fleshy crowns and roots
e.g. hosta, kniphofia.
Fleshy crowns are not easy to pull apart, so they are best cut with an old knife. The ideal time for division is spring, when plump buds are beginning to shoot and you can identify the pieces worth propagating.

For small clumps
● Lift and shake away loose soil.
● Divide with a knife so each piece has at least one developed bud.
● Dust fleshy cut surfaces with a fungicide such as sulphur or benomyl to prevent rotting.
● Replant or pot up at once to prevent drying out.

For large clumps
As above, but make initial division with a sharp spade or a half-moon edging iron or try the 2-fork method. Discard the worn-out centre and divide outer portions into smaller clumps with a knife.

Dividing rhizomes.

Plants with rhizomes
e.g. anaphalis, bergenia, physostegia.
A rhizome is a stem that grows horizontally, either on the soil surface or underground, producing roots and shoots at regular intervals.
● Lift, remove loose soil and cut back leaves to about 8cm (3in) above the roots.
● Cut away any of the old rhizomes with a knife, and cut young healthy rhizomes in sections, each one with a root and a shoot.
● Replant creeping underground rhizomes below the surface and surface rhizomes level with the soil with their roots pointing downwards. Irises should be planted on the surface.

Plants with fibrous crowns
e.g. geranium, hemerocallis.
These are best divided directly after flowering when the new shoots and roots are developing. Late-flowering plants such as asters would be best divided the following spring.

For small clumps
● Remove old flower stems and cut tall stems back to around 10cm (4in) before lifting to reduce water loss from the leaves and to encourage new growth.
● Lift with a fork and shake off the soil.
● Pull or cut into small pieces, each bit having at least one bud or shoot.
● Discard old, woody pieces. The young shoots around the outside will generally be quicker to establish.

For large clumps
● As above, but lift on to some sacking or a polythene sheet and try to shake off loose soil.
● Lie plants on their side and prise apart the clump with 2 forks (if you do it from above, the shoots are more likely to get broken) as necessary according to the size of clump.
● Clumps can be further subdivided with 2 hand trowels back to back or a half-moon lawn edger.

Plants that form loose clumps, such as Michaelmas daisies, can be divided by hand and separated into single stems with roots attached.

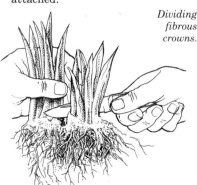

Dividing fibrous crowns.

Taking root cuttings

Some plants do not respond well to regular division and will not root from shoot cuttings. These plants can often be raised from small pieces of root.

If you want to take a number of root cuttings, it may be worth preparing the plant beforehand. Lift a healthy plant between November and early March and cut back any top growth. Cut off roots near the crown using a knife and replant. Grow on for a further year before taking root cuttings. Preparing the plants in this way should improve your chances of success.

● Lift the plant in winter during the dormant season, cut off top growth and put the roots in a bucket of water to wash off the soil.

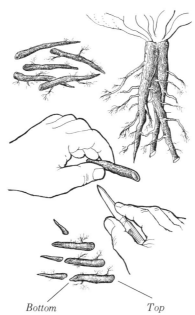

Bottom   *Top*

● Select young fleshy roots and cut them into sections using a sharp knife. Make a straight cut at the stem and a slanted cut at the base. Roots of pencil thickness are cut into 5cm (2in) sections and planted the right way up in pots so that they are just buried. Plants with thin roots are cut into 8cm (3in) sections and planted horizontally in trays of compost.

● Before inserting the cuttings, remove any fibrous side roots and place the roots in a plastic bag, sprinkle a fungicide such as benomyl over them and give the bag a good shake.

● Once strong shoots have developed, pot up individually for planting out in the autumn.

Taking stem cuttings

Quite a few perennials can be raised from cuttings and will produce small flowering plants within a year. Overwintering cuttings in the greenhouse or cold frame is also a good way of insuring against winter losses.

Basal cuttings are taken in spring from the new shoots that arise from the base of the old stems. These can be removed when they are 5–8cm (2–3in) long and inserted into pots or trays of 2 parts moss peat and 1 part sand. Cuttings taken early in the year are best rooted in a propagator or on the windowsill in a pot covered with a plastic bag.

Soft cuttings can be taken throughout the summer. Remove tips of side shoots with about three pairs of leaves attached. Non-flowering shoots are best; otherwise remove any flower buds. Trim the cutting to below a leaf joint and remove the lower leaves. Most cuttings should be about 5cm (2in) long. Cover pots or trays with polythene and keep well shaded until the cuttings have rooted.

Heeled cuttings are produced by pulling side shoots from the main stem so that a strip of the parent stem comes away with the cutting. The 'heel' is then trimmed (see page 12) before cuttings are potted up.

Whatever type of cutting you take, move into pots of potting compost as soon as they have rooted. With cuttings taken in September, leave this until the following spring. Feed plants with a liquid fertiliser during the growing season if in their pots for more than 6 to 8 weeks.

Removing a basal cutting.

Saving seed

With most herbaceous plants you can remove the seed stalk up to a week before the seeds disperse naturally and keep them in a dry airy room to finish ripening. The easiest method is to put the seed heads in open paper bags so that the seeds can easily be collected. Some plants such as geraniums (cranesbills) eject their seeds, and it is best to tie a paper bag over the seed heads to collect the seed when it ripens. Some seeds must be sown fresh, but most can be stored in a cool dry place until required. Remember that seed from most named varieties won't produce plants identical to the parents.

> **FOR LOTS OF CUTTINGS**
> Pot up a plant in autumn, trim all the shoots right back and keep in the greenhouse or cold frame over winter. By spring the plant should have produced lots of lush new growth. You can use all the shoots for cuttings and then replant the parent plant in the garden. Plants actually seem to benefit from the spring pruning.

species	how	when	what to do
A			
Acaena (New Zealand burr)	division	late Spr	Divide before flowers and burrs form. Can be invasive unless divided every few years. Lift a portion of roots and gently tease into small clumps. Replant 45cm (18in) apart.
	stem cuttings	Sep	For a number of plants from a small clump, take cuttings from stem tips with 3 leaves attached. Plant out in spring.
Acanthus (bear's breeches)	root cuttings	Nov to Feb	Best undisturbed unless overcrowded, but you can take a few root cuttings by gently scraping away the soil around the base. Insert 3cm (1in) sections right way up into pots of sandy compost in a cold frame. Plant out 60cm (2ft) apart in late May. They should flower in a year or 2. Plants raised this way may have less jagged leaves.
	seed	Aut	Collect seed heads about a week before ripening. Ripen off in a warm dry place and sow in a cold frame. Grow on for 2 years before planting out. Flowering takes 3 to 4 years.
Achillea (milfoil, yarrow)	division	Aut or Spr	A 3-year-old clump can yield up to 10 plants. Replant 30–40cm (12–18in) apart.
	seed	Spr	Worthwhile for species such as *A. millefolium* or *A. filipendulina*, but seed from hybrids such as 'Moonshine' produces poor plants. Sow bought seed in spring (or saved seed in autumn when ripe) in the cold frame and grow on in pots or a nursery bed for autumn planting.
	basal cuttings	Spr	Root 5–8cm (2–3in) cuttings in a cold frame and plant out once established.
Agapanthus (African lily)	division	Spr or July to Sep	Best undisturbed, but can be divided every 3 to 4 years. Split the clump carefully.
	seed	Aut or Spr	Either buy seed (look for variety 'Headbourne Hybrid', which is sturdier than most) and sow in spring or collect the shiny black seed and sow fresh in the cold frame. Plant out in spring. Flowering takes 3 to 4 years.
Ajuga (bugle)	division	any time	Best divided every 2 years. Replant the young offsets 20–30cm (8–12in) apart and discard the old centres.
	cuttings	July to Aug	Take 8cm (3in) stem tips and root in the cold frame. Pot up in spring and plant out in autumn.
	seed	Spr	Not worthwhile, as seed of coloured varieties forms green seedlings.
Alchemilla mollis (lady's mantle)	division	Mar	Clumps can be divided every 3 to 4 years. Occasionally offsets can be removed without disturbing the whole plant. Replant divisions 45cm (18in) apart.
	seed	Spr	Sow saved or bought seeds in trays in the cold frame, prick out into pots or boxes and grow on for autumn planting. Self-sown seedlings can also be transplanted.
Alstroemeria	seed	Mar to Apr	Pick off seed before dispersed in late summer. Ripen indoors. Sow 2 seeds to 1 8cm (3in) pot in spring and cover with a polythene bag. Keep warm – 20°C (68°F) is ideal – for 3 weeks and then transfer pots to fridge for a further 3 weeks. Seeds should germinate in 10 to 14 days once brought back into warmth. Flowering takes 2 years.
Althaea rosea (hollyhock)	seed	May to June or Jan to Feb	Short lived, so best raised from seed every few years. Sow in May to June in final positions for flowers the following year, or in trays in January to February for flowers the same year (plant out in April). Young seed-raised plants are just as susceptible to rust as older ones.

species	how	when	what to do
Anaphalis (pearl everlasting)	division	Spr	Divide into small pieces every few years to give a few extra plants and prevent overcrowding.
	seed	Mar to Apr	Sow in the cold frame and prick out into boxes or nursery rows. Move to border in October or March. Will also self-seed.
	basal cuttings	Apr to May	Take 5–8cm (2–3in) cuttings. Plant out into nursery bed when well rooted and into final positions in October or March.
Anchusa (alkanet)	seed	May to June	Often best treated as a biennial (see page 66). Self-seeds freely.
	root cuttings	Oct or Feb	To propagate named varieties, take a few root cuttings from edge of clump, cut into 5cm (2in) sections and plant the right way up in pots in the cold frame. Plant out in mid- to late spring. They will flower the next summer.
Anemone x hybrida (*A. japonica*, Japanese anemone)	seed	Aug to Sep	Sow seeds once ripe in trays in the cold frame, prick out the seedlings into boxes and nursery rows in autumn. They will flower in the second year. Plants can be very variable, so grow them on to flowering size and plant only the best ones in the border.
	division	Aut or Spr	Plants resent disturbance, but as they spread so freely it is worth trying to move a few.
Anthemis tinctoria (golden marguerite) (For chamomile, *A. nobilis*, see Herbs, page 124)	basal cuttings	Spr	Take 5–8cm (2–3in) cuttings and root in the cold frame. Move to pots or boxes once rooted and keep in the cold frame for first winter. Plant out 38cm (15in) apart in spring.
	seed	Spr	Hybrid varieties, such as 'E.C. Buxton' and 'Wargrave Yellow', are far superior to species and cannot be raised from seed.
Aquilegia (columbine)	seed	Apr to May	Best to buy seed, as aquilegia hybridise freely and can produce very variable plants. Look for 'McKana Hybrids' in catalogues. Four to six weeks in fridge prior to sowing should improve germination. Sow outdoors and move to final positions in autumn or, for sowing after June, in March.
	division	Aut or Spr	Worthwhile only if you have a good plant. Carefully split crown into single stems and replant 30cm (12in) apart.
Armeria (thrift, sea pink)	division	Spr	Remove small rooted portions from around the edge of older plants and replant 25cm (10in) apart.
	seed	Aut	Collect ripe seeds and sow in trays in the cold frame. Prick out into boxes or pots in spring and plant out in autumn. Flowering takes 1 to 2 years.
Artemisia (herbaceous)	cuttings	Aut	To guard against winter losses, take 8cm (3in) heel cuttings and root in a well-ventilated cold frame. Pot up in spring and plant out in early summer 38–45cm (15–18in) apart.
	division	Spr	Large plants can be lifted every 3 years, and any side shoots that have formed roots can be detached and planted separately.
Arum italicum (Italian arum)	offsets (as soon as leaves turn yellow)	Sum	A congested clump can yield as many as 20 to 30 offsets, which can be detached from the tubers and replanted 15–23cm (6–9in) apart. The best garden variety is the marble-leaved *A. italicum* 'Pictum', which does not come true from seed.
Aruncus sylvester (*A. dioicus*, goat's beard)	division	Spr or Sep to Oct	Divide every 3 to 5 years. Use a sharp spade or lawn edger to get through the woody crown. If self-sown seedlings are a problem, propagate only the male plants and throw away the females. The male plants have more feathery plumes and don't bear seed heads. Replant 60cm (24in) apart.

species	how	when	what to do
Aster (Michaelmas daisies)	division	Spr	Split the clumps into individual stems and replant about 15cm (6in) apart. Do this every year with *Aster novi-belgiae*, every 2 years with *A. novae-angliae* and every 3 to 4 years with *A. x frikartii*.
	basal cuttings	May to June	Worthwhile for *A. x frikartii*, which doesn't require such frequent division. Take 5–8cm (2–3in) cuttings and root in the cold frame. Pot up in September and plant out in spring. Seed-raised Michaelmas daisies are inferior to bought plants of named varieties.
Astilbe (false goat's beard)	division	Spr	Divide roots every 2 or 3 years to maintain vigorous plant. Each piece should have 2 or 3 developing shoots. Plant out about 38cm (15in) apart. Keep moist at all times. Seed-raised plants are likely to be poor.
Astrantia major (masterwort)	division	Aut or Spr	Divide regularly for a few extra plants or every 3 to 5 years to rejuvenate clumps. Pull clumps apart with your hands and replant divisions up to 45cm (18in) apart.
	seed	Aut	Cut off umbelliferous seed heads in autumn, leave to dry for up to a week and sow in trays in the cold frame. Prick out in spring and grow on in a nursery bed or pots for autumn planting. Variegated forms don't come true from seed, and the flowers are best removed to retain good leaf colour.
B			
Ballota pseudodictamnus (horehound)	cuttings	July to Sep	Not reliably hardy, so take cuttings every year to guard against winter losses. Take 8–10cm (3–4in) nodal or heeled cuttings and root in the cold frame. (Do not cover with polythene or cuttings liable to rot.) Pot on once rooted and overwinter under glass.
Bergenia	division	Aut or Spr	In autumn or after flowering, cut off all the healthy young rhizomes and discard old centre and any old leaves. Trim the cut pieces to just below a cluster of fibrous roots. Each one should be at least 5–8cm (2–3in) and have at least 2 buds. Remove any stumps or pieces of rotten stem and replant 30cm (12in) or so apart. This should be done about every 3 years. You can dice up the unused sections of young rhizomes into 2cm (¾in) sections, so long as each piece has a bud. Plant in trays of compost in the cold frame. By mid-summer these should be ready for potting up or planting out.
Brunnera macrophylla	division	Spr or Oct	Divide every 2 or 3 years to keep it under control and replant 45cm (18in) apart. With variegated forms, such as 'Langtrees' or 'Variegata', remove any green shoots or you'll lose the variegation.
	root cuttings	Nov to Feb	Cut the black, bootlace-like roots into 8cm (3in) sections and plant horizontally in trays in the cold frame.
	seed	Spr	Let it self-seed and transplant the seedlings to form a new clump. If self-seeding is a nuisance, dead-head regularly. Variegated forms don't come true.
C			
Campanula, perennial species (bell flower)	division	Aut or Spr	*C. persicifolia* needs to be divided every 3 years to rejuvenate plants. Other species, such as *C. latifolia* and *C. eriocarpa*, have creeping roots, and you can detach small portions from around the edge without disturbing the clump if you want a few extra plants.
	seed	Mar to Apr	Sow in trays in the cold frame and prick out into small pots or boxes and grow on for autumn planting. They will flower the following year. *C. latifolia* will freely self-seed in the border.
	basal cuttings	Apr to May	Root 3–5cm (1–2in) shoots in the cold frame. Treat as for seedlings once rooted.

species	how	when	what to do
Carex morrowii 'Evergold' and 'Variegata' (variegated sedges)	division	Aut or Spr	Divide clumps every 2 to 3 years or they will die out in the centre. Take care to minimise damage to tangle of fibrous roots and cut foliage right back to encourage new growth. Replant 30cm (12in) apart.
Catananche caerulea (cupid's dart)	seed	Feb to June	Short-lived perennial best raised from bought seed every few years. Early sowings in the greenhouse at 13°C (55°F), planted out in May, will flower the same year. Alternatively, sow *in situ* April to June for flowers the following year.
	root cuttings	Mar	Worthwhile if you have a good form. Plant 8cm (3in) sections the right way up in pots in the cold frame and plant out 38cm (15in) apart when they have a sturdy set of leaves.
Centaurea, perennial species (hardhead, knapweed)	division	Aut or Spr	Divide every 3 years to maintain vigour and replant 30–38cm (12–15in) apart. Divisions are quick to establish.
	seed	Apr	Sow *C. dealbata* in the cold frame in spring. Prick out into pots, plunge outdoors for the summer and bring back into the cold frame over winter. Although this is more effort, it should give you much stronger plants. Plant out the following year, when they will flower. *C. gymnocarpa* is best sown in autumn.
	heeled cuttings	Sep to Oct	Good insurance against winter losses for less hardy species such as *C. cineraria* and *C. ragusina*. Take 5cm (2in) cuttings with a 3cm (1in) heel of old wood, dip in a benomyl solution and root in a shaded cold frame. Plant out in June to flower the same summer.
Centranthus (valerian)	seed	Aut or Apr to May	Sow ripe seed in autumn or bought seed in spring where they are to flower. Does best on poor, limey soils. Saved seed often gives a mixture of colours. Flowers following year. Best not divided, as roots brittle.
Chrysanthemum (hardy types including pyrethrum, *C. coccineum;* Shasta daisy, *C. maximum;* and Korean chrysanthemum, *C. nipponicum*)	division	Spr	To maintain health and vigour divide fibrous roots into small clumps every 3 years. Replant 30–45cm (12–18in) apart.
	basal cuttings	Spr	Root 8cm (3in) cuttings in pots in the cold frame. Line out in nursery bed once rooted and move to final position in autumn.
	seed	June to July	Sow outdoors in seedbed and move to final position in autumn. Korean chrysanthemums and pyrethrums are well worth raising from seed, but Shasta daisies can be very variable.
Cimicifuga (bugbane)	division	Oct to Mar	Can be divided every 4 years or so, but best left undisturbed.
	seed	Aut	Sow ripe seed in the cold frame and pot up in spring. Flowering takes 3 to 4 years.
Convallaria majalis (lily of the valley)	division	Oct or after flowers	Divide long underground roots into 20cm (8in) sections each with at least 1 bud, and replant 3cm (1in) deep and 8–10cm (3–4in) apart.
Coreopsis (tickseed)	division	Aut or Spr	Divide every 2 years to rejuvenate clump and replant 45cm (18in) apart.
	seed	Mar to June	*C. grandiflora* is best raised annually from bought seed as it is short lived and will flower in same year from a spring sowing. Other species can be raised from early summer sowings to flower the following year.
Cortaderia (pampas grass)	division	Apr	If you want several plants, divide regularly when young with a sharp knife. Plants over 5 years old become very woody, so you may need an axe to divide them, and you risk killing the plant.
Corydalis (fumitory)	seed	Spr	Sow *in situ* for flowers the same year. Self-seeds freely once established.

species	how	when	what to do
Crambe cordifolia (ornamental seakale)	root cuttings	Dec to Feb	Take 5cm (2in) pencil-thick root cuttings and root in pots in the cold frame. Plant out in spring once they have strong shoots. Flowering takes 3 to 4 years. Can also be divided, but best undisturbed.
Crocosmia (montbretia)	division	Mar or Sum*	*After flowering. Divide every 3 to 4 years and replant 15–23cm (6–9in) apart.
	seed	Aut	Sow in pots in the cold frame as soon as ripe. Flowering takes 1 to 2 years. Colours will be variable.
D			
Delphinium	division	Spr	Divide every 3 to 4 years once flowering deteriorates. Split fleshy crowns with a sharp knife and dress wounds with a fungicide before replanting about 45cm (18in) apart.
	basal cuttings	Mar	Best method for 'Belladonna' and 'Elatum' types. Use 8–10cm (3–4in) shoots and root in the cold frame. For early cuttings that will flower the same year, box up crowns in autumn and treat as for dahlias (see page 105). Cuttings also root easily in water.
	seed	Feb to Mar or July	Bought seed of 'Pacific Hybrids' or 'Blue Fountains' will flower in same year if sown under glass in February to March. Otherwise sow in seedbed outdoors in July and move to final positions in autumn. These varieties are short lived and are best replaced every 3 years or so. Other types can be raised from seed sown as soon as ripe, though results from named varieties will be variable.
Dianthus (pinks and carnations)	pipings (pinks)	June to July	Pull out tips of non-flowering shoots at a joint and trim to below a node. Rooting hormone, though not essential, will hasten rooting, which takes 3 to 4 weeks. Plant out in autumn.
	layering (border carnations)	July to Aug	Layer a few side shoots from each plant. Sever rooted layers from parent plant after about 6 weeks and transfer to final position after a further 3 to 4 weeks.
	seed	Spr	Seed-raised varieties tend to be short lived and are generally raised as bedding plants (see page 59).
Diascia	seed	Feb to Mar	Raise as for bedding plants at 15–18°C (60–65°F) and plant out 38cm (15in) apart after frosts. They may flower same year.
	stem cuttings	Spr or late Sum	Only method of propagating hybrids such as *D. cordata* 'Ruby Field'. Late summer cuttings are best taken as routine with 'Ruby Field' as it is less hardy than the others. Root 5–8cm (2–3in) cuttings in sandy compost in the cold frame. Pot on and overwinter under glass.
Dicentra (bleeding heart)	division	Mar	Divide every 4 to 5 years to rejuvenate plants, but take care not to damage the fleshy, brittle roots.
	basal cuttings	Mar to Apr	Take 5–8cm (2–3in) cuttings and root in the cold frame. Grow on in pots or boxes for autumn planting. Will flower the following year.
	root cuttings	Nov to Mar	Cut root into 5cm (2in) sections and insert in pots in the cold frame. Flowering takes 2 years.
Dictamnus (burning bush, dittany)	root cuttings	Nov to Feb	Carefully scrape away soil to remove a root without disturbing the plant. Plant 8cm (3in) sections in pots in the cold frame. Pot and grow on for autumn or spring planting.
	seed	late Sum	Sow seed when ripe in trays in the cold frame. Germination may take 6 to 12 weeks (dried seed may require chilling over winter). Pot up carefully (seedlings do not transplant well) in spring and grow on for a few years before planting out. Flowering can take 5 years or so.

Erigeron – these attractive daisy-like flowers are easily raised from seed to flower the following year.

species	how	when	what to do
Dierama (wand flower)	division	Mar	Remove offsets from bulbs and plant out in a nursery bed. They take about a year to reach flowering size. Divide every 3 to 4 years.
	seed	Aut	Before seed ripens, cut off stems and hang them upside down in paper bags in a warm dry room. Sow in spring, prick out into pots in July and plant out the following spring. Flowering takes 3 to 4 years.
Digitalis grandiflora (perennial foxglove)	division	Spr	Best left undisturbed.
	seed	Apr to June	Seed very fine, so best started in trays and planted out in final position. They should flower the following year. Throw away poor colour forms once they flower. See also Biennials, page 67.
Doronicum (leopard's bane)	division	Sep or Spr	Divide every 3 to 4 years and replant 30cm (12in) apart. If divided in autumn, cut down foliage first. Seed is not worth the effort as the best varieties, such as 'Miss Mason', are hybrids and won't be true.
E			
Echinacea purpurea (purple cone flower)	division	Spr or Aut	Divide every 2 to 3 years for a few more plants, or else when centre starts to become bare.
	root cuttings	Feb	Best method for a number of plants of named varieties. Place in peat and sand mixture in the cold frame, pot up once leaves appear and plant out in May or June.
	seed	Spr	Sow under glass at 13°C (55°F), prick out into boxes and grow on for planting out in September. Will flower the following year.
Echinops ritro (globe thistle)	seed	Apr to June	Use bought seed or collect your own in paper bags before the seed head disintegrates (usually October). Sow outdoors in a seedbed and move to final position in autumn. Will flower the following year.
	division	Aut or Spr	Divide every 3 to 4 years and replant 60cm (24in) apart. Wear gloves, as they are usually prickly. Take care not to damage the roots.

species	how	when	what to do
Epimedium (barrenwort)	division	Aut or early Sum*	*After flowering. Only necessary every 8 to 10 years, though you can divide every few years for propagation. Separate clump into single stems and replant about 30cm (12in) apart.
Eremurus (foxtail lily)	division	Aug to Sep	Divide every 3 to 4 years as soon as leaves have died away. The roots are fleshy and easily damaged, so gently prise crowns apart, leaving each with some roots. Sit on grit with nose just above soil level.
Erigeron (fleabane)	division	Spr or Aut	Can be divided every 2 to 3 years. Replant 45cm (18in) apart.
	seed	Apr to July	Sow in seedbed outdoors and move to final positions in autumn. Will flower the following year.
Eryngium, perennial species (sea holly)	root cuttings	Nov to Mar	Plant 5–8cm (2–3in) sections in pots in the cold frame. Pot up in autumn and overwinter in the cold frame. Plant out the following May.
	seedlings	Spr	Self-sown seedlings can be transplanted carefully.
Euphorbia	division	Aut or Feb to Mar	Most species can be divided every 3 years. *E. characias* and *E. wulfenii*, however, resent any disturbance.
	seed	Aut or Spr	Tie a paper bag over stems before seeds ripen as the capsules explode. Sow in autumn or spring in the cold frame. Plant out in nursery rows in early summer and move to final positions in autumn. Should flower the following year.
	basal cuttings	Apr to May	Root 8cm (3in) shoots in peat and sand in the cold frame and plant out once well rooted. **Note**: Euphorbia stems exude a milky sap when cut, and the stem should be quickly passed through a flame to seal the stem. The sap contains an irritant, so wear gloves and keep away from your eyes and mouth.
	stem cuttings	late Sum	Take 3cm (1in) cuttings from stem tips and root in the cold frame as above. A useful precaution against winter losses for evergreen types.

F–G

species	how	when	what to do
Festuca glauca (sheep's fescue)	division	early Aut or Spr	Divide at least every other year or else it will lose its blue coloration. Replant 15–20cm (6–8in) apart.
	seed	late Mar or Sep	Sow in the cold frame in March. Plant out in tufts of 3 or 4 seedlings in a nursery bed; by autumn you'll have small clumps for planting in final positions. Alternatively, sow direct in the border and thin seedlings to form small clumps.
Filipendula (meadow sweet)	division	Spr or Aut	Divide every 3 to 4 years and replant 45–60cm (18–24in) apart. Keep divisions well watered through the first summer.
	seed	Aut or Feb to Mar	Collect ripe seed and sow in the cold frame in autumn or in the greenhouse at 10–13°C (50–55°F) the following spring. Flowering takes 2 to 3 years.
Gaillardia aristata (blanket flower)	seed	Feb to July	Early sowings (up to March) under glass at 15°C (60°F) and planted out in May will flower the same year. Alternatively, sow in seedbed outdoors and move to final positions in autumn or spring for flowers the following year. Best raised afresh every few years. Can also be raised from root cuttings in winter and stem cuttings in summer, but worthwhile only if you want to be sure of a particular colour.
Gentiana asclepiadea (willow gentian)	seed	Aut	Sow ripe seed before October in the cold frame. Sow thinly on the surface of the compost and cover with a thin layer of sand. Some will breed true from seed, others produce interesting variations. Flowering takes at least 2 years.
	basal cuttings	Spr	Take 3–5cm (1–2in) cuttings and root in the cold frame. Pot up once rooted and keep in the cold frame over first winter.

species	how	when	what to do
Geranium species (cranesbills)	division	Aut or Spr	Divide every 3 to 5 years. Some types, such as *G. endressi* and *G. macrorrhizum*, can be split up into a number of small pieces. Replant 20–30cm (8–12in) apart.
	seed	Sep to Mar	Tie a bag over stems to catch ripe seeds. Sow in September or March in a greenhouse or cold frame. Some species may take several weeks or months to germinate. Scarification (see page 33) before sowing helps. Will flower in first summer if planted early.
Geum (avens)	division	Spr	Divide every other year to maintain vigorous plants. Replant 30–45cm (12–18in) apart.
	seed	late Sum or Spr	Either sow in the cold frame in late summer, once seed is ripe, and plant out in spring or sow in spring and plant out in autumn. Will flower in the year after sowing. Named varieties such as 'Mrs Bradshaw' and 'Lady Stratheden', will come true from seed.
Gunnera	division	Spr	Divide every 4 to 5 years.
Gypsophilla paniculata (baby's breath, chalk plant)	seed	Feb to Mar	Sow bought seed under glass at 13°C (55°F) and plant out in May for flowers the same year. Alternatively, sow outdoors from April to June for flowers the following year.
	basal cuttings	Apr to May	Root 8cm (3in) shoots in peat and sand in the cold frame. Pot up once rooted and plant out in autumn or spring.
	stem cuttings	July	Take stem cuttings as above and overwinter in the cold frame for spring planting.
H			
Helenium autumnale (sneezewort)	division	Aut or Spr	Divide every 3 years to improve flowering. The crown can be split into single buds. Discard old woody centre and replant divisions 45cm (18in) apart.
	stem cuttings	Apr to May	Root 8cm (3in) cuttings in the cold frame. Pot up once rooted and plant out in autumn. Can also be raised from seed, but plants generally very poor.
Helianthus decapetalus (perennial sunflower)	division	Aut	Replant every 3 years. Double forms, such as 'Loddon Gold', may revert to singles if not divided regularly. After lifting, remove any rooted suckers and replant these at least 30cm (24in) apart.
	seed	Mar to Apr	Use saved seed or, for hybrid varieties such as 'Loddon Gold' or 'Soleil d'Or', bought seed. Sow in a seedbed outdoors, thin to 15cm (6in) and plant in border in autumn.
Helichrysum angustifolium (curry plant)	stem or heel cuttings	Apr to July	To insure against winter losses, root 3–5cm (1–2in) cuttings in 3 parts sand to 1 part peat. Pot on once rooted and overwinter in the cold frame for planting out in late spring or early summer.
	division	Mar	Can be divided every 4 to 5 years, though best undisturbed.
Heliopsis scabra (orange sunflower)			Though not a true sunflower, can be raised in exactly the same way as *Helianthus decapetalus*, above.
Helleborus (including Christmas and Lenten roses)	seed	mid-Sum	Tie a paper bag over the stems to catch the shiny black seed. Sow immediately 12mm (½in) deep in pots of seed compost and cover with a plastic bag. (If seed dries it may take several years to germinate.) Grow on for a year before planting out. Flowering takes 2 to 3 years. *H. orientalis* can produce fine colour variations from seed.
	division	*	*After flowering. Young plants can be divided into single shoots with a good root system. Replant 45cm (18in) apart. Plants over 5 years old resent disturbance and are likely to be killed by division.

species	how	when	what to do
Hemerocallis (day lily)	division	Oct to Apr	Can be divided every 3 to 4 years for a few extra plants, though will thrive undisturbed.
	seed	Spr	Sow under glass at 15–18°C (60–65°F), prick out into boxes and grow on for autumn planting. Will flower the following year. Seed saved from hybrids will give mixed results.
Hesperis matronalis (sweet rocket)	basal cuttings	June to July or Sep	Root 8cm (3in) shoots in the cold frame. This is the best way to propagate double forms that can't be raised from seed.
	division	Spr	Double forms should be divided every 2 years to maintain vigour, though this is not easy as they have a brittle taproot. Replant 38cm (15in) apart.
	seed	Apr to June	Single forms are short lived and are best treated as biennials (see page 67). They will self-seed in the border.
Heuchera sanguinea (alum root, coral bells)	division	Aut or Spr	Divide once rosettes appear to be raised above the ground. Split into individual rosettes and replant 25–30cm (10–12in) apart. Rooted offsets can also be removed in autumn.
	seed	Spr	Sow in the cold frame and prick out into a nursery bed. Select seedlings with good foliage markings and move to border in autumn (needs a well-drained soil). Should flower the following year.
Hieraceum (devil's paintbrush, hawkweed)	division	Aut or Spr	Divide every 3 to 4 years. Replant about 15cm (6in) apart.
	seed	Spr	Self-seeds in the border; these can easily be moved in spring.
Holcus mollis 'Variegata'	division	Spr	Uninvasive relation of 'Yorkshire Fog' with slowly creeping rhizomes. Can be split into small clumps or short sections of rhizome (down to 8cm/3in). The smaller the divisions, the longer they will take to re-establish. Replant about 15cm (6in) apart. May die back after division, but new shoots will emerge after several weeks.
Hosta (plaintain lily, funkia)	division	Mar	Divide every 3 to 4 years. Fleshy crown can be cut into 4 or 5 sections. Replant 45–60cm (18–24in) apart. Old plants can be split into up to 20 pieces.
	seed	Feb to Mar	H. albo-marginata is the only variegated species that will come true from seed, so may be worth trying. Pull off papery seeds in late summer and sow in a cool greenhouse in early spring at around 10°C (50°F). Germination may be poor and erratic, taking up to 3 months. Pot on as necessary, and plant out in autumn or spring when they reach a reasonable size. If you are successful, flowering will take 2 to 3 years.

Cut off the top third of a bud from a hosta division.

Make two cuts right down the bud and replant.

Try topping hostas from November to February
This is not an easy method but it is worth trying if you want a number of plants quickly. Lift the plant, clean off the roots and divide into sections, each with a plump bud. Cut off the top third of the bud and discard. Make two cuts (to make a cross) in the remainder of the bud right down to the woody base plate. Place in a shallow trench and cover lightly with 5cm (2in) of potting compost. By May, each division should have developed 6 to 8 buds. Once these are 3cm (1in) or so long, separate by cutting through the base plate. Dip each one in a solution of systemic fungicide such as benomyl and then pot up or plant out. Plants should reach flowering size by the following year.

species	how	when	what to do
I–K			
Iberis sempervirens (perennial candytuft)	seed	Apr to May	Sow *in situ*. Will flower the same year. Use bought seed, as plants are best trimmed back after flowering to keep them neat and tidy.
	stem cuttings	June to Aug	Only worthwhile for named hybrids. Take 5cm (2in) cuttings from non-flowering shoots and root in the cold frame. Pot on once rooted and overwinter in the cold frame for spring planting.
Incarvillea	division	Spr	Divide carefully every 4 to 5 years. You may need a bread knife to get through the crowns. New growth may not appear until late May or June or even the following year.
	seed	Spr	Pick ripe seed off split pods. Sow seed thinly 5cm (2in) deep in pots in the cold frame. Pot up and grow on for planting in the second spring. Flowering takes 2 years. Hard frost and wet soil may kill them.
Inula (elecampane)	division	Aut or Spr	Divide every 3 to 5 years and replant 30cm (12in) apart.
	seed	Spr	Not worthwhile for *I. helenium*, as named varieties are much better plants.
Irises, bulbous	division	once leaves die down	Split up large clumps and grow on offsets in a nursery bed for a year or two until they reach flowering size.
Irises, rhizomatous	division	After flowering or Sep	For those that form large surface rhizomes, cut off pieces from the outside of the clump, each with 1 or 2 fins of leaves attached, and discard the centre. Clump-forming irises can be divided into several pieces.
	seed	Aut	Best sown fresh in autumn in pots in the cold frame. Flowering takes 3 to 4 years for bulbous species and 2 to 3 years for rhizomatous species.

Cut back the leaves to prevent plants blowing over before the roots take hold. Replant divisions of rhizomatous irises so that the roots are just covered but the top of the rhizome is above the soil.

After lifting the clump, separate the tangled roots of bulbous irises with a hand fork.

species	how	when	what to do
Kniphofia (red hot poker, torch flower, tritona)	division	Spr	Carefully divide fleshy roots when necessary. Replant 30–50cm (12–20in) apart.
	basal cuttings	Spr	For quick results cut off the top of the crown. The new shoots that appear can be turned into 8cm (3in) cuttings. Root in the cold frame and grow on for autumn planting.
	seed	Jan to Feb or June to Aug	For flowers the same year, sow in greenhouse at 15–20°C (60–68°F) and plant out in April. For flowers the following year, sow seed outdoors in summer and move to final positions the following spring. Either buy seed or pick it from the plants between June and September.

Kniphofias are easy to raise from seed, but if you have an unusual variety such as this one with yellow flowers the best method of propagation is from basal cuttings in spring.

species	how	when	what to do
L			
Lamium (dead nettle)	division	Sep to Mar	The smallest piece of underground stem will form a new plant so long as it has a bud.
Lathyrus latifolius (everlasting pea)	seed	Mar to Jun	Sow in trays and grow on in individual pots for autumn planting. Division risky.
Liatris (blazing star, gayfeather snake root)	division	Spr	Divide every 3 to 4 years. Dig up the potato-like root clumps and cut them into sections, each with a few developing shoots. Replant 30cm (12in) apart in poor soil.
	seed	Spr	Sow in the cold frame, prick out into boxes and plant out small plants into nursery beds. Move to border in autumn or spring. Will flower the following year.
Ligularia (golden groundsel)	division	Spr	Every 3 to 4 years. Replant divisions 45cm (18in) apart in moist or boggy soil.
	seed	Aut	Collect ripe seed in late summer/early autumn and sow in the cold frame. Seed will most likely germinate in spring and can be grown on for autumn planting. Flowering takes 2 years. Named varieties, such as 'Desdemona', are best dead-headed as they self-seed freely and produce inferior plants.
Limonium (sea lavender, statice)	division	Spr	Divide carefully every 4 years and replant 30cm (12in) or so apart.
	root cuttings	Nov to Mar	*L. latifolia* only. Take 5cm (2in) root cuttings and insert in sandy compost in the cold frame. Flowering takes 2 years.
	seed	Spr	Collect ripe seed in late summer and sow in the greenhouse in spring at 18–21°C (65–70°F). Germination can be erratic. Pot on as necessary and plant out in autumn or spring. Flowering takes 2 to 3 years.
Linaria purpurea (purple toadflax)	seed	Spr or Sep	Sow *in situ* (or in trays in spring and prick out *in situ*) and thin to 30cm (12in) apart. Will flower the summer after sowing. Best garden form is 'Canon Went' (pink), which comes true from seed. Self-seeds freely in border if not dead-headed.

species	how	when	what to do
Liriope muscari (lily turf)	division	Spr	Divide every 4 to 5 years. Replant 25–30cm (10–12in) apart.
	seed	Oct	Collect seed as soon as it turns black and sow in the cold frame. Plant out in nursery bed the following year. Flowering takes 3 years.
Lobelia cardinalis (cardinal flower)	division	Spr	Not really hardy, so can be lifted annually in autumn and stored in boxes of peat in a frost-free place over winter. Large clumps can be divided before replanting in spring.
	seed	Spr	Collect ripe seed in late autumn (before frosts). In spring sow on the surface of compost in trays in the greenhouse. Select those with best foliage colouring for growing on. Flowering takes 1 to 2 years.
Lupinus polyphyllus (lupin)	seed	Jan to Feb or Apr to June	Good mixtures and single colours available from seedsmen. Letting the plants seed weakens them, so don't save your own. Nick seed coat and/or soak for 24 hours prior to sowing. Sow in greenhouse in January or February at 13–18°C (55–65°F) and plant out in May for flowers the same year. Alternatively, for flowers the following year sow outdoors April to June and move to final positions by August.
	basal cuttings	Spr	Remove young shoots when 8–10cm (3–4in) long, preferably with a little root attached. Insert in sandy compost in the cold frame and plant out in nursery bed in May or June. Move to border in autumn for flowering the following year. Plant 23–30cm (9–12in) apart.
Lychnis (campion)	seed	May to June	Sow bought or saved seed in outdoor seedbed. Plant in border in autumn or spring. Short-lived species, such as *L. coronaria* (dusty miller), are best raised as annuals started under glass in February.
	basal cuttings	Apr to May	Worthwhile for *L. chalcedonica* (Maltese cross) and *L. flos-jovis*. Root 5–8cm (2–3in) shoots in the cold frame. Plant out in nursery rows once rooted and into final positions in autumn.
	division	Aut or Spr	Divide every 3 to 5 years and replant 30–45cm (12–18in) apart.
Lysimachia nummularia (creeping jenny)	stem cuttings	Apr or Sep	8–10cm (3–4in) lengths of stem can be inserted direct into final position.
Lysimachia punctata (yellow loosestrife)	division	Aut or Spr	Very vigorous, especially in moist conditions, and may need to be divided every year. Replant 45cm (18in) apart.
	seed	Spr	Sow in trays in the cold frame and prick out into final positions. Will flower in the same year if sown early.
Lythrum (purple loosestrife)	root cuttings	Feb to Mar	The method to use for named varieties. Place 5cm (2in) sections of root in the cold frame and plant out once they have strong roots. Will flower the following year.
	seed	Apr	Sow in the cold frame, prick out into nursery rows and move to the border in autumn to flower the following year. Mixed shades only.
	basal cuttings	Spr	Root in the cold frame, line out in nursery rows and move to border in autumn. Will flower the following year.
M			
Macleaya (plume poppy)	division	late or early Spr	Resents disturbance, but suckers that form around base of plant can be severed with a spade and transplanted.
Malva moschata (musk mallow)	seed	Spr	Save seed in autumn and sow in the cold frame in spring. Prick out into nursery rows and move to the border in autumn. Will flower the following year. Not suitable for the white variety *M. moschata* 'Alba'.
	basal cuttings	Apr	Root 8cm (3in) shoots in sandy compost in the cold frame and grow on in pots for autumn or spring planting.

species	how	when	what to do
Meconopsis	seed	when ripe	Sow in small pots and keep in the cold frame or greenhouse over winter. *M. cambrica* (Welsh poppy) will self-seed freely.
	division	Aut	*M. betonicifolia* (Himalayan blue poppy) and *M. regia* are short-lived perennials and should not be divided. Division is the only way to propagate named varieties of *M. grandis*, such as 'Brooklyn' and 'Slieve Donard', and double forms of *M. cambrica*.
Mertensia (Virginian cowslip)	division	Sep	Divide every 4 to 5 years to maintain vigour, taking care not to damage the tuberous black roots. Foliage dies right back in summer, so mark the spot with a cane.
	seed	July	Sow ripe seed in a shaded cold frame. Germination may be slow (up to 2 months). Prick out into pots and grow on for a year before planting out. Never let compost dry out. Flowering takes 2 to 3 years.
Miscanthus	division	Spr	Divide plants while they are young (up to 4 years old) if you want a few extra. Older plants are difficult to divide and you may need an axe. Will happily thrive for 10 years or more without division.
Molinia (moor grass)	division	Spr	Divide every 5 to 6 years.
Monarda (bergamot, bee balm)			See bergamot under Herbs, page 124.
N – O			
Nepeta (catmint)	root cuttings	Nov to Mar	Insert 5cm (2in) sections in pots in the cold frame. Pot once strong shoots formed and grow on for autumn planting.
	seed	June to Aug	Sow in nursery rows and move to final position in spring. Plants are unlikely to be as good as named varieties.
Oenothera missouriensis (evening primrose)	seed	Apr	Sow in trays in the cold frame and prick out into final position. May flower in first year. Needs a well-drained soil. Plant 20cm (8in) apart.
	division	Spr	Not easy, but only way to propagate varieties such as 'Fireworks'. On established clumps only, cut the plant right back to ground level in autumn. In spring, carefully divide the brittle woody roots.
Omphalodes	division	Spr	Divide every 3 to 4 years and replant. Roots are very sensitive to drying out.
	seed	Spr	Pick off green seed in June and sow in the cold frame in spring. Prick out into pots or boxes and plant out the following spring. May also self-seed.
Ophiopogon planiscapus nigrescens (black-leaved lily turf)	division	Spr	Divide every 4 years and replant 15–20cm (6–8in) apart.
	seed	Spr	Saved seed can be sown in the cold frame in spring. Grow on in nursery rows for planting out the following spring. Most of the seedlings will have dark leaves.
P			
Paeonia (paeony)	division	Spr	Best left undisturbed for 15 to 20 years, though can be divided carefully every 4 years or so if you want more plants. Remove a section of the fleshy roots with 1 or 2 buds using a sharf knife. Treat cut surfaces with fungicide before replanting and take great care not to damage the plump buds.
	seed	Aut	Pick black seeds out of pods in autumn and sow immediately in the cold frame. Flowering takes 3 to 4 years. A bit of a gamble with named varieties as you never know what flowers will be like.

species	how	when	what to do
Papaver orientale (oriental poppy)	division	Mar	Divide every 3 to 4 years. Carefully cut up hard roots with a knife. Planting distance depends on variety.
	root cuttings	Nov to Feb	Cut roots into 8cm (3in) sections and place in pots in the cold frame. Pot up individually once strong shoots appear and plant out in autumn.
	seed	June to Aug	Most will self-seed. Alternatively, collect ripe seeds and sow in seedbed outdoors from June to August and move to final positions in October or April. They will flower the following year. Seed from varieties may give a mixture of colours.
Penstemon	stem cuttings	Sep	Insert 5cm (2in) cuttings in the cold frame and plant out the following April or May. A good way to insure against winter losses as well as obtaining more plants.
	seed	Feb to Mar	It is worth collecting seed from *P. x gloxinoides* (ripens June to August), as it will flower in first year if sown in early spring in the greenhouse at 15°C (60°F). Can also be sown outdoors in June or July for flowering the following year.
Phlomis russeliana (herbaceous Jerusalem sage)	division	Aut or Spr	Divide every 4 to 5 years and replant 45cm (18in) apart.
	stem cuttings	Spr	Root 5cm (2in) cuttings in the cold frame, pot up once rooted and grow on for planting out the following spring.
	seed	Spr	Collect seeds from July onwards when almost ripe and ripen in a paper bag indoors. Sow in the greenhouse at 15°C (60°F) the following spring and grow on for a year in pots before planting out. Flowering takes 3 to 4 years.
Phlox paniculata	root cuttings	Nov to Mar	Phlox can be prone to eelworm, but propagating from root cuttings will guarantee healthy plants. Use 8cm (3in) sections of thin roots and plant horizontally in trays in the cold frame. Plant out once they have strong shoots. Don't use this method for variegated types such as 'Harlequin' or 'Norah Leigh', as they will revert to green.
	division	Aut or Spr	Healthy clumps can be divided every 3 to 4 years. Replant 40cm (16in) apart.
Physalis (Chinese lantern, cape gooseberry)	seed	Spr	Seed needs light to germinate at above 15°C (60°F) but will germinate in darkness below this temperature.
	division	Spr	Divide every 3 years. Split into individual stems and replant 38cm (15in) apart.
Physostegia (obedient plant)	division	Aut or Spr	Divide younger plants in spring, older ones in autumn, every 4 to 5 years. Replant 30cm (12in) apart.
	stem cuttings	June to Aug	Root 8cm (3in) cuttings in the cold frame, overwinter under glass and plant out in spring.
Platycodon grandiflorum (balloon flower)	seed	Spr	Collect ripe seed pods in autumn and sow in the cold frame in spring. Best sown several to a pot as seedlings are very fragile. Plant out in October. Flowering takes 2 years.
	division	Spr	Best undisturbed, but can be done carefully every 4 to 5 years.
Polemonium (Jacob's ladder)	division	Aut or Spr	*P. foliosissimum* is a longer-lived species that rarely sets seed. Divide every few years once flowering starts to deteriorate and replant 23cm (9in) of root in a different part of the garden.
	seedlings	Spr	*P. caeruleum*, the most commonly grown, self-seeds freely. Seedlings are easily moved and will flower the following year.

Poppies self-seed so freely that even the annual types such as Papaver somniferum *behave virtually as perennials.*

species	how	when	what to do
Polygonatum (Solomon's seal)	division	Oct to Feb	Rhizomes can be cut into pieces with a single bud and replanted 23cm (9in) apart. Variegated forms are slow to spread and are worth propagating this way.
Polygonum (knotweed)	division	Aut or Spr	Divide every 3 to 4 years and replant 30–45cm (12–18in) apart, depending on the species.
	basal cuttings	Spr	Suitable method for *P. affine*. Root 5cm (2in) cuttings in the cold frame and plant out once rooted.
Potentilla, herbaceous	division	Aut or Spr	Easiest method for longer-lived hybrids, such as 'William Rollinson'. Replant 45cm (18in) apart.
	seed	Spr	Best method for short-lived species, such as *P. warrenii*. Sow in trays in the cold frame, prick out into a nursery bed and move to final positions by October.
	basal cuttings	Apr	Best method for species and short-lived hybrids, such as 'Miss Wilmott' and 'Roxana'. Root 5–8cm (2–3in) cuttings in the cold frame and treat as for seedlings.
Primula, hardy species	division	*	*After flowering. Divide every 2 to 4 years. Soak divisions in a fungicide, such as benomyl, before replanting.
	seed	June to July	Pick off seed when capsules split and sow immediately in trays in the cold frame on the surface of the compost. Prick out into pots and plant out the following spring. Named varieties will produce mixed colours.
	root cuttings	Nov to Feb	Suitable for *P. denticulata* (drumstick primula). Plant 5cm (2in) root sections in trays in a cool greenhouse. Plant out once they have strong shoots.

species	how	when	what to do
Prunella (self-heal)	division	Aut or Spr	Divide every 2 to 3 years to keep under control. Replant only small pieces 38cm (15in) apart.
	seedlings	Spr	Will self-seed freely in the border and should be dead-headed regularly if they become a nuisance.
Pulmonaria (lungwort, soldiers and sailors)	division	Aut*	*Or after flowering. Divide every 3 to 4 years to rejuvenate clumps.
	seedlings	Spr	Plants will self-seed if not dead-headed, though tend to produce inferior plants.
R			
Rheum palmatum (ornamental rhubarb)	division	Dec to Mar	Divide every 4 to 5 years. Either split the crown with a spade or sharp knife into fist-sized pieces each with a bud or remove offsets from the outside of the crown. Remove any parts in the centre of the crown which are dead or blackened. Divisions can be planted straight into garden (February to March), but will establish much quicker if potted up in soil-less compost for a few months prior to replanting. Replant so that buds are just below surface. Best in a well-manured soil.
Rodgersia	division	Spr or Sep	Divide rhizomes every 4 to 5 years, taking care not to damage the growing tips. Replant 75cm (30in) apart with growing tips just below the surface. Divisions can take a year or two before they flower.
	seed	Spr	Collect ripe seed in late summer and sow in the cold frame in spring. Grow on in a nursery bed for 2 years. Flowering takes 3 to 4 years.
Rudbeckia	division	Oct to Nov*	*After flowering. Divide every 3 years to rejuvenate plants. Replant 38cm (15in) apart.
	seed	Apr to June	Sow in outdoor seedbed and move to final positions in autumn. Will flower the following year.
S			
Salvia superba	division	Aut or Spr	Lift and divide every 2 to 3 years when overcrowded, and replant 45cm (18in) apart.
Saponaria officianalis (soapwort)	division	Aut or Spr	Cut around clumps with a spade every year to keep them tidy. Replant outer portions 38cm (15in) apart if you want more plants. Can also be propagated from summer cuttings, but this is hardly worthwhile.
	seed	Spr	Sow *in situ* for flowers the same year. Saved seed can produce very variable plants.
Saxifraga fortunei	division	Aut*	*Or after flowering. Divide every 3 to 4 years and replant 30cm (12in) apart.
Saxifraga x urbium (London pride)	offsets	*	*After flowering. Remove rooted offsets and replant 20cm (8in) apart.
Schizostylis coccinea (Kaffir lily)	division	Apr	Divide every year to maintain flowering. Separate horizontal rhizomes into sections with at least 4 buds and replant 38cm (15in) apart on a well-manured plot. Not worth raising from seed, as plants unlikely to be as good as bought named varieties.
Sedum spectabile (ice plant)	division	Spr	Divide every 2 to 3 years when clumps become overcrowded. Can be divided into small pieces if you want a number of plants.
	stem cuttings	Mar to July	8cm (3in) cuttings will root very easily, even in garden soil, and flower the following year.
	seed	Spr	Not suitable for 'Autumn Joy'. Sow in the cold frame in spring and grow on in pots for autumn planting. Will flower the following year.

species	how	when	what to do
Sildalcea malviflora (Greek or prairie mallow, checker bloom)	division	Aut or Spr	Divide every 3 to 4 years to rejuvenate and replant 38cm (15in) apart.
	seed	Spr	Will self-seed. You can also sow saved seed in the cold frame in spring, prick out into nursery rows and move to final positions in autumn. Seed from named varieties will produce good plants, though not always identical to parents.
Sisyrinchium striatum (satin flower)	division	Aut or Spr	Divide every 3 years. Cut down foliage and break roots into several pieces. Replant 38cm (15in) apart.
	seed	Spr	Will self-seed, or seed can be saved and sown in the cold frame in spring.
Solidago (Aaron's rod, golden rod)	division	Aut or Spr	Divide every 2 years to rejuvenate and keep under control.
	seed	May	Can be sown in situ in May for flowers the following year. But beware – it can easily become a weed. It's best to stick to plants of less invasive dwarf varieties, such as 'Cloth of Gold' and 'Golden Thumb'.
Stachys olympica (S. lanata, lamb's ears, lamb's tongues)	division	Oct or Spr	Can be divided annually, if you want to establish a ground cover, otherwise every other year. Replant 45cm (18in) apart.
	seed	Spr	Flower heads look very untidy once over, so best removed. Bought seed can be sown outdoors if you want lots of plants, though best variety for ground cover is 'Silver Carpet' which does not flower.
Stipa gigantea (feather grass)	division	Mar or Apr	Only when necessary. Cut down foliage before dividing.
	seed	Apr	Sow saved seed in pots and plant out in June. Will take a few years to reach flowering size.
Stokesia laevis (Stone's aster)	division	Spr	Divide every 3 to 4 years and replant 38cm (15in) apart.
	seed	Feb to Mar	Collect seed in autumn for spring sowing in the cold frame. Grow on in nursery rows for a year prior to planting in border. Will flower in the second year. Seed from named varieties should produce good colour forms.
	root cuttings	Feb	Insert 3–4cm (1–1½in) root sections in a heated propagator at 18°C (65°F). Harden off once strong shoots are formed and grow on for autumn planting.
Symphytum (comfrey)	division	Aut or Spr	Divide every 4 to 5 years and replant 38cm (15in) apart.
	seed	Spr	Collect seed capsules when they turn brown (usually August) and sow seed in spring in the cold frame. Plant out in summer. Flowering takes 2 years. Variegated forms won't come true from seed.
T			
Tellima grandiflora	division	Aut or Spr	Divide every 3 to 4 years, gently teasing roots apart, and replant 38cm (15in) apart.
	seed	Spr*	*Or when seed ripe. Sow in the cold frame, prick out into boxes and plant out in a shady border in May. The purple-leaved form won't come true from seed.
Teucrium (germander)	stem cuttings	June to Sep	Take 3–5cm (1–2in) cuttings from tips of stems. Overwinter in a cold frame.
	seed	Spr	Cut off ripe seed heads and dry indoors. Store seed in a cool dry place over winter and sow under glass in spring. Flowering takes 2 years.

species	how	when	what to do
Thalictrum (meadow sweet, meadow rue)	division	Spr	Divide fleshy roots only when necessary, as the plants resent root disturbance and resulting divisions are slow to establish.
	seed	Spr	Collect seed in June or August and sow in the cold frame in spring. Prick out into nursery rows and move to final positions the following spring. Flowering takes 3 to 4 years. Seed from named varieties will produce a lot of variation. The double forms have infertile seed.
Tiarella (foam flower)	division	Aut or Spr	Divide carefully every 3 to 4 years and replant 38cm (15in) apart.
	seed	Spr	Collect ripe seed in July or August (rub the capsules between your fingers; the seed will fall out if ripe) and sow in the cold frame in spring. Plant out in a shady border. Will flower the following year.
Tolmiae menziesii (pick-a-back plant)	plantlets	any time	Peg down stalks of mature leaves on to the soil. This will induce formation of plantlets, if not already present. Young plants can then be moved to final positions once well rooted.
Tradescantia x andersoniana and T. virginiana (spiderworts, trinity flower)	division	Spr	Divide every 3 to 4 years and replant 38cm (15in) apart. Alternatively, remove a few bits from the edge of a clump.
	seed	Spr	Unless you have at least two clumps from different sources they may not set seed. Sow in the cold frame in spring, prick out into boxes and plant out into nursery bed for summer. Move to final positions in autumn. Should flower the following year.
Trillium	division	July*	*Once foliage withers. Carefully scrape away soil from established clump and remove 1 or 2 outer crowns. Grow these on in pots for 2 years before planting out. Paint all cut surfaces with methylated spirits and water plant with a fungicide after replacing the soil.
	seed	July to Aug	Collect ripe seed in July or August and sow immediately in the cold frame. Germination may take up to 2 years, so don't let compost dry out. Flowering takes a further 4 to 11 years.
Trollius	division	Spr	Divide every 3 years and replant 45cm (18in) apart.
	seed	July to Aug	Collect ripe seed from split capsule and sow immediately in trays in the cold frame (if allowed to dry out, it can take up to 2 years to germinate). Flowering takes 2 years.
V–W			
Veratrum (false hellebore)	division	Aut or Spr	Divide only when necessary. **Note**: roots are poisonous.
	seed	Sep to Oct	Sow seed as soon as ripe in the cold frame. Prick out into pots or nursery bed in spring and grow on for a year or so before final planting. Flowering takes 3 to 4 years.
Veronica	division	Spr	Most species can be divided every year or two. Divide V. gentianoides in autumn or after flowering.
Viola	basal cuttings	July to Aug	A good way to produce a number of cuttings is to cut down plants to near ground level and cover them with peat and sand. The new shoots will form their own roots and can be planted out individually in autumn. Cuttings can also be taken from 3–5cm (1–2in) non-flowering shoots in July and rooted in pots.
	seed	July to Aug or Mar	Sow in outdoor seedbed in summer and transplant in autumn or in trays in the cold frame in spring for planting out in early summer.
Waldsteinia	division	Spr	Does not require regular division, but you can do this every 3 to 4 years for propagation. Runners can also be cut into small pieces and replanted up to 30cm (12in) apart.

ROCK PLANTS: TECHNIQUES

Just like herbaceous perennials, alpines can be raised from cuttings, division or seed, but they generally require very different treatment from their larger border relatives. Details of how to propagate individual plants are given in the Tables on pages 97 to 102. The basic techniques involved are described overleaf.

All these alpines are quite easy to raise from seed or cuttings.

FROM SEED

Many alpines are easy to grow from seed, though quite a few species require winter chilling before they will germinate. This can be achieved by sowing in November and leaving the pots outside over winter. In some cases, notably primulas, pulsatillas and hepaticas, seed should be sown straight from the plant. Others require no special treatment and can be stored in cool dry conditions for sowing in the cold frame in spring. Details of special treatments for individual plants are given in the Tables on pages 97 to 102.

Sowing techniques

You need a well-drained compost for alpines – use 1 part horticultural grit to either 1 part John Innes or soil-less seed compost, or moss peat. Plastic pots 5–8cm (2–3in) in diameter are the most useful.

● Fill the pots to the brim with compost, level off and gently tamp down with another pot or a purpose-made wooden tamper.

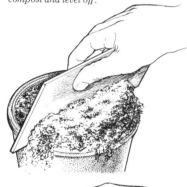

1 Fill pot to brim with well-drained compost and level off.

2 Tamp down compost to about 12mm (½in) below top of pot.

● Very lightly disturb the compost and sow the seed as thinly as you possibly can on the surface. Very fine seed is best mixed with sand to help you sow thinly.
● Cover the seed with 6–12mm (¼–½in) of grit and gently firm down with the tamper once more. Stand pots in a few centimetres of water and leave them until the grit at the top changes colour – usually overnight. If you are sowing dry seed, it is best to keep the pots in the warm for a few days before

3 Sow seeds on surface of compost.

4 Cover seed with grit and level off.

Saving your own seed

In general, it is worth saving seed only from plants of the original species. Named varieties will not come true from seed and can produce a very mixed batch of seedlings.

For most alpines, the simplest way to collect seed is to snip off the seed capsules once they turn brown, and keep them in labelled envelopes in a cool place. The seed can be cleaned up prior to sowing.

putting them outside for winter chilling so they can take up water.
● Once the seeds start to germinate, they can be put into the cold frame or cool greenhouse. If the seeds don't germinate, leave them for another year.
● Once the seedlings have developed their first two leaves (which are formed between the seedling leaves), let the pot dry out for a few days. You can then gently tip the whole pot out into a tray and then tease the seedlings from the compost.
● Pot on into 8cm (3in) pots using an equal mixture of John Innes No. 1 or 2, moss peat and horticultural grit. Top the pots with 6–12mm (¼–½in) of grit and water as when sowing. Keep the pot well watered and in a shady place until well established. Most plants are best overwintered in a cold frame or cold greenhouse and pricked out in spring, though the more vigorous ones may be ready for pricking out in autumn.

FROM CUTTINGS

Cuttings are usually the best way to raise named varieties. Some alpines, such as campanulas, are best propagated in February or March, just as new shoots appear. The majority of cuttings are best taken in June or July, once the shoots have started to ripen, and a few, such as aubrieta, root best once the growth becomes a bit woody in autumn.

Alpine cuttings are generally very small – 6–25 mm ($\frac{1}{4}$–1in) long – so need careful handling. They are best rooted in moist sand, either in trays or around the edge of a pot. The cuttings should be covered with a clear polythene bag secured with an elastic band, or a close-fitting propagator lid. Keep the cuttings in good light but out of direct sunlight or they will be scorched. Cuttings taken early in the year must be kept frost-free and will root best in a heated propagator at 13–15°C (55–60°F).

DIVISION

Most alpines take a long time to form large clumps, and it would be senseless to destroy the appearance of a rock garden by treating them like herbaceous perennials. The best method is to carefully dig out rooted pieces from the edges of clumps, pot them up and treat them as seedlings. You can make an exception to this rule for ground-hugging plants such as arenaria, thymus and raoulia, which are quick to settle in if replanted direct, and for more vigorous alpines such as *Geum reptans* and *Mazus reptans*.

If you grow autumn-flowering gentiana, such as *G. sino-ornata* (not the spring- and summer-flowering ones such as *G. verna* and *G. septemfida*), these should be lifted and divided every 3 years and replanted in a new part of the rock garden. If you don't do this, the soil can become 'gentian sick' and the plants will go downhill and eventually die out completely.

ROCK GARDEN PLANTS: A–Z

plant	how	when	what to do
A			
Acaena microphylla (New Zealand burr)	division	Aut or Spr	Replant direct in rock garden.
	seed	Mar to Apr	Sow in cold frame. Plant out in autumn.
Acantholimon (sea lavender)	cuttings	July to Sep	Cuttings are best taken with a heel of old wood. They can be slow to root. Best in a heated propagator.
	layering	Sum	Work peat and sand among stems (similar to stooling shrubs – see page 46) and pot up any that have formed roots in autumn or spring.
Achillea argentea, A. tomentosa	cuttings	June to Sep	Pot up in autumn and overwinter in the cold frame.
	division	Spr	Spring divisions can be replanted in the rock garden. Autumn divisions should be potted up and kept in a cold frame over winter.
Aethionema (candy mustard)	cuttings	June to July	Cut down stems after flowering. Pinch out growing tips before planting out in spring to produce good cutting material.
	seed	Feb to Mar	Sow in pots in the cold frame.
Alchemilla alpina	division	Spr	Replant direct in the rock garden.
Alyssum saxatile	cuttings	June to Aug	Pot up in autumn and pinch out growing tips to encourage bushy plants. Dwarf varieties such as 'Compactum' and 'Citrinum' are better for rock gardens.
	seed	July to Aug	Sow outdoors and move to final positions in autumn.
Anacyclus (Mount Atlas daisy)	seed	Nov	Sow fresh seed. Bring into cold frame once seeds start to germinate.
	cuttings	May to June	Grow on in pots for spring planting.
Anagalis (pimpernel)	cuttings	June to July	Overwinter a few cuttings in the cold frame to guard against winter losses.
	seed	Mar to Apr	Sow in pots in the cold frame or outdoors.

plant	how	when	what to do
Anchusa caespitosa	cuttings	Apr	Take cuttings with a small piece of old stem attached. Best in heated propagator at 13–15°C (55–60°F).
	seed	Nov to Feb	Sow in pots outdoors.
Andromeda (bog rosemary)	cuttings	July to Aug	Root in 2 parts peats, 1 part sand. Overwinter in rooting medium. Pot up in spring and grow on for a year before planting out.
Androsace (rock jasmine)	cuttings	June to July	Use individual rosettes. Pot up into lime-free compost.
	rooted runners	Sep	Pot up rooted runners in lime-free compost and keep in the cold frame over winter for spring planting.
Antennaria (mountain everlasting)	division	Spr	Individual rooted pieces can be pulled off and potted up or replanted.
	seed	Nov	Sow in pots outdoors
Arabis (rock cress)	cuttings	Aug to Sep	Take cuttings with a small heel of old wood.
	division	Sep to Mar	Divisions best potted and grown on for autumn or spring planting.
	seed	July	Species only. Sow in trays in the cold frame or outdoor seedbed. Move to final positions in spring. Flowers within a year.
Arenaria (sandwort)	mound layering	June to July	Cover the plant with peat so just the tips of the shoots are showing. Sever shoots once rooted and pot up.
	division	Spr	Replant direct into a shady position and keep well watered.
	seed	Spr	Best sown in soil-less seed compost.
Armeria caespitosa (thrift)	cuttings	June to July	Take cuttings with a tiny heel of wood.
Asperula (woodruff)	cuttings	June to July	Cuttings of alpine types are very small. Don't cover the cuttings. Leave potting up until spring.
Aster alpinus	division	Spr	Can be replanted direct in the rock garden.
Astilbe chinensis 'Pumila'	division	Spr	Divide clumps into 2 or 3 portions and replant in a shady spot and keep well watered until established.
Aubrieta (purple rock cress)	cuttings	Sep	Uncover once rooted and pot up in spring.
	division	early Aut	Pot up divisions and keep in the cold frame over winter.
C			
Calamintha	basal cuttings	May	Plant out once well rooted.
	seed	Nov to Jan	Bring into the cold frame once seed starts to germinate.
Calceolaria 'Walter Shrimpton'	side rosettes	May to June	Watch for aphids. Spray or wash cuttings before covering.
Campanula	basal cuttings	Feb to Mar	Root in sand at around 12°C (55°F) in a heated propagator.
	division	Spr	Easy method for clump-forming and spreading types. Small rooted pieces.
	seed	Nov	Collect ripe seed capsules and store whole until sown. It is easier to crush seed capsules and sow the lot as the seed is very fine.

plant	how	when	what to do
Cassiope	cuttings	June to July	Root in peat and sand as they take a long time to root and must not dry out. Don't pot up until spring.
Cotyledon	cuttings	July to Sep	Remove small rooted shoots. Overwinter in a cold frame.
	seed	Nov	Sow in pots outdoors.
D			
Dianthus alpinus, Dianthus deltoides (rock pinks)	seed	Feb to Apr	Seed saved from named varieties will give variable results. Will flower in the same year.
	cuttings	June to July	Remove the polythene cover after a few days and keep damp.
Diascia cordata	cuttings	June to July	Overwinter in frost-free conditions. Hardy once established.
Draba aizoides	seed	when ripe (Dec to Jan)	Leave pots outdoors and bring into the cold frame in March. Grow on in pots outdoors but keep in the cold frame for first winter and plant out the following spring. Flowering takes 2 to 3 years.
Draba bryoides	cuttings	June to July	Tiny rosettes take 2 years to make good plants.
Dryas octopetala (mountain avens)	cuttings	Aug to Sep	Best taken with heel of old wood attached. Uncover cuttings once rooted and pot up in spring.
	seed	Feb to Mar	Sow in pots in the cold frame.
E			
Edraianthus	basal cuttings	July to Aug	Remove any flowers that may appear on cuttings.
	seed	June to July	Sow as soon as ripe in pots in the cold frame.
Erigeron	seed	Nov	Plant out in summer. Self-seeds freely once established.
Erinus (fairy foxglove)	seed	Nov	Self-seeds freely.
Erodium (heron's bill)	basal cuttings	June to July	Take cuttings with a small heel of old wood attached.
Erysimum (alpine wallflower)	cuttings	June to July	Root in sand.
	seed	June to July	Self-seeds freely.
Erythronium	seed	when ripe	Ripens by end of June. Five years to flowering.
Euryops	cuttings	June to July	Best rooted in individual pots with potting compost below the sand as they resent root disturbance.
F–G			
Frankenia (sea heath)	cuttings	June to July	Plant out in autumn.
	division	Spr or Aut	Replant direct in the rock garden.
Gentiana acaulis	division	Sum	Replant in a new part of the garden every few years. Do best in heavy well-drained soil.
Gentiana septemfida	seed	Oct to Nov	Seed ripens late. Sow immediately. Seed can produce a range of blue flowers.
	cuttings	May to June	Take cuttings before flowering. Although easy from seed, worth trying if you have a good blue form.

plant	how	when	what to do
Gentiana sino-ornata	division	Spr	Divide every 3 years and replant in a new spot. If you leave them in one place for too long, the soil becomes 'gentian sick'.
Gentiana verna	seed	late Sum	Sow as soon as ripe. Prick out into clumps of 3–5 seedlings as it likes company. Replace plants every few years.
Geranium cinereum 'Ballerina'	basal cuttings	June to July	Take cuttings with a small heel of old wood attached.
	seed	Dec to Jan	Prick out in summer and plant out in autumn or the following spring. This variety comes true from seed.
Geum reptans (avens)	division	Spr	Replant direct in the rock garden.
Globularia (globe daisy)	division	Spr	Mat-forming types such as *G. cordifolia*.
	seed	Mar	Grow on in the cold frame for first year. Flowering takes several years.
Gypsophila repens	cuttings	May to June	Very easy to root.
H			
Haberlea	leaf cuttings	June to July	Select young leaves and insert the bottom third in sand and peat. Overwinter in the cold frame and pot on for autumn planting. Not easy.
	side rosettes	June to July	Treat as cuttings even though they may have a few roots attached.
	seed	Feb to Mar	Very fine seed. Needs frost-free conditions to germinate. Will take 3 years before seedlings are large enough to handle.
Helichrysum bellidioides	cuttings	June to July	Cuttings will be about 12mm ($\frac{1}{2}$in) long.
	division	Sum	Pot up and keep in the cold frame over winter.
Hepatica	seed	Sum	Collect and sow seed while still green before the capsule turns brown and sheds its seed. Seed may germinate in autumn or the following spring. They have a habit of sitting still for months once the first true leaves appear and should not be pricked out until the autumn. Flowering takes 3 years.
Hypericum polyphyllum (*H. olympicum*)	cuttings	June to July	Root in peat and sand.
	seed	Mar to Apr	Seed from varieties will produce variable results.
I–L			
Iberis sempervirens (perennial candytuft)	cuttings	June to Aug	Root in peat and sand.
	seed	Apr	Suitable for species only.
Leontopodium alpinum (edelweiss)	seed	Aut	Sow as soon as ripe or germination will be very poor.
Lewisia	seed	Sum	Seed heads ripen quickly, dropping shiny black seeds, so check plants regularly.
	side shoots	June to July	Remove these carefully and treat as for cuttings.
Linaria alpina (alpine toadflax)	seed	Mar to Apr	Sow in the cold frame or outdoors. Will flower the same year. Short-lived but self-seeds freely.

plant	how	when	what to do
Linum narbonense (flax)	cuttings	Aug to Sep	Pot up in autumn and keep somewhere frost free for first winter.
	seed	Mar to Apr	Sow in pots or trays in the cold frame.
Lithospermum diffusum	cuttings	July	Cuttings of 'Heavenly Blue' or 'Grace Ward' for some reason root best from cuttings taken in second and third week in July. Roots are very brittle, so submerge the whole pot in water and float out the rooted cuttings. If you break any of the roots they will die.
Lychnis alpina	seed	Mar to Apr	Plants can be short-lived, so raise new ones regularly.
M – P			
Mazus reptans	division	Spr	Replant direct. Can be invasive.
Morisia monantha	root cuttings	Dec	Insert 3cm (1in) root sections the right way in pots of moist soil in the cold frame (see page 76 for technique). Pot up once rosette forms.
Oxalis adenophylla and O. enneaphylla	division	early Spr	Remove bulblets and either pot up or replant direct.
Papaver alpinum	seed	Mar to Apr	Sow in pots or *in situ*. Self-seeds.
Parahebe	cuttings	July to Aug	Take cuttings annually to safeguard against winter losses.
Phlox	cuttings	July to Aug	Root in sand. Overwinter in a cold frame.
	seed	Nov to Feb	Colours will be variable as named varieties nearly always grown.
Polygala	cuttings	June to July	Pinch out growing tips once rooted to encourage a bushy plant.
Potentilla	cuttings	June to July	Very easy to root.
Primula auricula	cuttings	June to July	Remove small rooted shoots. Overwinter in a cold frame.
	seed	late Sum	Collect and sow seed while still green.
Primula marginata	seed	late Sum	Collect and sow seed while still green.
Pulsatilla (pasque flower)	seed	Sum	Sow seed as soon as it will come away from the capsules. Sow 'tail' upwards and snip off the tail after sowing or birds will pull seeds out. Seedlings are slow to develop, as with hepaticas, so don't prick out until the second autumn. Pulsatillas will also self-seed in the border, and seedlings can be carefully potted up in autumn without disturbing the soil around their roots and grown on until large enough for planting out. Flowering takes 3 years.
	leaf cuttings	June to July	As for Haberlea (page 100). Not easy.
R			
Ramonda	side rosettes	June to July	Treat as cuttings even though they may have a few roots attached.
	seed	Feb to Mar	Seeds are very fine and must be kept frost free to germinate. Will be 3 years before the seedlings are large enough to handle.
Raoulia australis	division	Aug to Sep	Pot up and overwinter in the cold frame to guard against winter losses.

plant	how	when	what to do
S – V			
Sagina	cuttings	June to July	Remove single tufts and root as cuttings.
Sanguinaria canadensis	division	Sep	Replant immediately in a damp shady position. Don't worry if stems weep.
Saponaria (soapwort)	cuttings	June to July	Pinch out growing tips once rooted and before planting in spring.
	seed	Feb to Apr	*S. ocymoides* is easy to raise from saved seed.
Saxifraga aizoon (encrusted)	rosettes	Aut	Put a single rosette in a small pot and root in a layer of sand above potting compost. Leave for at least a year before planting.
Saxifraga, mossy	cuttings	June to July	Can be divided but divisions tend to make untidy plants.
Saxifraga, kabschia	rosettes	Aut	Pot up several rosettes in a pot and leave until the second spring before planting out.
Sedum	leaf cuttings	any time	Insert bottom third of leaf into rooting medium.
Sempervivum	leaf cuttings	any time	As for Sedum.
	rosettes	any time	Rosettes can be potted up and treated like cuttings.
Silene	cuttings	June to July	Quite easy to root.
	seed	Oct to Nov	Prick out in January to February and keep frost free until planting out in April or May.
Sisyrinchium brachypus (satin flower)	seed	Spr	Self-seeds freely. Transplant seedlings in spring.
Soldanella	seed	when ripe	Very fine seed. Several years before seedlings large enough to handle.
	division	Sum	Pot up and grow on for a year before replanting.
Solidago brachystachus	division	Spr	Also from seed or self-sown seedlings, though these can be variable.
Thymus	cuttings	June to July	The best way of propagating a number of plants without disturbing a clump.
	division	Aut or Spr	Small portions can be potted up to avoid disturbing clump.
	seed	Spr	*T. serpyllum* is easily raised from bought seed.
Tunica	seedlings	Spr	Transplant self-sown seedlings.
Veronica prostrata	cuttings	July to Sep	10cm (4in) cuttings with a heel of old wood attached can be rooted direct in the cold frame. Other species of *Veronica* should be rooted in sand in the cold frame in the conventional way.
Viola	cuttings	June to July	Can root cuttings where wanted. Cover with a polythene bag or jam jar and shade from sun. Will root in days.
	seed	Spr	Sow in pots or trays of peat-based seed compost in the cold frame. They will also self-seed. Will flower in the same year.

SPECIAL INTEREST PLANTS

Chrysanthemums, dahlias, fuchsias and geraniums are quite easy to propagate, but you can save yourself a lot of time and effort by adopting the correct propagation strategy. As these plants are not hardy, keeping them over winter can be a real problem if you chose the wrong method.

Even if you can't heat your greenhouse, chrysanthemums will still produce a good display from cuttings taken in April.

CHRYSANTHEMUMS

From cuttings

Lift plants during October or November, three to four weeks after flowering has finished. Retain only healthy plants and burn any that have shown signs of disease or poor flowers, or any other unexplained trouble.

Before lifting, cut the stems to about 30cm (12in) – they can be shortened later when the sap has ceased to flow. Shake off as much soil as you can, then wash off the remainder in a bucket of lukewarm water. Immerse the plants in another bucket filled with a weak solution of a garden disinfectant to kill slugs' eggs, etc.

Label the stools and keep them in a cold greenhouse or cold frame (not a heated greenhouse) in boxes of peat with a little grit or perlite for drainage. Leave the stools at a slightly higher level than when in the ground and keep the compost just moist.

Stools brought into a heated greenhouse in January will produce an abundance of cuttings. A night temperature of 7°C (45°F) rising to 13°C (55°F) in the day is ideal. Without heating, cuttings will take longer to root and should not be started until mid-March. Use shoots growing from around the base of the stems and take 6–8cm (2½–3in) cuttings using a sharp knife or razor blade. Trim each cutting below a leaf joint and make sure there is at least one pair of leaves below the growing point.

Immerse the cuttings in a weak solution of fungicide, then dip the end in a hormone rooting powder. With a small pencil-sized dibber, make a hole about 12mm (½in) deep, insert the cutting and firm it gently with your fingers or with the dibber. A seed tray will accommodate two or three dozen cuttings without overcrowding. Keep cuttings shaded for the first few days and give them a light overhead spray with warm water every day (2 to 3 times a day in hot weather) to prevent wilting. Alternatively, cover the tray with a clear plastic lid or a polythene bag supported on a wire framework to maintain a humid atmosphere until the roots begin to form. If using a cold frame, the lights should remain closed and be covered with sacking at night.

FUCHSIAS

Spring cuttings

Fuchsias are very easy to root from cuttings throughout the growing season. The best time to take cuttings largely depends on what facilities you have for overwintering plants – or indeed if you want to bother at all. Cuttings taken in March and April will produce flowering plants by the summer. Established plants can be overwintered in frost-free conditions in the greenhouse or a spare room indoors, or even in boxes of peat in a shed. But as you can easily raise 30 to 50 new plants from a single specimen, you may find it easier just to buy a few new plants in spring.

To produce lots of cutting material, trim the plants back to within one or two buds of the main stem in late February or March and keep the greenhouse at a minimum temperature of 10°C (50°F). Once the shoots have three pairs of leaves, cut them off just above the lowest pair and insert the cuttings into a rooting medium (fuchsias are not fussy – sand and peat, plain sand or seed compost are fine). You can get 4 to 5 cuttings in a 8cm (3in) pot. Cover this with a plastic bag and the cuttings will root in 2 to 3 weeks at 10–15°C (50–60°F).

If you have a propagator, you could also try taking bud cuttings. Once the leaves are just starting to unfold from new buds, these can be broken off and inserted in moist peat and sharp sand. They should root in a week or two at 18°C (65°F).

Summer cuttings

Cuttings taken from June onwards won't be fully grown by the end of the season and need to be overwintered at 10°C (50°F) and kept just moist. You could overwinter a few on the window sill, but for large numbers of cuttings you will need to heat your greenhouse all winter. Summer cuttings are taken from tips of green shoots and should be about 8–10cm (3–4in) long. Where you cut the stem doesn't matter, but remove the lower leaves. Cuttings as for spring cuttings.

If you want lots of cuttings from one plant, you can trim the stems just above and below the leaf joint. These 'leaf-bud' cuttings can be rooted as above.

Autumn cuttings

The other option is to take semi-ripe heel cuttings (see page 12) in late September or October and root them in a frost-free greenhouse over winter. They can be potted up in spring once rooted.

Cuttings taken in autumn will often survive in an unheated greenhouse in milder areas, especially if it's insulated.

DAHLIAS

From seed

You can raise dahlias from seed in exactly the same way as other bedding plants (see page 58) and they should flower from late July from a March or April sowing. They need 10–15°C (50–60°F) for germination and 10–13°C (50–55°F) once pricked out.

The seed-raised types vary quite considerably, but most grow around 30–35cm (12–14in) in height and have single flowers. You will find some types in the seed catalogues with double flowers, maybe in the form of pompons or cactus dahlias. While these will give you a proportion of plants with double flowers, quite a few will be single or semi-double.

You can save your own seed from bedding dahlias but they are best dead-headed regularly to prolong flowering up until first frosts. Each plant will also form a tuber that could be saved, though it's probably easier to raise a new lot from seed the following year.

Dividing tubers

This is the simplest way to propagate named varieties. Overwintered tubers should be taken from store in March (in a frost-free greenhouse) or April (in an unheated cold frame), set up in trays of peat and watered well. Just push the tubers into the surface of the peat so that the junction of the old stem and the fat part of the tuber is just exposed. The new shoots will form within two weeks in a heated greenhouse, a little longer in a cold frame. Once the shoots are 3–5cm (1–2in) long, the whole tuber should be taken from the tray of peat and placed on a firm surface. Using a small saw or an old bread knife, make the first cut through the centre of the old stem so that two good shoots are separated cleanly. It may be possible to make further divisions. Each one should have at least one good growth point and some of the old tuber and the new roots.

To save money, look for large tubers at garden centres and divide before planting.

The divisions should now be boxed or potted up using a John Innes No. 1 compost or peat-based potting compost and grown on until planting time (end of May to early June). If the divisions are in a heated greenhouse, move the pots and trays into the cold frame in mid-May to harden them off before planting out. Divisions come into bloom very early – often 2 to 3 weeks in advance of plants propagated from cuttings or from seed.

Taking cuttings

This is the method to use if you want more than 2 or 3 plants of a particular variety. The tubers should be set up as for divisions. This can be done in February in a greenhouse heated to 10°C (50°F), but wait until April if you are using a cold frame. Water the tubers once the shoots appear, and when these are around 8–10cm (3–4in) long they can be separated from the parent. Take the cuttings just above the growing point so that further cuttings will be formed as a safeguard against initial losses.

Trim the cuttings with a sharp knife just below the lowest leaf joint, then dip in a hormone rooting powder. Insert the trimmed cuttings into peat and sand to a depth of 3cm (1in) and about 3–5cm (1–2in) apart. The cuttings are best rooted in a prop-agator. If you root them on an open bench, spray overhead with tepid water morning and evening.

Once rooted, pot them individually in 8cm (3in) pots or 8cm (3in) apart in deeper trays of potting compost and water them in. Newly potted cuttings can double their height and width in a week or so. Shade them carefully in the initial stages, and later harden them off in a cold frame prior to planting out, as for divisions. You can obtain 100 or more new plants from a single tuber, especially if you start in early February in a heated greenhouse.

Plants from cuttings will flower from early August until the first frosts and form fat tubers for the following year.

GERANIUMS

From cuttings

As with fuchsias, geranium cuttings are very easy to root if taken between late March and early September (cuttings taken later will probably need heat). And again the best time to take cuttings depends on your facilities for keeping them over winter. You could overwinter a few plants on the windowsill and trim them back to produce lots of cuttings in spring. If you are short of space, you could even cut back the tops and store them in boxes of peat in the shed or a spare room – or any other frost-free place. Cuttings, on the other hand, need at least 7°C (45°F) over winter, which means heating a greenhouse.

Whenever you take cuttings the method is the same. Cut the top 8–10cm (3–4in) off a strong healthy shoot, trim below a leaf joint and then remove all the leaves except for the immature ones right at the top. Any flower buds should also be removed. The cutting will root in water or even in the garden soil, but it's probably easier to root them in pots of peat and sand. Never cover geranium cuttings and don't leave them overnight to dry as is sometimes suggested.

Make your cut below a leaf joint.

Remove lower leaf and insert into a pot of compost. Do not cover.

From seed

Raising geraniums from seed is an alternative to overwintering cuttings, though it still involves heating your greenhouse. Geraniums have had a lot of attention from plant breeders over recent years, and seed-raised varieties are beginning to equal the quality of those available only as plants (with the exception of the ivy-leaved and cascade types). Seed of F1 varieties is very expensive, though the cheaper non-F1 varieties are perfectly adequate for bedding.

You can sow the seed in September and overwinter them at 7°C (45°F) or in January and maintain a temperature of at least 13°C (55°F), though 22°C (72°F) is ideal. Germination usually takes between 3 and 14 days. It is also best to keep seedlings at a higher temperature until they are potted on. Geranium seeds have a hard seed coat and required nicking or scarification (see page 33) to germinate. However, with bought seed you will usually find that the seedsman has already done this.

Seed-raised plants can be propagated further from cuttings, often resulting in stronger plants.

Most pond plants are quite vigorous, so it's unlikely that you are going to want large numbers of the ones you have already. However, you do need to divide plants regularly to keep them healthy and to prevent the pond from becoming overcrowded.

Waterlilies

Waterlilies are best divided between May and July so that they have a chance to become established before the winter. Remove the side shoots from the main root systems and cut them into sections about 8cm (3in) long. Each division should have 1 or 2 buds. Remove any old floating leaves. The rhizomatous types are continually branching and are easier to divide than the tuberous types, which produce side shoots from a single stem. Keep the waterlilies out of the sun while dividing as they can easily become scorched when out of the water. Replant the divisions singly in purpose-made waterlily pots (available from garden centres). Use a heavy soil which does not contain manure, compost or fertilisers and topdress with shingle. Place divisions a few inches under the water in a sunny part of the pond. As the plants grow, increase the depth of water (you can achieve this by standing the pot on a pile of bricks and removing them one at a time). By winter, ensure that they are

covered with sufficient water to prevent freezing.

The most vigorous varieties should be divided every other year, but the small *Nymphaea pygmaea* varieties need to be

divided only every 5 to 6 years.

Always wear rubber gloves when dividing waterlilies as nearly all varieties contain an inky blue dye that can stain your hands for several days.

Marginal plants

Most marginal plants can be propagated by simple division, replanting the young healthy outer sections and discarding the old woody core. This can be done any time from May to September, though May to June is best. The frequency of division depends on the vigour of individual plants, though it should not be done more often than every 3 to 4 years. Some types can be propagated from cuttings (as for herbaceous perennials – see page 74) or from seed if you want lots of plants.

Oxygenating plants

e.g. *Callitriche* (water starwort), *Elodea* (Canadian pondweed), *Ranunculus aquatilis* (water crowfoot)
Simply cut sections of healthy stems into sections up to 15cm (6in) long. Plant 5 to 6 cuttings to a pot, using heavy soil as for waterlilies, and topdress with pea gravel to prevent fish disturbing the soil. Place the pots in their final positions in the pond. Cuttings can also be planted in the same pots as waterlilies, but they are best in separate pots.

Floating plants

With some floating plants, such as *Lemna* (duckweed), it is just a matter of thinning them out with a net as required, but some of the choicer types are not hardy and need a bit more care if you are to keep them from year to year. See the Table on page 109 for details.

Water plants from seed

Seed from most water plants needs to be sown as soon as it is collected. Usually the seed pods turn yellow as the seed ripens, so check your plants regularly so the seed is not lost. Carefully remove any pulp or seed covering and keep them moist at all times. Sow thinly in trays of John Innes seed compost and cover with a thin layer of grit or shingle. Stand the trays in a bowl of shallow water to keep the compost sodden (*Aponogeton* and *Orontium* should be just submerged) and keep out of direct sunlight. Most seed should germinate within a few weeks, but some aquatic seed, most notably *Lysichitum*, may take up to 12 months. Heat is not required for germination. Unlike most seedlings, it is best to wait until the young plants fill the tray before they are pricked out. Pot up in heavy soil, top dress with shingle and place in the pond.

species	how	when	what to do
MARGINAL PLANTS			
Acorus	division	May to Sep	Seed of variegated varieties will produce all green seedlings.
Alisma plantago	seed	July or Spr	Self-sown seedlings can be a nuisance. Dead-head after flowering if you don't want to save seed.
Aponogeton (water hawthorn)	division	May to June	Cut creeping rhizomes into sections.
	seed	July	Sow as soon as ripe. Division much easier but not as interesting.
Butomus umbellatus (flowering rush)	division	May to June	Straightforward: see text.
	seed	Aug	Sow as soon as ripe.
Calla palustris (bog arum)	division	May to Sep	Straightforward: see text.
	nodal cuttings	Apr to June	Straightforward: see text.
Caltha palustris (marsh marigold)	division	May to Sep	Straightforward: see text.
	seed	Feb to June	Sow seed when ripe in summer or save seed for spring sowing. Flowers the following year. The double form, *C. palustris* 'Flore Pleno', produces infertile seeds.
Carex stricta 'Aureo-variegata' (Bowles' golden sedge)	division	May to Sep	Easier to divide if allowed to dry out a little.
Cotula coronopifolia	cuttings	May to June	Any bit of stem will root in shallow trays.
Cyperus longus (umbrella sedge)	division	May to Sep	Straightforward: see text.
Glyceria aquatica 'Variegata'	division	May to Sep	Straightforward: see text.
Iris kaempferi, I. laevigata	division	Apr to Sep	See page 86 for more details.
Lobelia cardinalis	division	May to Sep	Also grown as a border plant. See page 88.
Lysichtum (skunk cabbage)	seed	Aug	Sow as soon as ripe. Germination slow – up to 12 months. Flowering takes 3 to 5 years.
Menyanthes (bog bean)	division	May to June	Can become unwieldy if left too late.
	nodal cuttings	May to July	Sections of stem with a single node will root readily in pots in shallow water.

species	how	when	what to do
MARGINAL PLANTS			
Mimulus lutea (monkey flower)	division	Aut	Straightforward: see text.
	seed	Spr	Can be raised from bought seed. Sow in greenhouse in early spring to flower same year.
Myosotis palustris (water forget-me-not)	division	May to June	Straightforward: see text.
	cuttings	May to Sep	Simply break off small pieces with roots.
Nymphoides peltata (water fringe)	division	May to June	Straightforward: see text.
Orontium aquaticum (golden club)	seed	July to Aug	Sow as soon as ripe and submerge trays in water. Germination can take 6 to 12 months. Flowering takes 3 years.
	division	May to June	Can be difficult as forms very deep roots. Divide only if pot-grown.
Pontederia cordata (pickerel weed)	division	May to June	Straightforward: see text.
Ranunculus lingua	runners	May to June	Repot rooted offsets as required.
	seed	Aug	Sow when ripe or store for spring sowing.
Sagittaria (all sorts)	division	Sep	Frequently late to show growth, often not until July.
Scirpus	division	May to Sep	*Scirpus zebrinus* (zebra rush) becomes green with age but will regain variegation if divided.
Scrophularia aquatica 'Variegata'	division	May to Sep	Straightforward: see text.
	stem cuttings	Apr	Straightforward: see Herbaceous Perennials, page 76.
Typha latifolia, T. minima (reed maces)	division	May to Sep	Straightforward: see text.
Zantedeschia aethiopica 'Crowborough' (Crowborough lily)	division	Mar to Apr	Keep in 25-30cm (10-12in) of water over winter to protect from frost or pot up and bring into a frost-free greenhouse.
FLOATING PLANTS			
Azolla caroliniana (fairy moss)		Sep	May be killed in a bad winter so scoop a few plantlets out of the pond and keep in a bucket in frost-free conditions over winter.
Eichhornia crassipes (water hyacinth)		Sep	Increases freely from runners but will be killed outdoors in cold weather. Keep a few young plants frost free in a bucket.
Hydrocharis morsus-ranae (frog bit)		Sep	Retreats to a tiny bud in autumn and sinks to bottom of pond, not to reappear until early summer. Collect a few plants before this happens and keep them in a bucket over winter so you can start them off early in warm conditions in spring.
Stratoides alioides (water soldier)		May to Sep	Freely increases by runners that can be detached as required.
Trapa natans (water chestnut)		Aug to Sep	Annual that overwinters as a spiny seed that sinks to bottom of pond. Liable to be killed in cold winter, so collect a few plants in late summer and keep in a bucket in frost-free conditions until they reappear the following year.

A wild garden might seem appealing to a lazy gardener, but propagating wild flowers requires just as much effort as, if not more than, other garden plants. Many native plants are adapted to a particular type of soil, so the range you can grow in your garden will be limited by the conditions you can provide.

Creating a wild flower meadow is not simply a matter of letting the grass grow. You will need to control the more invasive weeds and introduce the choicer wild flowers as pot-grown plants.

TAKE NOTE
● Wild flower seeds should *never* be scattered in the countryside. A particularly aggressive species can push out the other native wild flowers, and related species can interbreed and alter the natural flora.
● *Never* collect seed from a rare plant as listed in the *British Red Data Book* (available from the Royal Society for Nature Conservation, The Green, Nettleham, Lincoln LN2 2NR). It is illegal to collect seed from plants protected under the Wildlife and Countryside Act 1981.
● It is also illegal to uproot *any* wild plant without the permission of the landowner. Even with permission, certain plants are still protected by law.

WILD FLOWERS IN GRASS

There are two ways to propagate a wild flower meadow, depending on whether you are starting from scratch or on an existing lawn.

Letting the lawn go wild

If you have been applying fertilisers to your lawn, the soil is likely to be too rich for the choicer wild flowers. You can reduce the fertility by letting grass grow to about 8cm (3in) and cutting it short, removing all the clippings. It may take up to 2 years of this treatment if you have been regularly feeding your lawn.

Another problem is that most lawns contain ryegrass, which is not an ideal companion for wild flowers, so you may be better off killing the existing grass and resowing with a fine mixture.

When you let the grass grow long, a number of wild flowers will grow naturally, though invasive species should be controlled by spot weeding. The best way to introduce new flowers is to raise them in trays or pots, or in a seedbed, like vegetables or spring bedding, and transplant them into the meadow. The best time to do this is in autumn, using a bulb planter to take out a core of turf. Sowing direct into the grass is unlikely to give good results.

Starting from scratch

Sowing a meadow is the same as sowing a lawn, and you first need to create a weed-free seedbed – but on no account apply fertilisers. It may also be worth removing the topsoil unless the soil is already very poor. You can buy mixtures of wild flowers and grass or make up your own. Whichever method you choose bear in mind the following points.

Grasses These can make up between 50 and 95 per cent of the mixture by bulk (most wild flower seed is very small compared with grass seed) and can either be fine lawn grasses (such as fescues and bents) or wild meadow grasses (such as meadow foxtail and meadow barley). Avoid perennial ryegrass as it will grow too well at the expense of the flowers. Go for fine lawn grasses if you don't want grass to grow too long or want to mow it short at some time during the year. Some of the meadow grasses are very attractive but can grow quite tall – 60–90cm (2–3ft) – and won't stand being cut short.

Flowers If you have acid clay soil, there is no point including wild flowers that grow naturally on chalk downs as they will never grow. The Table overleaf lists the conditions required and their suitability for grass. As a starting point, you could include about 20 species in your mixture. Grass and wild flower mixtures are often sold according to soil type.

It is also a good idea to concentrate either on spring or summer flowers to maximise the effect. Spring meadows can be cut down in July, once most of the flowers have seeded, and kept short for the rest of the year. Summer meadows should not be cut until autumn.

You can include some annual flowers, such as corncockles and field poppies. These will give a colourful display in the first year but are unlikely to reappear in any number. A good proportion of the perennial flowers should come up in the first year, but most won't flower until the second year.

COLLECTING SEED

You can collect seed from common wild flowers growing locally but not from rarer species (see Box). Most British wild flowers disperse their seeds in August and September (often up until November) and seed should be collected before this happens. Some plants, such as violets, shoot out their seeds as soon as they are ripe, so this is not always easy.

The easiest way to collect seed is to hold a paper bag under the seed head and snip it off with a pair of scissors. Spread the seeds out on newspaper and leave them to dry out for up to a week. You can either sow the seed in rows in a prepared seedbed or put the seed in manilla envelopes and store it somewhere cool (a sealed container in the fridge is ideal) for spring sowing.

Most of the larger seedsmen list wild flowers in their catalogues. There are also several seedsmen specialising in wild flowers (see Useful Addresses).

WILD FLOWERS IN THE BORDER

Many wild flowers make good border plants and can be used in conjunction with each other or with conventional border plants. The best way to propagate wild flowers for the border is either to raise them in seed trays or pots or in nursery beds for transplanting.

Germination rates for wild flowers can be very variable, so direct sowing is unwise. If you are unfamiliar with the plants, sowing in rows or trays will also avoid the seedlings being mistaken for weeds. When sowing wild flower seed, cover with no more than 3–6mm ($\frac{1}{8}$–$\frac{1}{4}$in) of soil.

Once established in a border, many will self-seed; otherwise they can be divided.

The best place to grow annual wild flowers is on a patch of very poor soil. Annuals such as corncockles, field poppies and corn marigolds can be broadcast in spring. These will provide a colourful summer display and, providing you rake over the soil in autumn, they should return again the following year.

	type	flowering period	uses	soil requirements	when to sow	notes
Achillea millefolium (yarrow)	P	June to Sep	SuM	any soil	Aug to Nov, Feb to May	Spreads locally by underground creeping stems.
Agrostemma githago (corn cockle)	A	June to Aug	SuM	moist, acid	Mar to May	Seeds are short-lived, so use fresh seed.
Campanula glomerata (clustered bellflower)	P	June to Sep	SuM	poor, dry, chalky	Aug to Nov, Feb to May	Sow outdoors in autumn or mix with sand and peat and keep in the fridge for 6 weeks prior to sowing.
Campanula rotundifolia (harebell)	P	July to Sep	SuM	poor, dry, chalky	Aug to Nov, Jan to Feb	As above.
Cardamine pratensis (lady's smock, cuckoo flower)	P	Apr to June	SuM	moist	Aug to Nov, Feb to May	
Centaurea cyanus (cornflower)	A	Mar to May	SuM	well drained	Apr to May	Won't reappear in any numbers unless soil disturbed in autumn.
Centaurea nigra (common knapweed)	P	July to Sep	SuM	any soil	Feb to May	
Centaurea scabiosa (greater knapweed)	P	July to Sep	SuM/B	dry, chalky	Feb to May, Aug to Nov	
Chelidonium majus (greater celandine)	P	May to July	SuM	any	Apr to May, Aug to Sep	Not invasive, unlike the lesser celandine.
Chrysanthemum leucanthemum (oxeye daisy)	P	June to Aug	SuM/B	any, dry	Feb to May, Aug to Nov	Stored seed deteriorates rapidly.
Chrysanthemum segetum (corn marigold)	A	Mar to May	B	acid, dry	spring	Self-seeds freely. Can be very slow to germinate.
Echium vulgare (viper's bugloss)	B	July to Aug	B	hot, dry, poor	July to Aug, Feb to Mar	Will flower the same year from early spring sowing.
Eupatorium cannabinum (hemp agrimony)	P	July to Sep	B	damp, not acid	Feb to May, Aug to Nov	Sow fresh or store, mix seed with peat and sand and keep in fridge for spring sowing.
Fritillaria meleagris (snakeshead fritillary)	P	Apr to May	B, Sum	moist, not acid	Apr to May	You can also buy bulbs.
Galium verum (lady's bedstraw)	P	July to Sep	SuM	poor	Aug to Nov, Feb to May	
Geranium pratense (meadow cranesbill)	P	June to Sep	SuM, B	chalky	Aug to Nov, Feb to May	Scarification (see page 33) aids germination.
Geranium robertianum (herb robert)	A*	Apr to Sep	B, on walls	any soil	Feb to May	Scarification (see page 33) aids germination. *P in milder areas.
Hypericum hirsutum (hairy St John's wort)	P	July to Sep	SuM, B	damp, alkaline	Jan to Feb	
Lamium album (white dead nettle)	P	May to Dec	M, B	any soil	Aug to Nov	Spreads locally by creeping underground stems.
Lamium purpureum (red dead nettle)	A	Mar to Oct	M, B	any soil	Feb to May	Will die out in meadow after first year.

	type	flowering period	uses	soil requirements	when to sow	notes
Leontodon hispidis (hawkbit)	P	June to Sep	SuM	chalky	Aug to Nov, Feb to Mar	
Linaria vulgaris (yellow toad flax)	P	June to Oct	SuM, B	average	Aug to Nov, Feb to May	Spreads locally by creeping underground stems.
Lychnis flos-cuculi (ragged robin)	P	May to July	SpM, by pool	needs damp soil	Aug to Nov, Feb to May	
Malva moschata (musk mallow)	P	July to Aug	SuM, B	any soil	Aug to Nov, Feb to May	
Medicago lupulina (black medick)	A or P	Apr to Aug	M	any soil	Aug to Nov, Feb to May	Leguminous and fixes nitrogen so it can make soil too rich for other wild flowers. Scarification (see page 33) aids germination.
Ononis spinosa (spiny restharrow)	P	June to Sep	SuM, B	dry	Aug to Nov, Feb to May	
Pentaglottis sempervirens (green alkanet)	P	Apr to June	B	any soil	Aug to Sep, Apr to May	
Poterium sanguisorba (salad burnet)	P	May to Aug	M	chalky, dry, poor	Feb to May	Stored seed deteriorates rapidly.
Primula veris (cowslip)	P	Apr to June	SpM, B	neutral or chalky	Aug to Nov	Sow outdoors or as for alpines (see page 96). Germinates best if exposed to light, but still irregular.
Primula vulgaris (primrose)	P	Apr to Aug	SpM, B	damp, neutral	Aug to Nov	As above.
Ranunculus acris (field buttercup)	P	Apr to July	SpM	damp, not acid	Aug to Nov, Feb to May	
Ranunculus bulbosus (bulbous buttercup)	P	Apr to June	SpM	dry, not acid	Aug to Nov, Feb to May	
Rhinanthus minor (yellow rattle)	A	May to Aug	SuM	any soil	Aug to Nov, Feb to May	Semi-parasitic on grass, so should always be sown with a grass seed.
Rumex acetosa (common sorrel)	P	May to June	SpM	moist	Aug to Nov, Feb to May	Self-seeds freely.
Silene droica (red campion)	B or P	May to July	SpM, B	any soil	Aug to Nov, Feb to May	S. alba (white campion) better on dry soils.
Veronica chamaedrys (germander speedwell)	P	Mar to July	SpM	any soil	Aug to Sep, Apr to May	
Viola tricolor (heartsease)	A*	Apr to Sep	SuM, B	neutral or acid	Aug to Nov, Feb to May	*P in milder areas.

Key to type
A Annual
P Perennial
B Biennial

Key to uses
SpM Spring meadow
SuM Summer meadow
M Spring or summer meadow
B Border

The techniques for propagating fruit are basically the same as for trees and shrubs. Details of what to do are given under individual fruits in the Tables, but if you need more advice on taking cuttings or layering turn to pages 12 and 42.

If you are starting a new fruit garden, it is a good idea to buy a number of different varieties and, once they have fruited, to propagate from the ones you like best. But think twice about propagating from old plants, especially blackcurrants, blackberries, loganberries and other hybrid berries, raspberries and strawberries.

The main problem with these fruits is that they are very prone to virus diseases, and these diseases will be carried to their offspring. The symptoms of virus diseases are not necessarily obvious to the eye, though they usually result in a steady decline in cropping over the years, and plants propagated from virus-infected plants may give poor crops.

If you have noticed a decline in your fruit yields, it may be worth throwing out all your old plants and starting again with certified virus-free plants. Strawberries should be replaced every 3 to 4 years in any case. Always plant new fruit in a different part of the garden to avoid problems with soil-borne diseases and pests such as eelworm. If you do propagate fruit from established plants, it is a good idea to spray them beforehand. This will have no effect on viruses, but it will control other pests and diseases. Never propagate from plants that don't look healthy.

Even for a small fruit garden, you can save a lot by buying one or two plants of each type to propagate from – the exceptions being apples, pears and plums.

> **Key to how easy**
> ●●● Quite easy   ●● More difficult
> ● Worth trying, but be prepared for failure
> **How long** Note times given are for first crops, which will probably be quite small. In most cases it will take another 1 to 2 years for plants to build up to full cropping potential

HARDWOOD CUTTINGS
It is often recommended that hardwood cuttings of fruit bushes can be taken from October right through to February. It is always better, however, to take hardwood cuttings as soon as the leaves fall.

Cuttings root much better in warm soil in autumn. Those taken once the soil has cooled down will remain dormant all winter and may form shoots before the roots in spring, putting the cuttings under stress and possibly killing them.

	how	when	hor-mone*	what to do	how easy	how long
B						
Black currants	hardwood cuttings	mid-Sep to Nov	no	Take 20–25cm (8–10in) cuttings from 1-year-old stems and remove any soft tips. Plant 15cm (6in) apart in trenches (line with sand on heavy soil) so top 1 or 2 buds show above ground level. Lift in the following autumn, plant out 30cm (12in) apart and trim back shoots to 1 bud. Grow on for a further year and plant in final positions.	●●●	3 yrs
Blackberries	tip layering	June to Aug	no	Insert the growing tips of new shoots into the ground about 10–13cm (4–5in) deep with tip pointing downwards. Rooting is very quick, and in a few weeks the tip will emerge and the process can be repeated. Move the layers to final positions in winter or spring.	●●●	2 yrs

To propagate blackberries and hybrid berries, just make a slit in the soil with a spade, insert the growing tip of a young cane and gently firm in with your foot. Water if the soil is dry.

	how	when	hor-mone*	what to do	how easy	how long
Blueberries	nodal cuttings	June	no	Take 10–20cm (4–8in) cuttings of soft growth and remove all but top 3 leaves. Root in a sandy compost, either in a pot covered with a polythene bag or, ideally, in a propagator at 20°C (68°F). After rooting (3 to 6 weeks), harden off and pot up into a *lime-free* compost.	●	3 yrs
Boysenberries	tip layering	June to Aug	no	See Blackberries, above.	●●●	2 yrs
F–G						
Figs	nodal cuttings	Aug	yes	Take 15cm (6in) cuttings of semi-ripe wood and insert to half their depth in rooting compost. Keep in the cold frame until rooted (4 to 6 weeks) and either pot on or plant out in a sheltered spot and grow on for 2 years before planting in final position.	●●	4 to 6 yrs
	hardwood cuttings	Oct to Nov	yes	Take 30cm (12in) stem cuttings of 1-year-old wood and plant in a well-drained soil in a sheltered spot. Transplant to final position after 2 years.	●●●	4 to 6 yrs
	layering	Spr	-	Select a 1-year-old shoot near ground level. Remove leaves for 13–25cm (5–10in) below the tip. Detach layer in winter or the following spring and grow on for 2 years.	●●●	4 to 5 yrs
	suckers	Oct to Nov	-	Carefully expose base of sucker and cut off close to main trunk. Grow on in a sheltered spot for 2 years before transferring to final position.	●●●	3 to 4 yrs

*Hormone means a rooting powder or solution

	how	when	hor-mone*	what to do	how easy	how long
Gooseberries	hardwood cuttings	mid-Sep to Oct	yes	Take 25–30cm (10–12in) cuttings from straight 1-year-old shoots of about half-pencil thickness. Treat with rooting hormone and plant out 15cm (6in) apart in a sand-lined trench. If you want a bush with several stems, bury the bottom two-thirds of the cutting. If you want a bush on a leg, remove all but the top 4 buds and spines and plant so lowest bud is 5cm (2in) above soil level to ensure no suckering can occur. See red currants.	● to ●●	3 to 4 yrs
	suckers	Win	-	If your bushes are not grown on a leg, you can detach rooted shoots and grow on as for cuttings. If you want a bush on a leg, remove lower buds and spines.	●●●	2 to 4 yrs
Grapes	hardwood cuttings	Dec	-	Take 20–25cm (8–10in) cuttings from 1-year-old shoots, each with at least 3 buds, and plant 15cm (6in) deep and 15cm (6in) apart in sand-lined trenches. New growth susceptible to frost damage, so may be worth protecting with cloches in May. Transplant to fruiting position the following autumn. 15cm (6in) cuttings with 2 buds can also be rooted in a cold frame in January. Pot on in June and plant out the following spring.	●●●	3 yrs
	single bud cuttings	Nov	no	Take cuttings about 8cm (3in) long with a bud in the centre. Remove a sliver of wood on the side opposite to the bud and insert horizontally into a peat and sand mixture. Root in a propagator at 18°C (65–68°F). Once rooted (4 to 6 weeks), harden off and pot up singly. Either plant out after worst frosts or grow on in a cool greenhouse for the first year.	●●	3 to 4 yrs

K – W

	how	when	hor-mone*	what to do	how easy	how long
Kiwi fruit (Chinese gooseberry, *Actinidia chinensis*)	layering	Spr	no	Layers should root by autumn and can be transplanted to final position. You need 1 male to 7 females for fruit.	●●	3 yrs
	hardwood cuttings	Dec	yes	Take 20–30cm (8–12in) cuttings of 1-year-old wood. Insert in a mixture of sand and peat and use propagator or soil-warming cables to provide a bottom heat of 20°C (68°F). After 3 to 5 weeks, calluses and tiny roots should form and the cuttings can then be transplanted into boxes or pots of sandy compost in a cool greenhouse over winter. Pot on into John Innes No. 2 in spring.	●	3 yrs
Loganberries	tip layering	June to Aug	no	See Blackberries, page 115.	●●●	2 yrs
Mulberries				See *Morus nigra* under Trees, page 40.		
Plums, Myrobalan (*Prunus cerasifera*)	hardwood cuttings	Nov to Dec	yes	Most plums are grafted or budded on to a rootstock, but Myrobalan can be grown on its own roots and produces acceptable fruit for jam or wine-making and can be a good hedge. Take 45–60cm (18–24in) cuttings of year-old wood and plant 8–10cm (3–4in) apart. Transplant to 30cm (12in) apart the following winter and grow on for further year before final planting.	●●●	6 to 7 yrs
	seed	July to Aug	-	Bury ripe fruits in a mixture of peat and grit and protect with netting. In autumn, sieve to remove the seeds and plant 5cm (2in) deep and 20cm (8in) apart in a seedbed. Cover with 1cm (½in) sharp sand and cover with netting. Grow on for 2 years before transplanting.	●	up to 10 yrs

*Hormone means a rooting powder or solution

	how	when	hor-mone*	what to do	how easy	how long
Raspberries	suckers	Nov to Feb	-	Lift young fruiting canes. Remove section of roots with dormant buds. Replant in another part of the garden.	●●●	1½ yrs
Red currants	hardwood cuttings	Oct to Nov	yes	Take 30cm (12in) cuttings of 1-year-old wood. If you want a bush on a leg, remove all but top 4 buds. Plant out 20cm (8in) apart in a sand-lined trench.	●●●	2½ yrs

20cm (8in)

With cuttings grown on a leg, prune back shoots by half in the first winter.

soil level

Remove buds for a bush grown on a leg; leave them on for a suckering bush.

buds

With suckering bushes, prune back all new shoots to one or two buds in the first winter.

	how	when	hor-mone*	what to do	how easy	how long
Strawberries, alpine (frais de bois)	seed	Sep to Oct or Feb to Mar	-	Sow thinly on surface of compost and cover seed tray with glass (not newspaper) and germinate at 18°C (65°F). When seedlings have 2 to 3 leaves, prick out 5cm (2in) apart in trays or individually into peat pots. Harden off and plant out in April or May. March sowings may not fruit until second year. Replace plants every 3 years.	●●●	1 to 2 yrs
Strawberries, summer and autumn fruiting	runners	June to Aug	-	Peg down runners into the surrounding soil or into 8cm (3in) pots of John Innes No. 2. Once rooted (4 to 6 weeks), plant in a different part of the garden.	●●●	1 yr

Strawberry runner rooted in an 8cm (3in) pot.

	how	when	hor-mone*	what to do	how easy	how long
	seed	Jan to Feb	-	'Sweetheart' is the only large-fruited strawberry that can be raised from seed. Sow thinly in trays of soil-less compost and lightly cover. Germinate at 18°C (65°F), prick out into small pots and grow on until early May in a cool greenhouse. Harden off for 3 to 4 weeks in a cold frame and plant out 30cm (12in) apart. First fruits should appear in late July to August (earlier in second year) and continue until October.	●●●	6 months
Strawberries, perpetual	division	early Spr	-	Lift and divide each plant into 2 or 3 portions, each having good crowns and buds as well as roots. Replant immediately in another part of the garden with the crowns just above soil level.	●●●	1½ yrs
Tayberries				As for Blackberries, page 115.	●●●	2 yrs
White currants				As for Red currants, above.	●●●	2½ yrs
Worcester berries				As for Red currants, above.	●●	3 yrs

*Hormone means a rooting powder or solution

VEGETABLES: TECHNIQUES

GETTING VEGETABLE SEEDS TO GERMINATE

Many gardeners blame the seed when vegetables don't come up. You may be unlucky enough to get a batch of poor seed, but it's more likely that you can attribute your failures to one of the following causes:

● Sowing too early, before soil has warmed up or dried out sufficiently.
● Sowing too deeply or taking insufficient care to cover the seeds to an even depth along the row.
● Letting a hard crust form on the seedbed before the seedlings emerge.
● Not taking precautions against pests and diseases – using old compost and dirty pots, for example.
● Leaving seedlings in their container too long without feeding them, resulting in pale, weak plants.
● Not hardening off seedlings properly before planting out.

Below we look at how you can overcome the problems of poor germination and failures at the seedling stage.

OLD OR STORED SEED

With a few vegetables, such as parsnips and onions, fresh seed is essential, but most vegetable seed can be stored at home for up to 3 years. However, it must be kept cool and dry, preferably in an air-tight container in the fridge. Put a bag of silica gel (from chemists) inside to absorb moisure.

Seed kept in warm, humid conditions, such as in the greenhouse, can lose its viability very quickly – in a matter of weeks with some seeds.

Temperature

Most vegetable seeds won't germinate until the soil temperature reaches 5°C (43°F). Celery, French and runner beans, outdoor tomatoes and sweet corn require a soil temperature of 10°C (50°F) to germinate, and cucumbers and marrows won't germinate until the soil reaches 13°C (55°F). Even hardy vegetables will germinate much more reliably once the soil reaches 10°C (50°F).

Sowing too early outdoors means that the seed will sit in the soil until it warms and will be more prone to rotting or being eaten by pests.

Water

A common cause of failure with seeds is that they take up some water and start to germinate and then are allowed to dry out.

With outdoor sowings, carefully trickle water along the bottom of the drill before sowing if the soil is dry. On light soils you can help prevent drying out by lining the drill with moist peat prior to sowing. A wind-break around the vegetable plot will also limit the effect of drying winds.

Sowing depth

A common fault with outdoor sowings is to sow too deep or burying some seeds deeper than others, resulting in uneven germination. Most small vegetable seeds require a covering of only 12–20mm ($\frac{1}{2}$–$\frac{3}{4}$in) of soil, and even larger seeds such as peas and beans don't need to be sown deeper than 50mm (2in).

Soil structure

Soils containing clay are very prone to form a hard crust on the surface (capping), and this can make it impossible for germinated seedlings to reach the light. You can prevent capping by working peat into the top few centimetres of the seedbed prior to sowing or covering the drill with a line of peat (or the contents of an old growing bag after sowing). Anti-capping gels may also be available from some garden centres. If capping occurs after sowing, water along the drill with a fine rose to moisten the soil in order to help the seedlings emerge.

On heavy clay soils it may be worth making a raised bed of improved soil so that you can start sowing earlier outdoors.

Air in the soil

Seeds need air to germinate, and this is the reason for working the soil into a good tilth before sowing outdoors. In heavy soils prone to waterlogging in the spring, seed will be starved of air and will be killed. Delay outdoor sowings until the soil has dried out sufficiently and make the earliest sowings under glass.

Pests and diseases

Indoor sowings The most common cause of failure is damping off, when seedlings collapse at soil level. To avoid problems, always use clean pots and trays and fresh seed compost, sow thinly and water from below. As a precaution, water the compost with a fungicide containing copper (such as Cheshunt compound or liquid copper) when sowing or when pricking out seedlings.
Outdoor sowings Most problems occur with early sowings, and it is worth treating the seed with a combined insecticide and fungicide dressing prior to sowing or buying pre-treated seed.
See also page 120.

Sweet corn can be sown outdoors in late April or early May under clear polythene. Make holes in the polythene to pull the seedlings through when they reach the four-leaf stage.

USING CLEAR POLYTHENE FOR EARLY CROPS

As a mulch

Sow seeds in furrows 8–10cm (3–4in) deep and 15cm (6in) wide and stretch thin polythene tightly over the soil, burying the edges or weighting them down with pieces of timber. Once the seedlings reach the polythene, make holes for them to grow through. The polythene will warm up the soil and keep the rain off, preventing waterlogging. The main disadvantage is that it also encourages weeds to grow, but you can lift up the sides of the polythene for weeding.
Suitable crops courgettes, runner beans, sweet corn.

As a floating cloche

Sow seeds in furrows 5cm (2in) deep and 8cm (3in) wide and cover as for mulches. Early in the year, young seedlings can be left to support the polythene, but be prepared to cover the plants with newspaper on frosty nights once they are touching the polythene. When the weather warms up, in about April, the cover should be removed. Wean the plants by making large slashes in the polythene 3 to 4 days before it is removed.
Suitable crops carrots, onions, radishes.

Hardening off

Plants raised under glass or polythene need to be weaned to outdoor conditions. Otherwise exposure to wind or a sudden drop in temperature can seriously weaken the plants and can prove fatal. Plants raised in the greenhouse are best placed in the cold frame for a week or so, gradually increasing the ventilation during the day. If plants are raised under a polythene film, gradually acclimatise them by making a few slits in the polythene before removing the cover altogether.

VEGETABLES THAT NEED TO BE STARTED IN THE GREENHOUSE

	when to sow	sowing temp.	grow on temp.	notes
Celery	Mar to Apr	18°C (65°F)	15°C (60°F)	Sow in pots or peat blocks and trim to one seedling. Plant out in May, under cloches if necessary.
Cucumbers, ridge	Apr to May	18°C (65°F)	15°C (60°F)	Sow singly in small pots. Plant out under cloches and protect until last frosts.
Melons	Apr to May	18°C (65°F)	15°C (60°F)	Plant out under cloches late May or June. Grow under cloches, but remove roof pane when in flower to allow pollination.
Tomatoes, outdoor	Mar to Apr	18°C (65°F)	15°C (60°F)	Plant out under cloches and protect until last frosts. See also fluid sowing.

OVERCOMING PROBLEMS WITH PARTICULAR VEGETABLES

Bean seed fly   (beans, onions, peas, shallots)
Lays eggs in freshly cultivated soil. Maggots feed on seeds and seedlings. Raise plants in containers and transplant or use soil insecticide, such as diazinon or phoxim, prior to sowing.

Birds   (onion sets, shallots)
To prevent birds pulling sets out of the ground, plant a little deeper so they are almost covered, cover with netting until rooted or start them off in pots.

Bolting   (beetroot, celery, Chinese cabbage)
Beetroot is liable to bolting if soil temperature is below 9°C (48°F), so choose a bolt-resistant variety such as 'Avonearly' or 'Boltardy' for first sowings or start round varieties in the greenhouse. Celery is liable to bolt if temperature falls below 15°C (60°F), so you'll need to raise them in a heated greenhouse. Chinese cabbage is liable to bolt below 10°C (50°F) or if it gets dry at any time. Varieties such as 'Sampan' and 'Nagoaka' are less prone to bolting.

Carrot fly   (carrots, parsley, parsnips)
Sow carrots before the end of April or in late June to miss main periods of attack. Try to avoid thinning. An 80cm (30in) high polythene barrier around the plot will keep carrot flies out. Alternatively, apply a soil insecticide such as diazinon or phoxim when sowing and

thinning, and again in September.

Cabbage root fly   (broccoli, cabbage, cauliflowers, turnips, swedes and radishes)
Maggots eat roots of seedlings and transplants, causing wilting, stunting and sometimes death. Problem worse in May, July and September (in South). Raise seedlings in 8cm (3in) pots or peat blocks to get them off to a good start, place brassica collars around stems of transplants or use a soil insecticide such as phoxim.

Clubroot   (as for cabbage root fly; also Brussels sprouts)
Symptoms similar to cabbage root fly, but roots distorted and no maggots present. If your soil is infected, raise seedlings in 8cm (3in) pots so plants get established before disease attacks. Alternatively, treat roots of seedlings in a clubroot dip before transplanting. Regular liming and crop rotation may help.

Cutworms   (lettuce)
Can affect all seedlings, biting them off at soil level, but can be a particular problem with lettuce sown in early summer when weather is dry. Raise seedlings in pots or peat blocks or use a soil insecticide prior to sowing.

Downy mildew   (cabbage, cauliflowers)
Can be a serious problem on seedlings overwintered in pots in a cold frame. Space plants so leaves not touching and ventilate when possible to avoid problems.

Germination slow or uneven   (carrots, parsnips)
Fresh seed is essential for parsnips. Never use seed left over from previous year. Best way to avoid problems is by pre-germinating the seed indoors and fluid sowing.

Flea beetle   (all cabbage family, including swedes, turnips and radishes)
Attacks leaves of seedlings, peppering them full of holes. Dust seedlings with derris powder.

Frit fly   (sweet corn)
Attacks seedlings, causing distorted leaves, later spoiling the cobs. To avoid attacks keep seedlings covered with clear polythene until the 4-leaf stage.

Thermal dormancy   (lettuce)
Summer sowings may fail to germinate if temperature reaches 25°C (77°F). Water seedbed well a couple of hours before you sow to lower the soil temperature and sow between 2pm and 4pm so that critical stages of germination take place in the evening. Alternatively, raise seedlings in small pots somewhere cool.

Seed rot   (courgettes, cucumbers, French and runner beans, sweet corn)
Seed in pots prone to rotting if compost too wet or greenhouse too cold. Keep a minimum temperature of 15°C (60°F) until seedlings appear. Sow flat seeds on edge.

See also Troubleshooting, page 132.

IMPROVING GERMINATION

Most vegetable seeds germinate quite readily without any special treatment. There are, however, a few techniques you can use to speed nature along.

Chitting

Worthwhile for cucumbers and melons, where you have only a few seeds to deal with and germination is best at quite high temperatures – around 24°C (75°F). Germinate the seed on moist blotting paper (as for fluid sowing) and sow individually in small pots. Sow flat seeds on edge to avoid rot. See also fluid sowing, opposite.

Soaking

Will speed up germination of large seeds and peas and beans. Soak overnight in warm water and sow once seeds have swollen. Soaking may also be worthwhile for beetroot, as the seeds contain a chemical that inhibits germination. Either soak overnight or keep under running water for about half an hour – in an old stocking tied to the cold tap, say.

SPECIAL SOWING TECHNIQUES

Sowing in peat blocks

By sowing in peat blocks, the seedlings can be planted out with the rootball intact and so preventing any check to growth. They are particularly useful for crops that don't transplant well, such as sweet corn.

Making the block.

● To make peat blocks you need a blocking tool and a special compost made from equal parts of sedge and moss peat.
● Fill the tool with compost and scrape off any excess. Put the tool down on a flat surface and press the plunger to compress the compost and get rid of any excess water. Remove the block by lifting the tool and pushing the plunger.
● Place a sheet of capillary

Sowing in peat blocks.

matting over a polythene sheet or in a seed tray. Thoroughly moisten and place the blocks on this so they are not touching. Sow the seed, cover with a sprinkling of silver sand and place a sheet of black polythene over the blocks to retain moisture.
● Remove the polythene once seedlings appear. If seedlings remain in blocks for more than 6 weeks, give them a liquid feed. Plant out as soon as roots emerge from the side of blocks. Water them in well outside and give plants a final liquid feed.

Multiple seeding

Multiple seeding is a variation on the peat block technique. A number of seeds are sown in the same block without thinning. The clumps of seedlings are then planted out at wider spacing than normal without thinning. The advantages are that it cuts down the number of peat blocks needed and saves greenhouse space. Worth trying are early beetroot (2 seed clusters a block), onions (6 seeds a block) and leeks (6 seeds a block). Plant out 30cm (1ft) apart.

Fluid sowing

Fluid sowing is a technique used for sowing pre-germinated or chitted seeds without damaging them. It has a number of potential advantages for certain crops.
● **Carrots and parsnips** Quicker and more even emergence of seedlings. Can save thinning carrots; earlier parsnips.
● **Lettuce** More reliable results from summer sowings.
● **Onions** Higher yields of bulb onions, earlier salad onions.
● **Parsley** Avoids delays in germination with early sowings.
● **Outdoor tomatoes** Quick-maturing varieties, such as 'Red Alert', can be sown direct outdoors in late April or May (under cloches in cold areas).
  You need a sandwich box, blotting paper, wallpaper paste (without fungicide), a tea strainer and a polythene bag.
● Place several layers of blotting paper in the bottom of a sandwich box, cover with water and drain.
● Keep the box somewhere warm – around 20°C (68°F) – until seeds

Removing chitted seeds from blotting paper.

start to germinate – a day for lettuce, 3 days for carrots and onions, up to 7 days for parsnips.
● As soon as tiny roots appear, gently wash the seeds off the paper into a tea strainer.
● Mix up wallpaper paste (around a heaped teaspoon to a half-pint of water), leave for 15

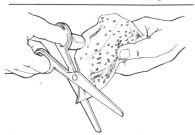

Remove the corner of the bag and sow the seed and paste mixture like icing a cake.

minutes and gently mix the seed with the paste. (Aim for around 50 to 80 seeds in a half-pint.)
● Pour the paste into a polythene bag, cut a small hole in one corner and sow in drills as if icing a cake. Finally, cover the seed with soil.

crop	when to sow	what to do	harvest
Beetroot	Feb to Mar	Sow 2 to 3 seeds a peat block. Germinate at 15°C (60°F). Use bolt-resistant varieties. Plant out under cloches or in open if soil temperature is over 10°C (50°F). Sow earlier only in mild areas.	late May to early June
	late Mar to Apr	Sow *in situ* under cloches or polythene film. Remove polythene film mid- to late May.	late June to mid-July
Broad beans	Feb to Mar	Sow in pots in a greenhouse. Plant outside or under cloches at 2 to 3 leaf stage. Remove cloches just before plants touch the glass. For slightly later crops, sow *in situ* under cloches or polythene film. Remove polythene when plants are 5cm (2in) high.	late June to early July
Cabbage, early summer	mid-Feb to early Mar	Sow at 15°C (60°F). Prick off into peat blocks or pots and grow on frost-free. Plant out in early April and, for earliest crops, keep under cloches until early May. Pointed varieties will be ready before round ones.	mid-May to mid-June
Carrots	mid- to late Oct	Sow *in situ* under cloches or polythene film. Suitable only for areas south of Wash to North Wales. Remove protection late April to mid-May.	mid- to late May
Cauliflower, early summer	late Sep to early Oct	Sow in a cold greenhouse. Prick off into 8cm (3in) pots. Plant out in February. For earliest crops keep under cloches until late April.	May to early June
	Jan to Feb	Sow as above but at 15°C (60°F). Grow on frost-free. Plant out in March to early April.	mid-June to early July
Courgettes and marrows (bush types)	early Apr to early May	Sow singly in small pots at 18°C (65°F). Grow on at 12–15°C (55–60°F). Plant out under cloches once first true leaf is size of 2p. Remove cloches once flowers form.	late May to mid-June
	late Apr to mid-May	Sow *in situ* under cloches or polythene film.	early to late June
French beans	mid-Apr	Sow in pots as for courgettes. Plant out under cloches when first leaves expanded. Remove cloches before plants touch the glass.	late June
	late Apr to mid-May	Sow *in situ* under cloches or polythene film. Remove polythene when first leaves expanded.	early July
Lettuce	early Sep to early Oct	Sow in a cold greenhouse. Prick off into small pots. Plant out under cloches mid-October to mid-November. Protect until harvest.	Apr
	Jan to Feb	Sow as above, but plant out in March. Without cloche protection, first crops ready late May or early June.	early to mid-May
Onions, bulb	late Feb to Mar	Sow 4 to 6 seeds per peat block. Germinate at 15°C (60°F). Plant out under cloches or outside if weather conditions are good.	late Aug to Sep
	late Feb to Mar	Sow *in situ* under cloches or polythene film. Remove cloches late April, polythene when second leaf shows.	early Sep
Peas	mid-Oct	Sow *in situ*, cover with cloches end December. Mild areas only.	June
	Feb to Mar	Sow 6 to 8 seeds per 8cm (3in) pot at 15°C (60°F). Grow on cold and plant out, without separating seedlings, 15cm (6in) apart under cloches.	late June to early July
Potatoes	mid-Feb to mid-Mar	Cover flat-topped ridges with clear polythene and make holes to plant through. Be prepared to cover the tops with paper on frosty nights.	mid-May to early June
Radishes	late Jan to mid-Mar	Sow *in situ* under cloches or polythene film. Ventilate (slit polythene) in warm weather, remove covers early April.	Mar to Apr
Runner beans	Apr	Sow singly in pots at 15°C (60°F) and plant under cloches or sow *in situ* through holes in clear polythene. Cover with paper on frosty nights.	mid-July
Sweet corn	late April to early May	Sow *in situ* under clear polythene. Pull leaves through holes in polythene after 4-leaf stage. Use an early variety such as 'EarliKing'.	early to mid-Aug

A lot of the plants we grow indoors are actually wild plants that grow rampant in the jungles, forests, deserts and scrublands all around the world. The fact they survive in the climates of our homes is testimony to their tough nature. All this is good news for the gardener, as it means that most indoor plants are very easy to propagate.

Useful techniques can be found on the following two pages and the table on pages 126 to 134 gives individual advice on over 100 widely grown indoor plants.

Most houseplants are very easy to propagate

LEAF CUTTINGS

A lot of indoor plants can be propagated from their leaves and there are a number of different techniques you can use.

Whole leaves

Technically, these are known as leaf-petiole cuttings, because you use a leaf with a stalk, or petiole. Select an undamaged leaf that has just fully opened and remove it together with its stalk. Trim the stalk about 5cm (2in) below the leaf using a sharp knife. Insert the cuttings into a cuttings compost or an equal mixture of peat and sharp sand. The cuttings should be at an angle of around 70 to 80 degrees. Water them in with a dilute fungicide and cover with a polythene bag supported on wires or sticks. After about five or six weeks, new plantlets will grow where the leaf stalk was cut. At

this stage give them a liquid feed and harden off before potting up.

This method is commonly used for African violets (Saintpaulia), begonias (except Begonia rex varieties) and stemless peperomias such as P. caperata and P. metallica. A variation commonly used for African violets is to root them in a dark-coloured medicine bottle filled with water. The top is covered with metal foil to support the cutting. The advantage with

Cut sansieveria leaves into 8cm (3in) strips

this method is that you don't need to cover the cuttings.

Leaf strips

The leaves of sansieverias and streptocarpus can be cut into horizontal strips around 8cm (3in) wide. The strips are inserted the right way up into the compost to a third of their depth. Otherwise, they are treated exactly the same as whole leaf cuttings. The difference being that you can get two or three plantlets from each leaf. It is likely that some leaf sections will die before the plantlets are formed and these should be removed immediately.

A slight variation with streptocarpus is to cut out the central midrib of the leaf and to inset the two halves cut side down into the compost. If it works, new plantlets will form at the points where each leaf was cut.

Leaf slashing

This is the method most commonly used for Begonia rex.

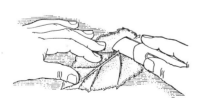

Cut slits in the veins of a Begonia rex leaf

New plants should grow from each leaf section

Place the leaf upside down on a smooth surface and make a slit through each of the prominent veins. Now lay the leaf face up in a tray of compost. Either peg it down with hairpins or weigh down with pebbles to ensure the cut surfaces are in good contact with the compost.

SHOOT TIPS

The most common method of propagating indoor plants is from the shoot tips. Simply remove 8–10cm (3–4in) of stem with a few leaves attached. With most plants, this will not only provide you with cutting material but will help to keep plants bushy, rather than tall and leggy.

OFFSETS

Some indoor plants, notably bromeliads and many cacti and succulents, have the obliging habit of producing miniature replicas of themselves that can be potted up and grown on into mature plants.

Place face up on compost and weigh down with pebbles

Succulents, such as sempervivums and echeverias, form offsets on creeping stems and these should be pulled from the parent plant, stem and all, to avoid any chance of rots. These offsets often have roots already and are quick to get established in well-drained compost.

Bromeliads (which include aechmeas, billbergias, cryptanthus, guzmanias, neoregelias and vriesias) die after

Be careful of the spines when removing echinopsis offsets

they have flowered but they replace themselves with offsets, which should be removed and potted up separately. Wait until the offsets are around half the size of the parent before removing them as this will give them the best chance of survival. To get them established quickly, cover with a polythene bag and keep them warm and shaded. A mixture of three parts peat-based compost to one part sharp sand is ideal for most bromeliads. Offsets can take anything from a year or two for billbergias, to three years for cryptanthus and five years for aechmeas and vriesias to come into flower.

Some cacti, like echinocereus, are easy to propagate from offsets. Use a strip of rolled up paper to

Tiny plantlets are formed where leaf veins are cut

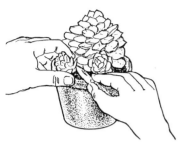

Remove the rosettes that form around the base of echeverias and pot up individually

get hold of them and gently tease them away with a knife if necessary. Let cut surfaces dry for a few days before potting up into a cactus compost.

PROPAGATING ORCHIDS

The easiest way to propagate orchids is by division. Orchids rhizomes have swollen bits from which the leaves appear called pseudobulbs. When dividing orchids, each section should have two or three healthy pseudobulbs. You can cut out and discard the old ones which are no longer producing leaves. The divisions should be potted up separately into orchid compost and kept slightly warmer than normal for the first month or so, while they get established. Water sparingly to avoid the risk of rotting.

CACTI FROM SEED

Growing from seed is a cheap and interesting way to grow cacti. Start in January or February if you have a heated propagator (late April/early May if you don't). Fill a seed tray with a mixture of one part John Innes Seed Compost, one part peat-based compost and two parts sharp sand or grit. Sow the seed on the surface, water from below and cover the tray with clinging film. Shade from direct sunlight and keep seeds at least 21°C (70°F) until they germinate.

The temperature can then be lowered to 17°C (65°F). For the first six months, keep the seedlings covered and make sure they don't dry out completely or catch the direct rays of the sun, otherwise, they'll turn pink and stop growing. In September, gradually remove the cover and harden the seedlings off. For quickest results, it is best to keep the plants warm and growing through the first winter. This means a minimum of 10°C (50°F). At this temperature, keep the plants moist, letting them almost dry out between waterings. At lower temperatures, let the plants dry out completely, so that they'll become dormant over the winter. If the seedlings still have room to grow, keep them in the same containers for the second year but liquid feed them through late spring and summer. Otherwise, repot into a cactus compost. By the end of year two, you should have decent-sized plants ready to go into 8cm (3in) pots the following spring.

Two-year old cacti seedlings ready for potting on

Key to how easy

●●● Very easy, expect 80–100 per cent success rates

●● Moderately easy, expect 50–60 per cent successs rates

● Difficult, be prepared for failure

species	how	when	what to do	ideal temp	how easy
A					
Acorus	division	Spr or early Sum	Tease grassy clumps apart with your hand. Split older clumps with a knife. Keep compost moist.	not critical	●●●
Aechmea (urn plant) – see offsets, page 124	offsets	Spr to Aut	Young plants form at base once flower dies. Remove these once they have 4–5 leaves using a sharp knife and pot up individually. Rooting takes 7–10 weeks.	17°C (65°F)	●●●
Agave	offsets	Spr and Sum	Remove offsets and pot up individually. Add grit to compost to improve drainage and keep on the dry side. Rooting takes 2–3 weeks.	17°C (65°F)	●●●
Aglaonema (Chinese evergreen)	division	Spr to Aut	Divide congested plants into smaller clumps or individual pieces of stem, each with two or three leaves attached.	17°C (65°F)	●●●
Aloe	offsets	Spr to Aut	Remove offsets and pot up individually. Add grit to compost to improve drainage and keep on the dry side. Rooting takes 2–3 weeks.	17°C (65°F)	●●●
Anthurium	division	Spr	Tease established plants into several clumps and repot each one in a 13cm (5in). Cover with a polythene bag for 6 to 8 weeks until well rooted.	21°C (70°F)	●●
Aphelandra (zebra plant)	stem cuttings	any time	After flowering, remove the old bracts. Feed and keep well watered to encourage new growth. Take cuttings from the tips of the stems with at least two pairs of leaves attached. Trim cutting about 3cm (1in) below the lowest leaf and dip in rooting hormone powder. Insert cuttings individually into 9cm (3½in) pots and cover with a polythene bag. Rooting takes 4 to 6 weeks.	17°C (65°F)	●●
Aporocactus (rat's tail cactus)	stem cuttings	Sum	Remove a rat's tail and cut into 5 to 8cm (2 to 3in) cylinders. Place them on kitchen towel to dry off for two days and then gently press the base into a sandy compost. Put several in a pot to create the effect of a mature plant. Rooting takes about 5 weeks.	15–17°C (60–65°C)	●●●
Araucaria (Norfolk Island pine)	tip cuttings	late Sum	Remove 8cm (3in) tips from young shoots, dip in rooting hormone powder and insert in sandy compost. Leave rooted cuttings until early summer the following year before repotting.	17°C (65°F)	●
Asparagus ferns (A. plumosus and A. spengeri)	division	Spr or Sum	Divide plant into sections and pot up only healthy outer portions.	17°C (65°F)	●●●
	seed	Spr or early Sum	Seed is widely available and quick and easy to grow. Sow as for bedding plants.	17°C (65°F)	●●●
Aspidistra (cast iron plant)	division	late Spr to early Sum	Tease apart young plants. Divide older ones with a knife or a saw. Divisions establish quickly.	15–17°C (60–65°F)	●●●
Azalea indica (florist's azalea)	cuttings	July to Sep	Take 10cm (4in) nodal cuttings (see page 13), dip in rooting hormone powder and insert into 3 parts peat and 1 part sand. Ideally, the air should be cool (around 13°C/55°F) and the compost warm (17°C/65°F). For best results, use a heated propagator, without the lid, in a north-facing room. Rooting may take 10 weeks or more.	see what to do	●

species	how	when	what to do	ideal temp	how easy
B					
Beaucarnea (pony tail palm)	cuttings	Spr and Sum	Older plants form tufts of arching leaves. Remove these with a section of stem, treat with rooting hormone powder and insert into an equal mixture of peat and sand. Rooting takes around 6 weeks.	17–21°C (65–70°F)	●●
Begonia, foliage types	leaf cuttings	Spr and Sum	See page 124 for details of the method. New plants will root in 4 to 8 weeks.	21°C (70°F)	●●●
	stem cuttings	Spr and Sum	Remove a stem tip with two or three leaves attached. Insert into a pot of compost and don't overwater as this leads to fungal problems. Rooting takes 2 to 3 weeks. Only suitable for foliage begonias which have stems.	21°C (70°F)	●●●
Begonia, flowering types	stem or leaf cuttings	Spr and Sum	Take cuttings from stem tips or use whole leaves and insert the stalk in to the compost. Non-flowering shoots are best for stem cuttings – otherwise remove the flowers. A rooting hormone will speed rooting, which takes 3 to 6 weeks. This method is suitable for both fibrous-rooted and tuberous begonias.	17°C (65°F)	●●●
	division of tubers	Spr	See page 69.	15°C (60°F)	●●●
	seed	Feb to Mar	Sow as for bedding types – see page 59.	21°C (70°F)	●●
Beleperone (shrimp plant)	cuttings	Spr and Sum	Take 15cm (6in) cuttings from the tips of fresh green shoots (remove any coloured bracts). Trim each cutting about 3cm (1in) below the lowest leaf. Treat with rooting hormone powder, insert six cuttings into a 10cm (4in) pot and cover with a polythene bag. Rooting should take about 6 weeks. Once roots are well established, pot whole clump into a larger pot to give you the effect of a mature plant.	17°C (65°F)	●●
Billbergia	division	any time	Remove all flowering shoots and divide plant into clumps of several stems using a strong knife. Throw away all old stems and dead material and repot the best bits individually.	not critical	●●●
Bryophyllum	plantlets	any time	Place pots of compost around the plant. The young plantlets that form round the leaf margins will drop off naturally and root themselves in the pots in a few days.	not critical	●●●
C					
Caladium (angel's wings)	division of tubers	Feb	Remove plant from pot before new growth appears and cut the tuber into sections, each with one or two shoots. Allow the cut surfaces to dry out for a day before repotting individually. Cover with a polythene bag until new growth well established.	17°C (65°F)	●●
Calathea (Maranta, prayer plant, peacock plant)	division	Spr	Split up established plant into two or three clumps and repot individually.	17°C (65°F)	●●●

species	how	when	what to do	ideal temp	how easy
Campanula isophylla (Italian bellflower)	cuttings	Spr	Take 8 to 10cm (3 to 4in) cuttings from stem tips, treat with rooting hormone powder. Insert in a cutting compost and cover with a polythene bag.	15°C (60°F)	●●●
	division	Spr	Split up plants when repotting.	15°C (60°F)	●●●
	seed	Spr	Sow as for bedding plants. See page 59.	17°C (65°F)	●●●
Capsicum annuum (Christmas cherry)	seed	Feb	Sow in a propagator. Difficult unless you have a greenhouse as seedlings tend to get leggy early in the year.	23–25°C (75–80°F)	●
Ceropegia woodii (rosary vine, string of hearts)	bulbils	Spr to Aut	Remove ball-shaped bulbils and place them on compost to root.	17°C (65°F)	●●●
	cuttings	Spr to Aut	Take cuttings from small sections of stem with a single leaf attached. Root 8 to 10 in a 8cm (3in) pot to give you a full, well-balanced plant.	17°C (65°F)	●●●
Chamaecereus silvestrii (peanut cactus)	stem cuttings	Spr and Sum	Remove a section, which resembles a peanut, and pot up in sandy compost.	not critical	●●●
Chlorophytum (spider plant)	plantlets	any time	Remove plantlet with small section of old stem (to anchor plantlet) and insert into a new pot.	not critical	●●●
Cissus (kangaroo vine)	stem cuttings	Spr and Sum	Take cuttings from stem sections with one or more leaves attached. Treat with rooting hormone powder and insert up to 5 cuttings in an 8cm (3in) pot. Cover with a polythene bag. Rooting should take 4 to 8 weeks.	17°C (65°F)	●●
Citrus (oranges, lemons and limes)	stem cuttings	Spr and Sum	Take cuttings from stem sections with three leaves attached and treat with rooting hormone powder. Cover with a polythene bag. Rooting should take 4 to 6 weeks. Bought plants are often grafted but most species grow satisfactorily on their own roots.	17°C (65°F)	●●●
Clivia (Kaffir lily)	division	after flower-ing	Remove offsets with a sharp knife and discard some of the old matted roots. Repot and water sparingly until established.	17°C (65°F)	●●●
Codiaeum (croton, Joseph's coat)	cuttings	Spr or Sum	Remove stem tips with 3 or 4 leaves attached and insert singly in 8cm (3in) pots. Cover with a polythene bag or place in heated propagator. Rooting takes 6 to 8 weeks.	23°C (75°F)	●●
	air layering	Spr or Sum	See page 44 for the technique.	21°C (70°F)	●●
Coleus	cuttings	Spr or Sum	Take 10cm (4in) cuttings from shoot tips, remove shoot tips and insert individually into 8cm (3in) pots. Cover with a polythene bag. Rooting should take 3 to 4 weeks. Don't let plant flower or it will drop its leaves and you won't have any cutting material.	17°C (65°F)	●●●
	seed	Spr	Sow as for bedding plants. See page 59.	17°C (65°C)	●●●
Columnea	stem cuttings	Spr and Sum	Take 8cm (3in) cuttings from stem tips and remove lower leaves. Root 5 to 7 cuttings in an 8cm (3in) pot to create a full-looking plant. Pinch out tips once cuttings are growing to induce branching.	17°C (65°F)	●●●

species	how	when	what to do	ideal temp	how easy
Cordyline	stem cuttings	Spr and Sum	Cut woody stems into 8 to 15cm sections using a hacksaw and place horizontally in sandy compost so that they are partially buried. Cover with a polythene bag or place in a propagator.	17°C (65°F)	●●
	offsets	Spr and Sum	Offsets at the base can be removed and rooted in sandy compost as above.	17°C (65°F)	●●●
	root cuttings	any time	If your plant has thick fleshy roots, cut these into 8cm (3in) sections. Place horizontally in peaty compost and cover with a polythene bag.	17°C (65°F)	●
Crassula (money plant, jade tree)	stem or leaf cuttings	Sum	Use individual leaves or sections of stem with leaves attached. Can be rooted. Let cuttings dry out for a day or more before inserting in sandy compost. Rooting should take 4 to 6 weeks.	17°C (65°F)	●●●
Crossandra (zebra plant)	stem cuttings	Sum	Use 8 to 10cm (3 to 4in) sections of stem with at least one leaf attached. Best rooted in a heated propagator with the vents open.	21°C (70°F)	●
Cryptanthus (earth star)	offsets	when avail-able	Remove offsets from base of parent plant and peg down into soil-less compost using a piece of bent wire. Cover with a polythene bag.	21°C (70°F)	●●
Cyclamen	seed	Aug to Sep or Feb (F1 varieties)	Soak seed for 24 hours or place in running water for ½ hour before sowing. Germination is often erratic so pinch out seedlings as soon as they are large enough to handle.	17°C (65°F)	●●●
Cyperus (umbrella plant)	seed	when flower-ing	Stand pot on tray of compost and it will self-seed itself.	17°C (65°F)	●●●
	division	Spr and Sum	Split up plant and repot individual clumps.	not critical	●●●
D–E					
Dieffenbachia (dumb cane) **WARNING** Always wear rubber gloves and wash your hands after handling this plant as sap is poisonous and an irritant	stem cuttings	Spr or Sum	Use tips of stems with 3 or 4 leaves attached or sections of woody stem which have at least one bud. Cover with polythene bag.	21°C (70°F)	●●
	offshoots	when avail-able	Detach offsets from base of plant, peg down into a pot of compost and cover with a polythene bag for 4 to 6 weeks.	21°C (70°F)	●●●
Dionea (Venus fly trap)	seed	Spr	Sow in a mixture of peat and sphagnum moss and cover with a polythene bag.	21°C (70°F)	●
	division	Spr	Split established plants into two or three and repot in peat and sphagnum moss. Cover with a polythene bag for 4 to 6 weeks.	17°C (65°F)	●●
Dizygotheca (false aralia)	root cuttings	Spr	Cut fleshy stems into 10cm (4in) sections and insert the right way up into compost with all but the top buried. Water in with a fungicide and cover with a polythene bag. Allow ten or more weeks for shoots to appear.	17°C (65°F)	●

species	how	when	what to do	ideal temp	how easy
Dracaena (dragon tree)	stem sections or offshoots	Spr or Sum	See under Cordyline for the method.	17°C (65°F)	●●
Echeveria	leaf cuttings	Spr or Sum	Insert individual leaves into sandy compost. Keep on the dry side and they should root in 4 to 6 weeks.	17°C (65°F)	●●●
	offsets	Spr and Sum	Remove rosettes that form around the base of the parent plant and pot up individually.	17°C (65°F)	●●●
Echinocactus (barrel cactus)	seed	Spr	See page 125.	17°C (65°F)	●●
Echinocereus (hedgehog cactus)	offsets	Spr and Sum	Remove offsets, allow to dry for a day and pot up in sandy compost.	17°C (65°F)	●●●
	seed	Spr	See page 125.	17°C (65°F)	●●
Echinopsis (sea urchin cactus)	offsets	Spr and Sum	As Echinocereus above.	17°C (65°F)	●●●
Epiphyllum (orchid cactus)	stem cuttings	Spr and Sum	Remove stem section, allow to dry for a day or two and pot into peat compost (they don't like lime).	17°C (65°F)	●●●
Euphorbia milii (crown of thorns) **WARNING** Sap is poisonous so wear rubber gloves and wash your hands after handling.	stem cuttings	Spr and Sum	Cut the top of a stem around 8cm (3in) long, allow to dry for 2 to 3 days and pot up in sandy compost.	17°C (65°F)	●●●
F					
Fatshedera × lizei (ivy tree)	stem tip or leaf bud cuttings	Spr and Sum	Take 10–15cm (4–6in) cuttings from stem tips or use section of stem with a single leaf attached, making sure there is a bud between the leaf stalk and the stem. Cover with a polythene bag after potting. Rooting should take 8 to 10 weeks.	17°C (65°F)	●●
Fatsia japonica (false castor oil plant)	stem tip cuttings	Sum	As above.	21°C (70°F)	●●
Ficus benjamina (weeping fig)	stem tip cuttings	Spr or Sum	Take 8 to 15cm (3 to 6in) sections from stem tips and cover with a polythene bag after potting. Rooting should take 8 to 12 weeks.	21°C (70°F)	●●
	air layering	any time	See page 44 for the method.	17°C (65°F)	●●
Ficus deltoidea (Ficus diversifolia, mistletoe fig)	stem tip cuttings	Spr or Sum	As above.	21°C (70°F)	●

species	how	when	what to do	ideal temp	how easy
Ficus elastica (rubber plant)	leaf bud cuttings	Spr and Sum	Make a cut just above a leaf and about 3cm (1in) below it, making sure there is a bud between the stem and the leaf stalk. Cover with a polythene bag. Rooting should take 8 to 12 weeks.	21°C (70°F)	●●
	air layering	any time	See page 44 for method.	17°C (65°F)	●●
Ficus lyrata (fiddle leaf fig)	leaf bud cuttings	Spr and Sum	As above.	21°C (70°F)	●●
	air layering	any time	See page 44 for method.	17°C (65°F)	●●
Ficus pumila (creeping fig)	stem tip cuttings	Spr and Sum	Take 8cm (3in) sections from stem tips, insert in compost and cover with a polythene bag. Rooting should take 2 to 4 weeks.	21°C (70°F)	●●●
Ficus radicans (trailing fig)	stem tip cuttings	Spr and Sum	As above.	21°C (70°F)	●●●
Fittonia	stem cuttings	any time	Almost any piece of stem will root in peaty compost. Cover with a polythene bag. Rooting should take 2 to 3 weeks.	21°C (70°F)	●●●
G–H					
Guzmania	offsets	when available	Detach well-established offsets and pot into 8cm (3in) pots. Cover with a polythene bag for 6 to 10 weeks until you see new growth.	17°C (65°F)	●●●
Gynura (purple passion vine) **WARNING** Remove any flowers that form because they stink	stem cuttings	any time	Insert stem sections with one or more leaves into compost. Root 3 or 4 cuttings in a small pot to give you an attractive full looking plant.	15°C (60°F)	●●●
Haworthia	offsets	Spr and Sum	Peel offsets away from plant and repot in sandy compost.	not critical	●●●
Hedera (ivy)	cuttings	Spr to Aut	Use method for nodal or leaf-bud cuttings described on page 49.	17°C (65°F)	●●●
Helxine (mind your own business)	division	any time	Pull a few bits off and put them in a new pot. Keep compost wet.	not critical	●●●
Heptapleurum (parasol plant)	stem tip or leaf bud cuttings	Spr	Take cuttings from stem tips with three leaves attached or cut just above a leaf and about 3cm (1in) below, making sure there is a bud between the stem and leaf stalk. Insert up to 3 cuttings in a 10cm (4in) pot and cover with a polythene bag. Rooting should take 8 to 12 weeks.	17°C (65°F)	●●
Hibiscus	stem cuttings	Spr and Sum	Take cuttings with 2 or 3 leaves attached, preferably from stem tips. Cover with a polythene bag after potting. Rooting should take 8 to 12 weeks.	17°C (65°F)	●

species	how	when	what to do	ideal temp	how easy
Hippeastrum (amaryllis)	bulbils	Spr or Aut	Remove bulbils from around parent bulb and repot individually. They will take around three years to reach flowering size. Unlike mature bulbs, don't let them dry out until they reach flowering size.	15 to 17°C (60 to 65°F)	●●
Hoya (wax flower)	stem tip or leaf bud cuttings	Spr or Sum	Take 8 to 10cm (3 to 4in) sections from stem tips or a single leaf with a section of stem attached. Cover with a polythene bag after potting. Rooting should take 4 to 8 weeks.	17°C (65°F)	●●●
	layering	any time	Peg down stem into pot of compost and sever once rooted, after 8 to 12 weeks.	not critical	●●●
Hypoestes (polka dot plant)	stem cuttings	Sum and Aut	Any part of stem with leaves attached should root within 2 or 3 weeks. Cover with a polythene bag. Pinch out tips of plants regularly to prevent legginess.	17°C (65°F)	●●●
	seed	Spr	Sow as for bedding plants. See page 59.	17°C (65°F)	●●●
I–M					
Impatiens (busy lizzie)	stem tip cuttings	any time	Stem tips root freely in water or compost.	17°C (65°F)	●●●
	seed	Spr	Sow thinly on surface of the compost and cover pot or tray with clinging film until seeds germinate.	21°C (70°F)	●●
Jasminum polyanthum	heel cuttings	Spr and Sum	Pull off side shoots so that they come away with a heel of the main stem attached (see page 12). Cover with a polythene bag. Rooting should take 6 to 8 weeks.	15°C (60°F)	●●●
	layering	Spr to Aut	Peg down shoot into a pot of compost and sever once rooted, after 2 to 3 months.	not critical	●●●
Jacaranda	stem tips	Sum	Root 8 to 10cm (3 to 4in) cuttings in peaty compost and cover with a polythene bag until well-rooted, after 8 to 12 weeks. Also easy from seed.	17°C (65°F)	●●
Kalanchoe	leaf or stem cuttings	Spr or Sum	Place individual leaves on surface of compost or take stem cuttings with a few leaves attached. In the latter case, let the cut surface dry for a few days before potting. Also easy from seed.	15°C (60°F)	●●●
Laelia	division	Spr	Split into two or three pieces and repot into orchid compost.	17°C (65°F)	●●●
Lobivia	offsets	Sum	Detach offsets and repot individually in a cactus compost.	15°C (60°F)	●●●
Mammilaria	offsets	Spr or Sum	Remove offsets with a pair of tweezers and a sharp knife. Allow to dry off for a few days before potting in cactus compost.	15°C (60°F)	●●●
Maranta (prayer plant)	stem cuttings	Spr or Sum	Use stem tips with three or four leaves attached. Treat with rooting hormone and insert individually into pots of moist peat. Best rooted in a heated propagator. Older plants can also be divided.	21°C (70°F)	●●
Monstera deliciosa (Swiss cheese plant)	stem cuttings	Spr or Sum	Shot tips with two or three leaves will root in peaty compost. Alternatively, use short sections of stem with no leaves but at least one bud. Bury to half their depth and root in a heated propagator.	21°C (70°F)	●●●

species	how	when	what to do	ideal temp	how easy
N–P					
Nerium oleander (oleander) **WARNING** All parts of this plant are highly poisonous	stem cuttings	Sum	Shoots up to 15cm (6in) long will root readily in compost or in water.	21°C (70°F)	●●●
Nidularium (bird's nest fern)	offsets	Spr	Remove offsets, pot up in peaty compost and cover with a polythene bag and keep warm until well rooted.	17°C (65°F)	●●
Notocactus	offsets	Spr or Sum	Pot up well-formed offsets in small pots of cactus compost. Also quite easy from seed.	17°C (65°F)	●●●
Opuntia	pads	Spr or Sum	Remove individual pads, allow to dry for a day or two and pot individually into cactus compost.	17°C (65°F)	●●●
Orchids	division	Spr or after flower-ing	See page 125.	keep slightly warmer than recom-mended for the species	●●●
Pandanus (screw pine)	offsets	Spr or Sum	Peel established offsets from base of plant. Pot individually in a well-drained compost and cover with a polythene bag until rooted.	21°C (70°F)	●●
Peperomia	stem or leaf cuttings	Spr or Sum	Stemless species can be propagated from whole leaves; others from stem tips with two or three leaves attached.	17°C (65°F)	●●●
Philodendron, climbing types	stem or leaf cuttings (also air layering –see page 44)	Spr or Sum	Take cuttings from stem tips with two or more leaves attached, or use single leaves with a short section of stem. Cover with a polythene bag and keep out of direct light. Non climbing types can be propagated by seed or division.	21°C (70°F)	●●●
Pilea	stem cuttings	Spr or Sum	Virtually any piece of stem will root in warm, moist conditions. Root several cuttings in a pot to give a full effect.	17°C (65°F)	●●●
Plectranthus (Swedish ivy)	stem cuttings	any time	Any piece of stem with a few leaves will root in compost or water.	10°C (50°F)	●●●
R–Z					
Rebutia	offsets	Spr or Sum	Remove offsets and pot individually in cactus compost. Also easy from seed.	15°C (60°F)	●●●
Rhipsalidopsis (Easter cactus)	stem sections	Spr or Sum	Break off a stem section at a joint, allow to dry out for a few days and pot up into a well-drained compost.	17°C (65°F)	●●●
Rhoeo (boat lily)	self-seeding or division	Spr or Sum	Stand pot on a tray of moist compost or gravel so that the seeds it scatters can germinate. Alternatively, split up older plants.	17°C (65°F)	●●●
Saintpaulia (African violet)	leaf cuttings	Spr to Aut	See page 123 for step-by-step instructions.	17°C (65°F)	●●●

species	how	when	what to do	ideal temp	how easy
Sansevieria (mother-in-law's tongue)	leaf cuttings, division or offsets	Spr or Sum	Leaves may be cut horizontally into 8cm (3in) sections and rooted in a heated propagator. However, variegated plants will revert to green if propagated this way. The alternative is to pot up established offsets or split older plants.	23°C (75°F) for leaf cuttings, 17°C (65°F) for others	●●
Saxifraga sarmentosa (mother of thousands)	plantlets	any time	Pot up plantlets individually.	not critical	●●●
Schefflera	seed	Spr	Buy in seed and sow in heated propagator. Unlike Heptapleurum, also known as the umbrella plant, this one is reluctant to root from cuttings.	21°C (70°F)	●●●
Schlumbergera (Christmas cactus)	stem sections	Spr or Sum	See Rhipsalidopsis on page 133.	17°C (65°F)	●●●
Scindapsus (devil's ivy)	leaf cuttings	Spr or Sum	Root individual leaves with a short section of stem attached in sand in a heated propagator.	21°C (70°F)	●
Sedum	stem cuttings	any time	Almost any piece of stem will root in well-drained compost.	not critical	●●●
Selaginella (creeping moss)	stem tips	Spr or Sum	Insert stem tips in moist peat and place in a heated propagator.	23°C (75°F)	●●
Sempervivum (house leeks)	offsets	Spr to Aut	Pot up offsets individually into well-drained compost. Seed mixtures are a cheap way of obtaining a range of type.	not critical	●●●
Senecio macroglossus (German ivy)	stem cuttings	Spr or Sum	Sections of stem with one or two leaves will root readily in peaty compost.	17°C (65°F)	●●●
Sonerila	stem cuttings	Spr or Sum	Root 10cm (4in) cuttings in peaty compost in a heated propagator.	21°C (70°F)	●●
Spathipyllum (peace lily)	division	Spr or Sum	Split up mature clumps and keep moist and shaded until well established.	15°C (60°F)	●●●
Stephanotis (Madagascar jasmine)	seed or leaf cuttings	Sum	Plants occasionally form large, plum-like seed pods. Allow these to ripen and split. Sow seed in an equal mix of peat and sand. Alternatively, take sections of stem with one pair of leaves attached, insert in moist peat and cover with a polythene bag.	21°C (70°F)	●●
Syngonium (goosefoot plant)	stem cuttings	Spr or Sum	Take 10cm (4in) sections of stem with one or more leaves, insert in peaty compost and cover with a polythene bag.	21°C (70°F)	●●
Tolmeia menziesii (piggy back plant)	plantlets	any time	Remove a leaf with a piece of stalk and press firmly into compost. The plantlet will then root readily.	17°C (65°F)	●●●
Tradescantia	stem cuttings	any time	For a full effect, insert five to seven stem tips in a 10cm (4in) pot. Rooting takes as little as three weeks.	not critical	●●●
Zebrina	stem cuttings	any time	As above.	not critical	●●●
Zygocactus	stem sections	Spr or Sum	See Rhipsalidopsis on page 133.	17°C (65°F)	●●●

Herbs may be annuals, perennials, shrubs or even bulbs, and so their propagation encompasses a wide range of techniques. Details for individual herbs are listed on pages 136 to 139, but you may also find it useful to consult the earlier chapters on techniques according to the type of plant you want to propagate. All the herbs are listed under their common names as that is what you will usually find them under in seed and nursery catalogues and other reference books.

You could create this combination very cheaply. Golden marjoram is easy to propagate from cuttings or by division, chives from seed or by division and purple sage from cuttings.

Angelica — Biennial
(*Angelica archangelica*)

If prevented from flowering or cut back early in autumn it behaves as a perennial
Seed is best sown fresh in late summer, although it can be stored in the fridge over winter and sown in spring. Harvest the seed once it turns brown. Sow either direct or in small pots or peat blocks, as seedlings don't transplant well, and plant out in spring in a moist, shady position. Outdoors, the seed should be lightly covered; in pots, sow on the surface of the compost as seed needs light to germinate. Self-sown seedlings can also be carefully moved.

Balm, Lemon — Perennial
(*Melissa officinalis*)

Seed Spring sowing allows plenty of time for plants to get established before winter. On heavy soils, however, it may be better to sow in late summer and overwinter the seedlings in pots in the cold frame for spring planting. Best sown in pans, as there may be intervals of several weeks before flushes of seedlings. Leave the pans out of doors and bring them into the warmth once the first seedlings appear to achieve a quicker and more even germination. Alternatively, germinate the seeds in a propagator at 13°C (55°F).
Division Lift and divide roots in autumn or spring.

Basil — Half-hardy annual
(*Ocimum basilicum*)

Seed Sow under glass or on the windowsill in March ready for planting out after frosts. Pinch out growing tip after planting out to encourage bushy plants. A second sowing *in situ* in May or June will provide a continuing supply until the first frosts. Basil grows best in a warm, dry border.

Bay, sweet bay — Evergreen
(*Laurus nobilis*)

Cuttings Take 15cm (6in) basal cuttings of ripened wood in September or October and root in the cold frame. The cuttings should be ready for potting on in early summer. Keep them in pots for the first 2 years and overwinter them under glass.

Bergamot — Perennial
(*Monarda didyma*)

Division In spring or autumn split outer shoots for propagation. Divide into quite small rooted pieces and plant in damp rich soil. Divide the clumps every 2 or 3 years, once they start to become bare at the centre.

Borage — Hardy annual
(*Borago officinalis*)

Seed Sow *in situ* in spring and thin out plants to about 30cm (12in) apart. It self-seeds freely and can become a nuisance. To overcome this problem, sow a few seeds every few weeks from spring to mid-summer and throw out the older plants once the flowers fade.

Chamomile — Perennial
(*Anthemis nobilis*)

Seed (flowering type only) Sow outdoors in late spring. The seed is very fine and it is advisable to mix it with sand to ensure even distribution. Do not cover, but water in with a fine rose and protect it from birds. Thin out the seedlings to 15cm (6in) apart. Alternatively, sow in trays under glass in May.
Cuttings Non-flowering clones such as 'Treneague' are propagated from rooted offsets or runners in spring or late summer. Plant 15cm (6in) apart and keep them well weeded and watered.
Note: On heavy soils, work plenty of peat and sand into the top 15cm (6in).

Chervil — Annual
(*Anthriscus cerefolium*)

Seed Fresh seed is best sown the same year. You can sow outdoors up to August. Make later sowings in trays in the greenhouse at 7°C (45°F) and plant out in spring. Thin outdoor sowings to about 15cm (6in) apart.

Chives — Perennial
(*Allium schoenoprasum*)

Division Split up old clumps in spring or autumn.
Seed can be sown successfully *in situ* in spring but, as seedlings are so flimsy, it is better to raise them in seed trays or peat blocks using the multiple seeding technique (see page 121). Plant out in clumps about 23cm (9in) apart.

Comfrey — Perennial
(*Symphytum species*)

Division In autumn or spring remove sections of root with at least one bud and plant out at 60cm (2ft) apart in rich or deeply worked soil in partial shade.

Coriander — Annual
(*Coriandrum sativum*)

Seed If grown for fresh leaves for use on curries, you can sow outdoors any time between April and August (or under cloches in October for use from February). Sow quite thickly in rows about 15–23cm (6–9in) apart. It is ready for cutting when it is 10–20cm (4–8in) high, about 6 to 8 weeks after sowing. Don't let it flower or the leaves will become tough and unusable. It is a cut-and-come-again crop and you can get about 4 cuttings from a single sowing. If you want to harvest the seed, sow in spring. The plants will bloom about 9 weeks later and produce seed from midsummer onwards. Harvest the seed when it turns pale brown.

Dill   Annual
(*Anethum graveolens*)

Seed If grown for its aromatic seed, sow in March or April; otherwise you can sow up until July. Sow thinly *in situ* in shallow drills and thin out to 20cm (8in) apart. The thinnings transplant badly and are better discarded. Harvest seed for the kitchen or for sowing next year, once seed heads turn brown. Lay the ripe seed heads over trays covered with paper or cloth (never plastic) and keep them in a dry airy place until the seeds fall out. Store in an airtight jar. If you want to sow your own seeds, don't grow dill near fennel as they cross-fertilise and produce inferior seedlings. Left to its own devices, dill will self-seed freely.

Fennel   Perennial
(*Foeniculum vulgare*)

Seed Sow in pinches about 60cm (2ft) apart along a shallow drill once the soil has warmed up in spring. Subsequently thin out to strongest seedlings. The thinnings can be transplanted if handled carefully. Harvest seed as for dill. Fennel self-seeds freely and, like dill, can become a nuisance.
Root division Divide in spring or autumn. Useful method if plants are cut back regularly. In autumn you can pot up a root and keep it indoors for use over winter.

Fenugreek   Annual
(*Trigonella foenum-graecum*)

Seed For continuity, sow from spring to late summer. Sow thickly in rows 23cm (9in) apart and keep well watered at all times. Harvest when about 20cm (8in) high, before it runs to seed (about 12 weeks from spring sowings and 6 weeks from summer sowings). Alternatively, you can grow for seed sprouts in a jam jar. Eat when sprouts are 1–2cm (½in) long (after about 2 days).

Garlic   Bulb
(*Allium sativum*)

Cloves Start with cloves bought from a seedsman as those bought in shops may be infected with eelworms (microscopic pests that can damage a wide range of crops). Plant in autumn, even in cold districts, as spring planting will produce much smaller bulbs. Plant individual cloves upright 10cm (4in) apart and about 3cm (1in) deep. On heavy soils or in wet seasons, incorporate dry sand along the base of the drill before planting to prevent rotting. Lift bulbs as soon as leaves start to turn yellow (don't wait until it topples). Dry in the sun or under cloches. Healthy-looking cloves can be planted again in the autumn.

Horseradish   Perennial
(*Cochlearcia armoracia*)

Root cuttings Lift in early spring and cut roots into 8cm (3in) sections and plant out 20–30cm (8–12in) apart the right way up.

Hyssop   Shrubby perennial
(*Hyssopus officinalis*)

Seed Sow in April in trays in a cold frame as they can be slow to germinate. When seedlings are about 5cm (2in), pot up and grow on for autumn planting.
Cuttings Take soft basal cuttings about 5–8cm (2–3in) long in May. Treat with a rooting hormone and root in equal parts peat and sand in a pot covered with a polythene bag (see page 16). If you want to root lots of cuttings, use the method described in the Box on page 9. By either method, roots should form in 4 to 6 weeks. Once rooted, pot up singly, protect from cold winds, and plant out in spring or late summer.
Root division Divide in spring or autumn as for Herbaceous Perennials. The simplest method if you just want 1 or 2 plants.

Lavender   Perennial
(*Lavandula angustifolia*)

Cuttings In spring root 5–8cm (2–3in) long cuttings in a sandy compost or pure sand in the cold frame. Spring cuttings can be potted on or planted out after rooting (4 to 6 weeks). In June take 5–8cm (3–4in) heeled cuttings, removing any flower buds. In mild areas with light soils, these can be rooted in the garden and transplanted in spring. Cuttings can be taken in September and October and rooted in the cold frame for spring planting.

Lemon verbena   Tender perennial
(*Lippia triphylla,* syn. *Aloysia triphylla*)

Cuttings Take 10–13cm (4–5in) stem cuttings from the side shoots in June or July. Treat with a rooting hormone and insert in a pot containing equal parts sand and peat then cover with a polythene bag. Once new leaves form (after about a month), pot up separately. Keep indoors or in a cold greenhouse or conservatory over winter. The plants may die down in winter but they will sprout again in late spring.

Lovage   Perennial
(*Levisticum officinale*)

Seed Sow from late July to early autumn as fresh seed becomes available. Alternatively, mix fresh seed with damp peat in a plastic bag and store it in the fridge over winter for April sowing. Cut the seed heads when they turn brown and lay them on trays covered with paper or cloth to collect the seed. Sow a pinch at 60cm (2ft) intervals and thin out to the strongest seedlings. In spring further thin out to about 1.5m(5ft).
Root division Divide in spring or autumn. Replant sections of fleshy root bearing a shoot.

Above: Common thyme (T. vulgaris) can be raised from seed, but take cuttings from or layer named varieties or those with golden or variegated leaves.

Above left: Coloured-leaved sages, such as Salvia officinalis 'Tricolour', are just as good in the kitchen as the plain one.

Left: Divide mints regularly to maintain a good supply of fresh leaves. Replant in a bottomless bucket to prevent them spreading too far.

Marigold, pot   Annual

(Calendula officinalis)

Seed   Treat as a hardy annual and sow in spring, either in trays in the cold frame or direct. The plants need a final spacing of about 25cm (10in). In mild areas you can sow in September for early flowering. You can save your own seed, though results may be variable compared with named varieties bought from seedsmen.

Marjoram   Perennial

(Origanum species)

Seed   The sweet or knotted marjoram (*O. majorana*) is a half-hardy perennial but is grown as an annual by sowing seed *in situ* in spring.

Division   The more commonly cultivated kinds are forms of *O. vulgare* and *O. onites* (pot marjoram), and these can be divided every other year in early

autumn. Either lift the roots and split into small clumps or detach rooted offsets from the plants with a sharp knife and plant out individually. On heavy or wet soils, pot up the offsets in a well-drained compost and overwinter them in a sheltered place. These perennial types can also be raised from seed sown in July or August

Mint — Perennial

(*Mentha* species)

Division from very early spring to autumn. Once buds show in spring, the creeping stems can be pulled away from the outside of the clump and replanted separately. To maintain a good clean stock with freshly aromatic leaves, replant every 3 years or so. Discard the old runners and propagate from the younger ones.

Parsley — Biennial*

(*Petroselinum hortense*)

*Grown as an annual

Seed Sow from late spring to late summer to provide a succession from summer through to the following spring (protect with cloches or pot up and take into the greenhouse over winter). Parsley seed won't germinate reliably until soil temperature reaches a steady 15°C (60°F), so don't sow too early. Soaking the seed is a waste of time.

Pennyroyal — Perennial

(pudding grass, *Mentha pulegium*)

Division Small rooted pieces can be detached in spring or early summer and replanted in a damp, shady spot. Established plants can be split up into as many pieces as desired so long as each bit has a root. Do not divide old roots in the autumn as pennyroyal is the least hardy of all the mints.

Rosemary — Evergreen

(*Rosmarinus officinalis*)

Cuttings can be rooted in the cold frame or in pots covered with a plastic bag throughout the summer, but it's easier to take cuttings in September or October. Take 13cm (5in) basal or heeled cuttings (see page 12) and root in the cold frame. No rooting hormone is necessary. Pot on or plant out in spring.

Sage — Shrub

(*Salvia officinalis*)

Cuttings taken in September or October are an insurance against winter losses. Take 10cm (4in) basal cuttings of semi-ripe wood and root in the cold frame. Pot on or plant out in spring.

Savory, summer — Annual

(*Satureja hortensia*)

Seed Sow *in situ* in spring or early summer and thin out to about 23cm (9in) apart.

Savory, winter — Perennial

(*Satureja montana*)

Seed Sow fresh seed *in situ* in April, barely covering the soil, and thin out to 15–23cm (9in) apart.
Cuttings Take 5cm (2in) stem cuttings in May, pot up once rooted and overwinter in the cold frame for spring planting.
Division In spring or autumn split up roots with a sharp knife and replant sections with a shoot.

Sorrel — Perennial

(*Rumex acetosa*)

Seed Sow in spring or autumn either *in situ*, later thinning to 25cm (10in) apart, or in pots or trays for transplanting later. Self-seeding can become a serious problem unless the flower heads are removed as soon as they appear. This is also necessary to maintain a supply of fresh tender leaves. Plants are best replaced every other year.

Sweet cicely — Perennial

(*Myrrhis odorata*)

Seed Sow *in situ* in early autumn. Sow in pinches about 90cm (3ft) apart and thin to strongest seedlings. Once established, it self-seeds freely.

Tarragon — Perennial

(*Artemisia dracunculus*)

Division French tarragon, the superior herb to Russian tarragon (*A. dracunculoides*), rarely sets seed so is propagated by dividing old plants in spring. In winter protect the crowns with bracken, straw, bark or even plastic sheeting held down with pegs to ensure a good supply of buds on the underground runners. In spring the runners can be divided into small sections, each with one or two buds. In harsh areas lift and pot up a root in autumn and over-winter under glass.

Thyme — Perennial

(*Thymus* species)

Seed Common thyme (*T. vulgaris*) can be raised from seed sown in spring. You can sow outdoors in a shallow drill, thinning out seedlings to about 25cm (10in) apart. However, germination is slow, so it is often better to raise seedlings in trays or pots in a cold greenhouse or cold frame. Seedlings take about 2 years to reach a usable size.
Cuttings All the thymes (including *T. vulgaris*) can be raised from cuttings of tip growth taken in early or late summer. They can be inserted *in situ*, so long as they are not allowed to dry out, and should root in 4 to 6 weeks.
Layering Best done in spring or summer. Weight down creeping stems of mat-forming types with small stones.

Wormwood — Perennial

(*Artemisia absinthium*)

Root division Lift the root stock in early spring and divide it into small sections, each bearing roots and one or two buds.
Seed Sow in autumn or spring. Best started in trays as it is slow to germinate. Seed germinates best in light, so don't cover trays.

TOOLS AND EQUIPMENT

You don't need a number of expensive tools or equipment in order to propagate your own plants, but it does pay to have a proper bench and the right bits and pieces to hand. Hygiene is vital to success in propagation, and blunt blades and messy working conditions can negate all your efforts.

The basic tool kit

Pots and seed trays See opposite page.
Composts and rooting media See page 143.
Secateurs for taking cuttings. You may find it easier to see where you are cutting with the bypass or scissor action type than with the anvil type, but the main requirements are that they should be sharp and clean.
Knives Most cuttings can be prepared with secateurs, though if you are preparing lots of cuttings, using a knife is a lot easier. Choose one with a straight blade as it will be easier to sharpen (for which you will also need an oil stone). Keep it just for cuttings – don't use it for string or compost bags. If you don't take enough cuttings to merit buying a proper knife, safety razor blades or a craft knife would be perfectly adequate. An old bread knife is useful for dividing plants.

Sieve Essential for covering seeds with compost – one with a 3mm (⅛in) mesh is ideal. A rectangular sieve the same size as a seed tray is convenient to use. You could make your own from wire mesh on a wooden frame.
Labels Always label seeds and cuttings with the full plant name and the date – it's very easy to forget what they are otherwise. It is also a good idea to keep a record book as a reference for future years as well as a standby in case the labels get lost.
Watering can with a fine rose Essential for watering cuttings and seedlings. Use it with the rose upside down.
Mist sprayer For perking up cuttings or moistening fine seeds.
Panes of glass Use a pane of glass to prepare your cuttings on as this will help avoid bruising and is easy to keep clean. Small panes of glass are also useful for covering

seed trays and pots, though you could use plastic clinging film instead.
Dibbers For inserting cuttings and transplanting seedlings. A few sharpened sticks and a lollipop stick with a notch cut in the end for easing out seedlings are all that are needed – though purpose-made ones are available.
Polythene bags Invaluable for maintaining humid conditions. The fairly thin ones are best. Buy a few packets of bags of different sizes from your local freezer shop rather than hunt around the house every time you need one.
Tampers for firming down compost. You could use any suitable-sized object with a flat bottom, but if you do a lot of sowing it is handy to have a set of tampers. Cut a block of wood to fit your pot or seed tray and screw on a smaller block of wood to act as a handle.

Other useful equipment

Cold frame This can prove invaluable for cuttings and seeds of hardy plants and hardening off plants raised at higher temperatures. Those with glass lids and timber or brick sides are best, as they can conserve most heat during the winter months. If you have an all-glass one, insulate the sides with polystyrene tiles in winter and seal all gaps. It's often recommended that you throw an old mat over your cold frame on nights when frost is forecast, but it is probably a lot easier to insulate it with bubble polythene firmly wired in place. At least your plants won't be left in darkness if you forget to remove the mat in the

morning. Cold frames should be well shaded in sunny weather or seedlings and cuttings will be cooked. Use a shading wash and supplement this with fine mesh netting in summer if necessary.
Polythene cloches can be a useful alternative to cold frames, especially if you want to root lots of cuttings. (See page 16.)
Polythene house Worth considering if you have a large garden to stock. Trees and shrubs raised from seed and cuttings will grow much more rapidly if kept under polythene for the first season or so than they would outdoors, as long as they are well watered and fed. For a small

investment you could save a year or two in getting your plants established.
Propagators See page 142 for how to make your own.

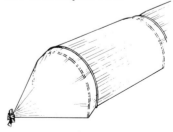

A cheap polythene tunnel is a good investment if you want to root lots of shrub cuttings, for ground cover or a hedge, say.

Chemicals

Rooting hormone Rooting hormones are available as powders or liquids. Murphy Rooting Hormone Powder did well in *Gardening Which?* tests.

Fungicide It is also wise to water the compost with a fungicide such as Liquid Copper or Cheshunt compound prior to seed sowing and after pricking out the seedlings as a precaution against damping off disease. If you are not using a rooting hormone, dip your cuttings in a fungicide solution (eg benomyl) to reduce problems with rotting and moulds.

Liquid fertilisers All rooted cuttings and seedlings will need regular feeding a month or so after potting on. Rooted cuttings or seedlings should also be fed if you have to delay potting on or pricking out for any reason. A balanced fertiliser (containing equal amounts of nitrogen, phosphorus and potash) should be suitable for most plants in their early stages.

Disinfectant Dirty pots and trays are a source of diseases. After use, wash them thoroughly and then sterilise them with a garden disinfectant such as Jeyes Fluid, ICI Clean Up or Murphy Mortegg.

POTS AND SEED TRAYS

Pots

Plastic pots 8cm (3in) pots are the most useful for propagation purposes as this size is ideal for potting on rooted cuttings or individual seedlings of all types prior to planting out. Smaller pots are not worth using as they dry out too quickly. For growing on trees and shrubs to a larger size, a range of pots up to 15cm (6in) will be useful. Half pots or pans are good for raising small numbers of seedlings or rooting cuttings. Plastic pots are generally better than clay as they are cheaper, more durable and less prone to drying out.

Peat pots are useful for raising seedlings that resent root disturbance, such as sweet corn and French beans, as they can be planted out pot and all. However, since they are not reusable the extra cost is probably not worthwhile for run-of-the-mill flowers and vegetables. Peat pots can dry out very rapidly and are best used in conjunction with capillary matting. The 8cm (3in) size is probably most useful.

Peat blocks are cubes made from a special compost using a blocking tool. Seeds can be sown direct into the blocks and planted out with their rootball intact. They are best used with capillary matting, otherwise watering can be difficult. They are also prone to crumbling apart if you try to move them before the roots have bound them together. Worth considering for seedlings that don't transplant well, such as sweet corn.

Peat pellets are blocks of compressed peat which swell up when watered. They have the same uses as peat blocks and are probably not worth the extra cost for seedlings that are easy to transplant.

Peat blocks.

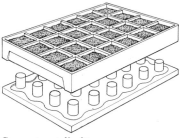

Compartmentalised tray.

Seed trays

Standard seed trays measure approximately 36 by 22cm (14 by 8½in) and are usually 5cm (2in) deep. Besides standard trays, it is useful to have a few half and quarter trays for sowing small numbers of seeds. Deep trays, which are 8cm (3in) deep, are useful for rooting small cuttings – though tomato trays lined with paper would be a cheap substitute.

Compartmentalised trays may be a collection of pots joined together or a set of dividers which fit into a seed tray. You can also get a polystyrene grid without a bottom which comes with a device for pushing out the plants once the roots fill the compost.

Compartmentalised trays are best used for larger seeds, where you only want to sow 1 or 2 per unit, or for seedlings after pricking out. The ones with dividers won't stop the roots matting together.

CHEAP ALTERNATIVES
Yoghurt pots are ideal for pricking out seedlings or potting on small cuttings, especially if you want to give away the plants. But remember to make drainage holes in the bottom. However, they are useless if you want to water your plants by capillary matting as they invariably have concave bottoms.

A HOME-MADE PROPAGATOR

The propagator on this page takes a 6.1m (20ft) soil-warming cable and is fitted with a thermostat. It measures 90 by 60 by 15cm (approx 36 by 24 by 6in).

How to make it

1. Cut the polystyrene with hot wire or a sharp saw. Wrap the polystyrene in polythene film and seal it with tape to extend its life.
2. Glue and nail the wooden sides together and drop the base into position.

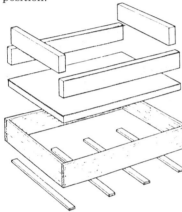

How the pieces are assembled.

3. Nail the battens tightly across the base.
4. Drop in the polystyrene sides.
5. Place the propagator frame in position in the greenhouse. Spread a 2.5cm (1in) layer of sand over the base using pieces of 2.5cm (1in) thick wood to gauge the correct depth.

Levelling the sand.

6. Drill a hole large enough to take the soil-warming cable and another to take the rod thermostat. Remember the rod should be at right-angles to the cable and the hole drilled 10cm (4in) from the bottom. Make sure the connection between the cable and the supply cord is inside the sand – not the polystyrene.

Cables and thermostat fitted.

7. Arrange the cable in the sand so that the runs are evenly spaced. Avoid sharp bends that may damage it. Pieces of wood pushed into the polystyrene base at the ends of the cable (as shown) can be used to hold it in position.
8. Fix the rod thermostat in position. The rod should be 2.5cm (1in) above the cable.
9. Cover the cable with sand, making sure the runs remain straight. Level off the sand about 2.5cm (1in) above the rod.
10. The cover is made by bending

Wire hoops in position to hold polythene tent.

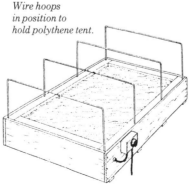

Materials and cutting list

(Use either metric or imperial units throughout).
Expanded polystyrene sheet 1.2m (4ft) square by 2in (5cm) thick. This is available from insulating or packaging firms or builders' merchants. Some will cut to size for a small extra charge.
Base 90 by 60cm (36 by 24in)
Two sides 90 by 10cm (36 by 4in)
Two ends 50 by 10cm (20 by 4in)
Wood 12mm ($\frac{1}{2}$in) thick exterior or marine-grade plywood.
Two sides 90 by 15cm (36 by 6in)
Two ends 62.5 by 15cm (25 by 6in)
Wooden battens Four pieces 12mm ($\frac{1}{2}$in) thick, 7.5cm (3in) wide and 62.5cm (25in) long.
Polythene Large sheet of transparent polythene at least 1.2 by 1.5m (4 by 5ft).
Heavy-gauge wire (8-gauge) Four pieces at least 1.2m (4ft) long.
Sand At least 2 cu ft.
Soil-warming cable 6.1m (20ft), 75 watts, with thermostat.

the wires as shown and covering them with clear polythene film – the corners of the tent can be stapled to maintain a high humidity.

BE SAFE WITH ELECTRICITY

● If you use a propagator in your greenhouse, make sure you have a proper moisture-proof control unit and use a residual current device (RCD). If in doubt, consult a qualified electrician or your local electricity board.
● Never try to open a propagator to expose the thermometer or heating element, and don't use it if it becomes damaged.
● Always switch off the propagator while attending to the seedlings or cuttings.

CHOOSING A COMPOST

Composts are formulated in different ways according to their use.

Seed and cutting composts contain few nutrients as too much fertiliser can inhibit seed germination and the rooting of cuttings. Once seeds have germinated and cuttings take root, they must be moved into a potting compost.

Potting composts contain more nutrients than the seed and cutting composts. Loam-based John Innes composts are graded according to how much fertiliser they contain. No. 1 contains the least fertiliser and is ideal for potting on cuttings and seedlings; No. 3 contains the most fertiliser and is best for growing established plants in containers. Peat-based potting composts can hold only a limited amount of fertiliser, and rooted cuttings or seedlings should be fed with a liquid fertiliser if they are to remain in the pots more than about 6 weeks (or according to the instructions).

All-purpose composts (sometimes called universal, multi-purpose or seed and potting composts) are a compromise between the different needs of seed and plants and can be used for both sowing and potting on. These are generally peat-based, and you must start feeding plants about 4 to 6 weeks after potting on or they will suffer.

For cuttings

All you need to root cuttings is a medium that will hold moisture but also allow aeration. The most widely used rooting medium for cuttings is a mixture of moss peat (don't use sedge peat) and sharp sand or grit. For most woody cuttings, 2 parts sand to 1 part peat (by volume) is best, while most herbaceous plants root well in an equal mixture. For alpines, use pure sand or grit.

There are also a number of other rooting mediums you might like to experiment with:

Perlite is a very light volcanic material that looks very much like expanded polystyrene. It can be mixed with 2 parts or equal parts moss peat for rooting cuttings or as a substitute for sharp sand or grit in seed and potting composts. You can also root cuttings in just perlite, but you will need to water it very carefully to keep it moist. As it contains no nutrients and, unlike peat, cannot hold nutrients from any liquid fertiliser you may add, cuttings have to be potted on as soon as they are rooted.

Vermiculite is a silvery-beige, light spongy material that can be used in the same way as perlite. (Vermiculite is sometimes sold for insulation but only the horticultural grade is suitable for plants.) It can hold large amounts of water or air. Unlike perlite, it can absorb nutrients from liquid fertilisers, and it also contains small amounts of potassium and manganese. Vermiculite on its own is good for rooting cuttings, particularly softwood cuttings. Thoroughly water the vermiculite before and after inserting the cuttings and do not compact it around the stem. As with perlite, pot up the cuttings, or start feeding them, as soon as they have rooted. You can also topdress light-sensitive seeds with a fine topdressing of vermiculite to help prevent them from drying out.

For seed

The simplest solution for most seed is to use an all-purpose compost. In *Gardening Which?* trials these have proved to be just as good as using a separate seed and potting compost. For seeds that take a long time to germinate, a John Innes seed compost or a mixture of sharp sand and peat may be better. To avoid pricking out seeds that are very sensitive to fertilisers, fill a pot with potting compost and cover it with a thin layer of seed compost in which to sow the seeds.

The geranium on the right was fed regularly; the other wasn't.

TROUBLESHOOTING

If your cuttings fail to root and your seeds do not germinate, or if you are troubled by pests or diseases in the early stages, the Charts on the next 3 pages should lead you to the cause of the problem.

CUTTINGS

Did cuttings wilt?

YES

Did you insert the cuttings straight away?

YES   NO

All leafy cuttings should be collected in a polythene bag (or a bucket of water for softwood cuttings) and prepared in a cool place. The bag may be kept in the salad compartment of the fridge.

Was the compost sufficiently moist?

YES   NO

Stand pots and trays in shallow water for about 15 minutes and leave to drain before inserting cuttings.

Did you provide a humid atmosphere?

YES   NO

Most cuttings do better if covered with a polythene bag or propagator lid – or at least misted frequently. Cover is essential for softwood cuttings and those with delicate leaves.

Did cuttings have large leaves or a lot of foliage, or were they in direct sunshine?

YES   NO

Cuttings difficult to root or taken at wrong time of year.

Keep all leafy cuttings shaded until rooted. Large leaves can be cut in half or rolled up and secured with an elastic band. Most cuttings should not have more than 2 or 3 leaf pairs.

Did cuttings rot below compost level?

YES

Did you treat cuttings with a fungicide?

YES   NO

A benomyl dip is a wise precaution for all cuttings – see page 15.

Did you use fresh compost?

YES   NO

Always use a sterile medium for leafy cuttings – not garden soil.

Was the compost very wet? Was the weather cold?

NO   YES

Wrong rooting medium. Incorporate extra sand and don't overwater. Cold and wet conditions can prove fatal.

Did you use a sharp knife or razor blade to prepare the cuttings?

NO

Ragged cuts can lead to infections.

Did the cuttings fail to root and slowly die?

YES

Did you take the right type of cutting? At the right time?

YES   DON'T KNOW

Check with relevant section of this book.

Did you provide sufficient heat at rooting level?

YES   DON'T KNOW

Cuttings may root better in a heated propagator at 18–21°C (65–70°F).

Was the weather very hot?

NO   YES

High temperatures may induce shoots to grow before any roots have formed, putting the cutting under stress.

Did you use a rooting hormone or try wounding the cuttings?

NO

Worth trying if cuttings prove difficult to root (see page 15). Rooting hormones are essential for some plants.

INDOOR SOWINGS

Did the seeds fail to germinate?

YES

Did the compost get too wet or dry out?

NO   YES

Check the compost daily. Mist if it dries out.

Did you use the right compost?

YES   NO

Use fresh seed or all-purpose compost.

Was the temperature high enough or too high?

YES   NO

Do not rely on thermostats if rooting cuttings in a heated propagator.

Are you sure you sowed at the right depth?

YES   NO

Dig up the compost to see if the seedlings started to grow but failed to reach the surface.

Was seed fresh? Or are you trying out unusual seeds? Perennials, trees, shrubs, perhaps?

NO   YES

Find out if the seed needs special treatment. See relevant section of book. Otherwise complain to shop or seedsman.

Buy fresh seed.

Was germination patchy?

YES

Did the compost look patchy due to uneven wetness?

NO   YES

Firm and level the compost before sowing. Prior to sowing stand seed tray in shallow water for 15 minutes and allow to drain.

You are probably sowing the seed unevenly. Mix very small seeds with fine dry sand before sowing. Some seeds, such as cyclamen, naturally germinate unevenly.

Were seedlings poor quality?

YES

With yellowing leaves?

NO   YES

Overwatering or possibly starvation with older seedlings. If latter, pot on, plant out or give liquid feed.

Straggly and lopsided?

YES

Uneven lighting. Turn daily (especially if grown on windowsill). Insufficient light – move to a brighter spot.

Did seedlings die after emerging?

YES

Did the stems turn brown and shrivel at soil level?

NO   YES

Damping off fungus. Thin out seedlings sooner, improve ventilation, and don't water from above. Remove affected seedlings and spray others with a liquid copper fungicide or Cheshunt compound. Water compost with liquid copper or Cheshunt compound prior to sowing.

Did the seedlings wilt then shrivel, leaves first?

YES   YES

Too much sun – keep seedlings out of direct sunlight until well established. Shade on clear sunny days.

Did the seedlings die suddenly?

NO   YES

It is likely that the compost was too wet or dried out at some stage. Alternatively, sudden low temperatures in the greenhouse could be to blame.

Try again.

OUTDOOR SOWINGS

Did seedlings fail to appear or only a few germinate?

YES

Did you sow early in the year?

NO   YES

Seed may have rotted in cold wet soil or been eaten by soil pests. Don't sow too early (see map on page 59) or when soil is very wet. Treat early sowings with a combined fungicide/insecticide seed dressing.

Was the soil dry? Or did a dry period follow sowing?

NO   YES

Flood seed drills several hours prior to sowing and keep soil moist with a fine spray until seeds germinate. If your soil is prone to forming a hard crust, this will prevent seedlings emerging. See page 118 for what to do.

Did you sow in summer?

NO   YES

A few seeds, notably lettuce, won't germinate above 25°C (80°F). See page 120 for how to overcome this.

Did you sow too deep?

NO   YES/DON'T KNOW

Dig up part of drill to find out whether seed germinated but failed to surface. Follow directions on packet in future.

Does seed require special treatment to germinate?

NO   DON'T KNOW

Turn to relevant section of book to find out. Many trees and alpines, for example, need chilling.

It is likely that you've got old seed or that it was stored in adverse conditions. Keeping seed in warm, moist conditions, such as the greenhouse, can reduce viability in a matter of weeks.

Were seedlings damaged or did they suddenly die after they emerged?

YES

Were stems and leaves eaten back to ground level?

NO   YES

Slugs and snails – look for slime trails – or mice – look for droppings. Use slug pellets or mouse traps.

Did seedlings collapse and look as if they had been cut off at ground level?

NO   YES

Cutworms, leatherjackets, wireworms. Work in a soil insecticide such as diazinon or phoxim before future sowings.

Use a stick to help you make straight, even drills. Graduations on the stick make spacing easier and reduce the need for thinning later.

Take care to cover seeds to an even depth to avoid problems with patchy germination.

Were there lots of small holes in leaves?

NO   YES

Flea beetles – affect cabbage family, including turnips, radish, swedes, wallflowers and beets. Dust seedlings with derris powder.

Were seedlings nibbled around the edge?

NO   YES

Slugs, snails or caterpillars.

Was seedbed disturbed? Leaves torn?

YES

Cats or, if leaves torn or seedlings pulled up, birds. Cover rows with netting or hoops of chicken wire.

Was germination patchy?

YES

Did you prepare the seedbed carefully?

YES   NO

Lumps in the soil or stone could be to blame. Be more persistent with the rake next time. Too much or uneven distribution of fertiliser could also be to blame.

Did you take care to make the drills even all the way along?

YES   NO

It is a lot easier if you use a bit of timber as a guide and make drills with a sharp stick or the corner of a hoe:

Is your soil prone to forming a hard crust?

NO   YES

Cover seed drill with a line of peat or work in moist peat to top few centimetres of soil prior to sowing.

Was the seedbed previously a lawn or a neglected weedy plot?

NO   YES

It is likely that soil pests are to blame. Work in a soil insecticide such as diazinon or phoxim prior to sowing.

Were there any signs of soil disturbance?

NO   YES

Mice (particularly with early sown peas and beans), birds or cats. Start seeds indoors or use mousetraps and netting.

Is seed prone to uneven germination?

DON'T KNOW

Carrots and parsnips are known for this – try fluid sowing (see page 121). Trees, shrubs, and some perennials may need special treatment – see relevant sections of this book.

If mice are a problem or the soil is still cold and wet, get peas and beans off to an early start by sowing in pots or trays.

Protect seedlings and seedbeds against birds and cats by using hoops of wire mesh.

USEFUL ADDRESSES

MAIL-ORDER SEED COMPANIES

Samuel Dobie & Son Ltd, PO Box 90, Broomhill Way, Torquay, Devon TQ2 7QJ

D T Brown & Co. Ltd, Station Road, Poulton-le-Fylde, Blackpool, Lancashire FY6 7HX

Kings Crown Quality Seeds, Monks Farm, Coggleshall Road, Kelvedon, Essex CO5 9PG

Mr Fothergill's Seeds, Gazeley Road, Kentford, Newmarket, Suffolk CB8 7QB

S E Marshall & Co. Ltd, Regal Road, Wisbech, Cambridgeshire PE13 2RF

Suttons Seeds Ltd, Hele Road, Torquay, Devon TQ2 7QJ

Thompson & Morgan (Ipswich) Ltd, London Road, Ipswich, Suffolk IP2 0BA. Large range of unusual varieties

Unwins Seeds Ltd, Histon, Cambridge CB4 4ZZ

SMALLER AND SPECIALIST SEEDSMEN

General
J W Boyce, 67 Station Road, Soham, Ely, Cambridgeshire CB7 5ED. Strong on traditional varieties

Seeds-by-Size, 45 Crouchfield, Boxmoor, Hemel Hempstead, Hertfordshire HP1 1TB. Flower and vegetable seeds sold by weight (multiples of 1g). Large ranges of cabbages, lettuce, tomatoes, wallflowers, petunias and stocks

Vegetables
Chase Organics (GB) Ltd, Coombelands House, Coombelands Lane, Addlestowe, Weybridge KT15 1HY. Seeds for organic gardeners and farmers, mostly vegetables

Down-to-Earth, Cade Horticultural Products Ltd, Streetfield Farm, Cade Street, Heathfield, East Sussex TN21 9BS. Small quantities of commercial varieties

Genetic Resources Dept, Henry Doubleday Research Association, Ryton-on-Dunsmore, Coventry, West Midlands CV8 3LG. Seed library for vegetable varieties no longer sold

W Robinson & Sons Ltd, Sunny Bank, Forton, nr Preston, Lancashire PR34 0BN. Varieties of mainly exhibition vegetables and some unusual tomatoes available

Unusual plants
Chiltern Seeds, Bortree Stile, Ulverston, Cumbria LA12 7PB. A very large range of ornamental plants, including exotic trees and shrubs, wild flowers, some oriental and unusual vegetables

Wild flowers and herbs
John Chambers, 15 Westleigh Road, Barton Seagrave, Kettering, Northamptonshire NN15 5AJ. Wild flowers/grasses, conservation mixtures, herbs

Emorsgate Seeds, Terrington Court, Terrington St Clement, King's Lynn, Norfolk PE34 4NT. Wild flower seeds and plants, grass/wildflower mixtures

Seeds-by-Post, Suffolk Herbs, Sawyers Farm, Little Cornard, Sudbury, Suffolk CO10 0NT. Wild flowers, conservation mixtures, herbs, cottage garden flowers, vegetables (less usual varieties and unusual vegetables)

INDEX